ALL THAT IS W

WRITING WALES IN ENGLISH

CREW series of Critical and Scholarly Studies
General Editors: Kirsti Bohata and Daniel G. Williams (CREW, Swansea University)

This CREW series is dedicated to Emyr Humphreys, a major figure in the literary culture of modern Wales, a founding patron of the *Centre for Research into the English Literature and Language of Wales*. Grateful thanks are due to the late Richard Dynevor for making this series possible.

Other titles in the series

Stephen Knight, *A Hundred Years of Fiction* (978-0-7083-1846-1)
Barbara Prys-Williams, *Twentieth-Century Autobiography* (978-0-7083-1891-1)
Kirsti Bohata, *Postcolonialism Revisited* (978-0-7083-1892-8)
Chris Wigginton, *Modernism from the Margins* (978-0-7083-1927-7)
Linden Peach, *Contemporary Irish and Welsh Women's Fiction* (978-0-7083-1998-7)
Sarah Prescott, *Eighteenth-Century Writing from Wales: Bards and Britons* (978-0-7083-2053-2)
Hywel Dix, *After Raymond Williams: Cultural Materialism and the Break-Up of Britain* (978-0-7083-2153-9)
Matthew Jarvis, *Welsh Environments in Contemporary Welsh Poetry* (978-0-7083-2152-2)
Harri Garrod Roberts, *Embodying Identity: Representations of the Body in Welsh Literature* (978-0-7083-2169-0)
Diane Green, *Emyr Humphreys: A Postcolonial Novelist* (978-0-7083-2217-8)
M. Wynn Thomas, *In the Shadow of the Pulpit: Literature and Nonconformist Wales* (978-0-7083-2225-3)
Linden Peach, *The Fiction of Emyr Humphreys: Contemporary Critical Perspectives* (978-0-7083-2216-1)
Daniel Westover, *R. S. Thomas: A Stylistic Biography* (978-0-7083-2413-4)
Jasmine Donahaye, *Whose People? Wales, Israel, Palestine* (978-0-7083-2483-7)
Judy Kendall, *Edward Thomas: The Origins of His Poetry* (978-0-7083-2403-5)
Damian Walford Davies, *Cartographies of Culture: New Geographies of Welsh Writing in English* (978-0-7083-2476-9)
Daniel G. Williams, *Black Skin, Blue Books: African Americans and Wales 1845–1945* (978-0-7083-1987-1)
Andrew Webb, *Edward Thomas and World Literary Studies: Wales, Anglocentrism and English Literature* (978-0-7083-2622-0)
Alyce von Rothkirch, *J. O. Francis, realist drama and ethics: Culture, place and nation* (978-1-7831-6070-9)
Rhian Barfoot, *Liberating Dylan Thomas: Rescuing a Poet from Psycho-Sexual Servitude* (978-1-7831-6184-3)
Daniel G. Williams, *Wales Unchained: Literature, Politics and Identity in the American Century* (978-1-7831-6212-3)
M. Wynn Thomas, *The Nations of Wales 1890–1914* (978-1-78316-837-8)
Richard McLauchlan, *Saturday's Silence: R. S. Thomas and Paschal Reading* (978-1-7831-6920-7)
Bethan M. Jenkins, *Between Wales and England: Anglophone Welsh Writing of the Eighteenth Century* (978-1-7868-3029-6)

All that is Wales

The Collected Essays of M. Wynn Thomas

WRITING WALES IN ENGLISH

UNIVERSITY OF WALES PRESS
2017

www.uwp.co.uk

British Library CIP Data
A catalogue record for this book is available from the British Library

ISBN   978-1-7868-3088-3
          978-1-7868-3089-0
eISBN   978-1-7868-3090-6

THE ASSOCIATION FOR
WELSH WRITING IN ENGLISH
CYMDEITHAS LLÊN SAESNEG CYMRU

Typeset in Wales by Eira Fenn Gaunt, Cardiff
Printed by CPI Antony Rowe, Melksham

Er cof am fy mam

CONTENTS

SERIES EDITORS' PREFACE

The aim of this series, since its founding in 2004 by Professor M. Wynn Thomas, is to publish scholarly and critical work by established specialists and younger scholars that reflects the richness and variety of the English-language literature of modern Wales. The studies published so far have amply demonstrated that concepts, models and discourses current in the best contemporary studies can illuminate aspects of Welsh culture, and have also foregrounded the potential of the Welsh example to draw attention to themes that are often neglected or marginalised in anglophone cultural studies. The series defines and explores that which distinguishes Wales's anglophone literature, challenges critics to develop methods and approaches adequate to the task of interpreting Welsh culture, and invites its readers to locate the process of writing Wales in English within comparative and transnational contexts.

Professor Kirsti Bohata and Professor Daniel G. Williams

Founding Editor: Professor M. Wynn Thomas (2004–15)

CREW (Centre for Research into the English Literature and Language of Wales)
Swansea University

ACKNOWLEDGEMENTS

Most of the essays in *All that is Wales* have been previously published over the last two decades in a range of publications, the details of which have been carefully recorded at the conclusion of each piece. I am very grateful indeed to all concerned for permission to reprint here, as I am to the many authors and publishers the particulars of whose works have been duly cited throughout in my textual notes.

Yet again, thanks beyond measure go to the wholly indispensable University of Wales Press, and most particularly to the following members of staff with whom I have liaised so profitably closely: Sarah Lewis, Helgard Krause, Siân Chapman, Dafydd Jones, Elin Williams, Elisabeth Edwards and Eira Fenn Gaunt. And, of course, friends and colleagues such as Helen Vendler, Tony Brown, Neil Reeve, Glyn Pursglove, Kirsti Bohata and Daniel Williams, who share my interests and have provided me with invaluable companionship and intellectual sustenance:

As always, the present volume is, in its way, as much the product of my close family – Karen, Elin, Bob and, yes, little Joseph and littler Elliott too – as it is my 'own' work.

But in the end this book – probably one of my last – is – indeed *had* to be – dedicated to the memory of my mother, who sadly died (as did my beloved father so very much earlier) before any publications of mine had seen the light of day. In my end is my beginning. But for my mother's unstinting devotion, long outlasting my childhood and adolescence, I am acutely conscious I would have come to nothing: in her beginning, therefore, was this my end.

The University of Wales Press gratefully acknowledges permissions granted for use of the following materials:

New Directions Publishing Corp., for the following works by Dylan Thomas:
'The Peaches', 'Old Garbo' and 'Return Journey' by Dylan Thomas, from *The Collected Stories of Dylan Thomas*, copyright © 1940 by New Directions Publishing Corp. Reprinted by permission of New Directions Publishing Corp.
'After the Funeral' by Dylan Thomas, from *The Poems of Dylan Thomas*, copyright © 1938 by New Directions Publishing Corp. Reprinted by permission of New Directions Publishing Corp.
'The Force That Through the Green Fuse Drives the Flower' and 'Especially When the October Wind' by Dylan Thomas, from *The Poems of Dylan Thomas*, copyright © 1939 by New Directions Publishing Corp. Reprinted by permission of New Directions Publishing Corp.
'The Hunchback in the Park' by Dylan Thomas, from *The Poems of Dylan Thomas*, copyright © 1943 by New Directions Publishing Corp. Reprinted by permission of New Directions Publishing Corp.
'Do Not Go Gentle Into That Good Night' by Dylan Thomas, from *The Poems of Dylan Thomas*, copyright © 1952 by Dylan Thomas. Reprinted by permission of New Directions Publishing Corp.

David Higham, for the writings and poetry of Dylan Thomas in the following works:
Walford Davies (ed.), *Dylan Thomas: Early Prose Writings* (London: Dent, 1971).
Paul Ferris (ed.), *Dylan Thomas: The Collected Letters* (London: Dent, 1985).
Walford Davies and Ralph Maud (eds), *Dylan Thomas: Collected Poems 1934–1953* (London: Dent, 1988).
Dylan Thomas, *Quite Early One Morning: Poems, Stories, Essays* (London: Dent, 1974).
Leslie Norris (ed.), *Dylan Thomas: The Collected Stories* (London: Dent, 1983).
Vernon Watkins, *Dylan Thomas: Letters to Vernon Watkins* (London: Dent, 1957).
The Dylan Thomas Omnibus, Under Milk Wood, Poems, Stories and Broadcasts (London: Phoenix, 2000).

Carcanet Press Limited, for material in:
Lynette Roberts, *Collected Poems*, ed. Patrick McGuinness (Manchester: Carcanet, 2005).
Lynette Roberts, *Diaries, Letters and Recollections*, ed. Patrick McGuinness (Manchester: Carcanet, 2008).
Gillian Clarke, *Letter from a Far Country* (Manchester: Carcanet, 1982).
Meic Stephens (ed.), *The Bright Field: An Anthology of Contemporary Poetry from Wales* (Manchester: Carcanet, 1991).

Meic Stephens, as literary estate, for copyright permission to use the work of Leslie Norris in the following publications:
Leslie Norris, *Albert and the Angels* (New York: Farrar, Straus and Giroux, 2000).
Leslie Norris, *Recollections* (Provo: Tryst Press, 2006).
Leslie Norris, *Collected Poems* (Bridgend: Seren, 1996).
Leslie Norris, *Translations* (Provo: Tryst Press, 2006).
Leslie Norris, *Glyn Jones* (Cardiff: University of Wales Press, 1973).

Seren Books, for permission to use material from the following publications:
Margiad Evans, *The Old and the Young*, ed. Ceridwen Lloyd-Morgan (Bridgend: Seren, 1998).
Tony Curtis (ed.), *How Poets Work* (Bridgend: Seren, 1996).
Colin Edwards and David N. Thomas (eds), *Dylan Remembered, Volume One, 1914–1934* (Bridgend: Seren, 2003).
Leslie Norris, *Collected Poems* (Bridgend: Seren, 1996).

W. W. Norton & Company, for permission to use material from the following work:
Eavan Boland, *Object Lessons: The Life of the Woman and the Poet in Our Time* (Manchester: Carcanet, 1995).

The University of Wales Press gratefully acknowledges the kind permissions granted to include essays in this volume published in their original form in the following:

'"There's words": Dylan Thomas, Swansea and Language', in *The Transactions of the Honourable Society of Cymmrodorion* (New Series, 21).

'"A huge assembling of unease": Readings in *A Man's Estate*', in Katie Gramich (ed.), *Mapping the Territory: Critical Approaches to Welsh Fiction in English* (Cardigan: Parthian, 2010).

'Vernon Watkins: Taliesin in Gower', in *The Journal of the Gower Society* (64).

'"Staying to mind things": Gillian Clarke's Early Poetry', in Menna Elfyn (ed.), *Trying the Line: A Volume of Tribute to Gillian Clarke* (Llandysul: Gomer, 1997).

Er bod hi'n fach mae hi'n ddigon.

Introduction:
Microcosmopolitan Wales

When, over thirty years ago, Jan Morris elected to write, with her customary brio, a highly personal history of Wales, she intriguingly sub-titled it 'epic views of a small country'.[1] This collection of essays has been fashioned in a similar spirit, and is an attempt to trace, in however preliminary a fashion, the surprisingly extensive and intricate cultural contours of a tiny area of negligible land. To foreground that ambition, and bring it into appropriate contemporary focus, I have ventured to title this introductory chapter rather grandiosely 'microcosmopolitan Wales', a term borrowed from a seminal essay by Michael Cronin, Ireland's leading scholar of translation practice.

Cronin's declared aim in coining the term was to deliver 'intellectuals from [small, "marginal"] nations such as Ireland, Scotland and Wales' from 'the facile dualism of macro perspectives'.[2] 'Macrocosmopolitanism', in Cronin's terms, encapsulates the unexamined supposition that only large politico-cultural units can nurture a tolerant, fluid, humane pluralism and a hospitable openness to others. From this perspective, small units are to be condemned for the inevitable narrowness of their mental horizons, the fixity of their essentialist identities, and their bigoted hostility to cultural variety. Cronin's introduction of the concept of 'microcosmopolitanism' is therefore designed to break up this barren dualism.

> Microcosmopolitan thinking is not an approach which involves the opposition of smaller political units to larger political units (national or transnational), but one which in the general context of . . . cosmopolitan ideals . . . seeks to diversify or complexify the smaller unit. In

other words it is a cosmopolitanism not from above but from below. (191)

What he is advocating is a 'defence of difference, not beyond but within' even such small units as Wales. To this end, he mobilises the concept of 'fractal differentialism', a

> term [which] expresses the notion of a cultural complexity which remains constant from the micro to the macro scale. That is to say, the same degree of diversity is to be found at the level of entities judged to be small or insignificant as at the level of large entities. (192)

The exploration of this micro-diversity could therefore be roughly described as the cultural equivalent of nanotechnology. To illustrate the point, Cronin borrows from the thinking of the French mathematician Benoir Mandelbrot, who in 1977 came up with an intriguing answer to the question he'd posed: 'how long is the coast of Britain?' Mandelbrot's point was that 'at one level the coast was infinitely long', since a satellite's estimation of it would differ exponentially from that of, say, an insect, traversing it laboriously pebble by pebble. The more fine-grained one's mapping of the coast's contours, the more, not the less, complex the whole process became. Much the same law, Cronin argues, applies in the case of cultural studies. Accordingly, 'the micro-cosmopolitan movement . . . situat[es] difference and exchange at the micro-levels of society', rather than at the 'macro' level customarily supposed to be the exclusive location of such progressive cosmopolitan practices.

Instead, therefore, of engaging in current debates, fashionable but futile, about the respective merits of centripetal and centrifugal models of society, with attendant misgivings about such 'loaded' terms as 'cosmopolitanism', Cronin proposes we think instead in terms of equal – and equally rewarding – levels of complex sociocultural organisation at every supposed 'level' of a large geo-social unit. In his lexicon, 'cosmopolitan' is not a privileged term, an honorific reserved for the 'centre' and signifying a sophisticated mingling of international elements, but rather a signifier of a richness born of a constant process of cultural exchange wherever that is to be found and whatever distinctively local forms it takes.

Thus defined, the microcosmopolitan approach mirrors the intentions that have prompted me to publish a series of English-language studies of the Welsh cultural scene over the last thirty years or so. As its title indicated, *Internal Difference,* the first of these, set out to show that what characterised Welsh identity was the distinctive, and constantly shifting, constellation of widely differing cultural practices and constituencies of which it was actually composed.[3] In other words, Wales actually existed as a distinctive pattern, or system, of differences (or rather, as Derrida might have it, as a dynamic process of constant *differencing*).

The different elements were in many respects competing as much as co-operating, and so Wales was defined as well by its distinctive pattern of internal conflicts and tensions, none of course greater than those associated with Wales's two primary languages and cultures. And one of the most crucial aspects of that particular issue was obviously the grotesque asymmetry of sociocultural power between the two respective sectors. These perceptions were therefore further developed in *Corresponding Cultures* (as in my Welsh-language study *DiFfinio Dwy Lenyddiaeth Cymru*) primarily through an exploration of the largely taboo subject of the dynamic rivalries and interactions between Wales's two linguistic cultures, but attention was also paid to the way in which Welsh imagining of the US provided a fascinating mirror to the constantly shifting, fractured condition of Wales itself.[4] Through other publications, I also set out to consider the different ways in which Continental Europe had functioned, during the twentieth century, as the 'Eutopia' of many Welsh writers and intellectuals. Indeed, a simplified but fruitful cultural history of modern Wales could, I suggested, be written in terms of the division between those who favoured an 'American Wales' and those who were conversely attracted to the ideal of a 'Welsh Europeanism'.[5] A concern to understand Wales's embeddedness in the wider world is, of course, a natural feature of the 'microcosmopolitan' approach, as is a respect for the complex inner dynamics of a myriad other small cultural units world-wide routinely overlooked by 'macrocosmopolitan' zealots.

But it also manifests itself in my interest in exploring some of the, frequently competing, images of themselves the Welsh had, at different periods, inwardly digested and projected outwards. *In the Shadow of the Pulpit*, which I published in 2010, was accordingly an attempt to demonstrate how a whole, seminal chapter in the evolution of modern Wales – that relating to its nineteenth-century self-fashioning as a 'Nonconformist nation' – had been largely obliterated from cultural memory, with the resultant serious deficit in Wales's awareness not only of its history, but of its own richly diverse potentialities as a nation.[6] And finally, and most recently, *The Nations of Wales, 1890–1914* concerned itself with the restless cultural pluralism of a period in which a Wales still (however belatedly) transitional between the pre-industrial and the industrial, the religious and the secular, the Welsh language and the English language, spawned a fertile number of rival versions of Welsh identity.[7]

From the beginning until the present, my researches into the anglophone literary culture of Wales have consciously avoided foregrounding the work of Dylan Thomas. Contrary to erroneous supposition, this has not been for want of deep admiration of Thomas's multifaceted genius. Rather, it is a strategy that was first consciously adopted, and has ever since been consistently implemented, with a view to correcting popular misconception (so revealing of the plight of the Welsh psyche) that Wales had never succeeded in producing any significant English-language writers, save for 'Dillon'. Therefore my entire career, insofar as it has related to 'Anglo-Welsh literature', has been consciously devoted to the excavation and rehabilitation of the neglected writers of Wales. Moreover, whenever I have had occasion to address Thomas's work directly, I have done so from a Welsh angle that some have deemed marginal, perverse and provincial, choosing to examine such topics as the Welsh-language reception of his poetry; the influence of Gwilym Marles and Welsh Unitarianism on his work; the similarities between his cultural situation and that of certain Welsh-language writers; and his relation to the culturally divided world of his Swansea. The reason for this is quite simple: I feel equipped by my own cultural background to explore these particular dimensions of Thomas's output that remain very largely inaccessible to 'mainstream' criticism. And in addition, such an approach has enabled me to 'reclaim' Thomas for Wales – a necessary counterbalance, I would further argue, to the 'international bias' of so much contemporary Thomas scholarship.

* * *

As beguiling as it is no doubt misleading, personal retrospection suggests to me that the version of the culture of Wales that has gradually formed itself in my writings bears the imprint of my own early circumstances. To register that is also implicitly to admit that both the range and the likely appeal of my academic work have inevitably been limited in part by the particular personal conditions of its production. But there is one advantage of having been raised partly in a minority culture. It saves one from the arrogant presumption of supposing oneself to be the authoritative voice of 'majority experience' – a voice that in fact gives expression only to what John Stuart Mill famously termed 'the tyranny of the majority' – and it sensitises one to the extraordinary plurality (as well as the accordingly conflicted character) of any sociocultural collective. Wales is not only a community of communities; it is also a bewildering nexus of different cultures and of sub-cultures, which is not to deny that most of us inhabit several of these simultaneously. Such an awareness is implicit, wherever it is not explicit, in my own primary concentration on a single, dominant primary division between a Wales that is English-speaking and a Wales that is Welsh-speaking.

To return briefly therefore to those early circumstances whose importance for my own development I have noted. Evening always reached us early in Ferndale as the sun abruptly disappeared behind the mountain high on whose slopes our terraced house was situated. But its light continued to grace the opposite slopes of our narrow valley of the Rhondda Fach, illuminating tiny Blaenllechau and etching, clear against the sky, the great spoil tip on the horizon where trams toiled steeply uphill like some Sisyphean ants only to roll back empty and exhausted. Although my own well-worn paths were always downwards – once I'd left the infants school directly behind our house I headed daily downhill to the primary school situated next to the pit-head and railway sidings at valley bottom – my fearful imagination was periodically haunted by tales of the *bwci-bo* whose distant figure I occasionally glimpsed stalking the hillside above. And from time to time I'd be thrilled by the exotic sound – and fleeting sight – of a hunt pursuing some poor fox high on the mountain ridge.

My tiny personal world was, then, full of dualities from the very start, and now, as I look back, my whole environment seems studded with allegory. A stone's throw from home was Darran Park with its swings, roundabout and public swimming pool, where I watched Ferndale play on a red-ash pitch that decidedly discouraged rugby – a rough game I therefore only came to know and very gradually to love much later. Consequently, one of the most pleasurable dualities in my life has involved the sharing of my passion equally between soccer and rugby, unlike some of my compatriots, who remain as obstinately monocultural in this sporting realm as they do in matters cultural!

Particularly precious to me in memory – for reasons I don't understand – is the native woodland that rises gently behind the park's
beautiful natural lake, ancient, still and deep. Only much later did I
learn it was magically called Llyn y Forwyn and realise that the
language so largely confined to my own little family was actually the
original language of my whole native environment and that it had a
history there that was every bit as deep as the lake itself. It had certainly
not seemed so when I was growing up. By some quirk of good fortune,
my best friend was golden-locked Gareth Jones who lived just a few
doors away and spoke Welsh just like me. But we were exceptions.
It was the English I learned at the late age of five that was to be heard
everywhere – apart that is from the Welsh diffidently spoken in chapel
by a few of the nostalgic older generation to whom I, therefore, was
a permanent wonder. I well remember intriguing our friendly grocer
by suddenly asking for 'sudd cwrens duon' – his residual Welsh no
longer encompassed such an exotic term for Ribena. It seemed at
that time so absurdly unlikely that my infants school would end up
a Welsh-medium institution, a development that naturally gives me
immense pleasure. But my early experience of speaking a language
not understood by the majority of my contemporaries makes me
apprehensively sympathetic to today's generation of Rhondda youngsters who are subject to the same potentially alienating experience,
except now sadly in reverse. Coming from English-speaking homes
and neighbourhoods they are in danger of becoming distanced from
their family, friends and neighbours by learning Welsh – an experience
that could easily lead to a lifetime of resentment that would be hugely
damaging both to them and to the language.

The fact that my first world mainly spoke English meant I grew up
never doubting that English was fully a Welsh language and furious
whenever it was suggested otherwise. But nor did I suppose that Welsh
was somehow an 'illegitimate' language of Valleys experience that
had no right to speak of Rhondda life. The removal of Welsh to the
margins, if not entirely from the scene, common in so much supposedly
authoritative academic writing and popular imaging of 'the Valleys'
makes me extremely angry, as if a vital element in my own identity
were being casually erased. It was such a feeling that made me an
ardent regular contributor to the late Hywel Teifi Edwards's groundbreaking series recording the rich Welsh-language culture of the south
Wales valleys, a culture that included the working class every bit
as much as the bourgeoisie.[8] I can therefore understand the feelings

of innumerable minorities that daily suffer the same fate on an un-
imaginably greater scale – as also the feelings of monoglot English-
speakers of Wales who are still occasionally susceptible to similar
treatment by Welsh-speakers. And never in largely anglophone Ferndale did I feel the resentment at, or condescension to, my 'other'
language. That was felt only after I'd left the Rhondda just before my
tenth birthday and moved to my second home district of Gorseinon
and its environs, which was, compared to the Rhondda, much more
bilingual in character, and it was an experience of disinheritance
augmented by my aggressively anglophile education both at Gowerton
Grammar School and at University College, Swansea.

There is one further aspect of my Rhondda experience that, I feel,
was to have profound consequences for my cultural development.
Shortly after I had entered infants school, the first Welsh-medium
primary school in the Rhondda Fach was opened just down the valley
in Pontygwaith. As my mother, in particular, had long been a Plaid
Cymru supporter (and had attended Plaid's early summer schools)
and had also been educated by the culturally enlightened and admirably
pioneering Principal of Barry Training College, Ellen Evans, to value
her Welsh-language heritage, and as the headmistress of the new
school was an old friend of my father's and lived just down the road
from us in Rhondda Terrace, it seemed inevitable that I would be
moved from my monoglot English school in Ferndale to Pontygwaith.
But appreciative as ever of my neurotic anxieties as a little boy, and
therefore unwilling to uproot me from a school into which I had
begun happily and comfortably to settle, my considerate parents
decided against any such move – an act that was totally contrary to
their usually mild and accommodating natures. The result was that
throughout my school days, as of course thereafter, I never experienced
a Welsh-medium education. The consequences were long-lasting and
mixed. On the one hand, I was left with a lifelong feeling that, while
Welsh was my mother tongue and the language ever closest to my
heart, my mastery of it as a medium for sophisticated intellectual
discussion was imperfect, since English had so very early become
the first language of what might be termed my 'educated' self. Decades
later, it took a considerable effort on my behalf to improve my Welsh
sufficiently to allow me – in response to the promptings of my conscience and in accordance with cultural choice – to produce articles
and books in that language, although I remain frustrated by the relative
lexical narrowness, idiomatic poverty, grammatical uncertainty, and

limited range and register of my written Welsh, compared to that of
more accomplished writers.

But if it is convenient, at least, for me to blame such lamentable
shortcomings on my English-medium education, I also have to admit
that I owe it a debt of gratitude for enabling me to feel so thoroughly
at home amongst the English-only speakers of Wales, whose company,
after all, I have mostly kept, and whose Welshness I have so strongly
asserted throughout my personal and professional life. And while my
rather precarious 'interstitial' cultural position between two cultures
has resulted in a misgiving, from time to time, that I am viewed as
suspect by both Welsh-speaking and English-speaking Wales, it has
also undoubtedly helped me gradually to mediate between my two
cultures, exploiting my biculturalism in an attempt to demonstrate
the complex, if deeply conflicted, unity of Wales as manifested by its
writers on both sides of the major language divide.

As I approached ten, I left the Rhondda for Penyrheol, Gorseinon,
a locality I already knew extremely well from visits every school holiday
without fail, as it was my mother's home patch. But moving there was
nevertheless an introduction to a very different Wales, even though it
too, like Ferndale, was an industrial conurbation within the great
South Wales coalfield – my maternal grandfather was a colliery
winderman, just as my paternal grandfather had been a Rhondda
miner, and my youth in the Gorseinon area was lived night and day
to the accompaniment of the chug of the tinplate mills and the wailing
sound of the works' hooters. The coalfield writers of industrial Wales
came naturally, therefore, to appeal to me in due course, and it never
occurred to me to regard that extensive, internally diverse region that
stretches, after all, as far west as the Gwendraeth valley, as the exclusive
preserve of 'Anglo-Welsh' authors, as was strongly implied, I came
eventually to realise, in the writings of several highly influential cultural
historians.

At that time, the village of Penyrheol was an entity totally distinct
from the neighbouring township of Gorseinon that was in time to
engulf it before in its turn being engulfed by the expanding city of
Swansea. In character, it represented (as did so many of the industrial
villages of the western coalfield) an intermediate zone between the
rural and the industrial – although change was already physically
evident when I arrived, in the form of the large council-house estate
then in process of being built on many of its fields. Nevertheless,
throughout the twenty or so unmarried years I lived there, several

of the small side-roads were still attractively lined with hedges and many of the houses were detached, their extensive back gardens entirely given over to the vegetables the workmen managed to tend even after a day's gruelling manual labour in mine or tinplate works. These plots guaranteed them a small degree of self-sufficiency. The thriving local farms were solidly integrated into community life, and the little local school was set amongst fields through which I daily made my way. There was an enchantment attaching to the place that won my immediate and lasting affection. As for the community of miners, tinplate workers and steelworkers, it was at that time largely Welsh-speaking, although children of my own age had already stubbornly begun to refuse to speak the language, with dramatic sociocultural consequences, and the residents of the new council houses were almost exclusively speakers of English only.

In short, this was a transitional world, one corner of which had as much in common with the Welsh-speaking, chapel-going, rural communities of the *gwerin* as it did with the industrial world of the proletarian Rhondda. And Rhondda residents – many of whose grandparents had after all fairly recently arrived fresh from the Welsh countryside – recognised this difference. This was evident from their habit (so puzzling to me as a child) of referring to my family's holiday visits to the Swansea area as 'going down the country'. The great distance and difference this implied was amply confirmed by my tiring experience of travelling between the two localities. The journey to Penyrheol from the Rhondda (nowadays completed in an effortless three-quarters of an hour) used to take all day and involved taking a bus up through 'Little Moscow', Maerdy, and over the mountain to Aberdare – a tortuous route that to this day affords the most spectacular view in Wales – a long wait before the next long-haul bus journey down the Neath valley to Swansea, and then patient queuing for the final journey, again by bus, to my grandparents' house. Once there I was – so unlike the Rhondda – lovingly entangled in a network of extended family, since quite a few in the village were related to me directly or indirectly. For good and no doubt for ill I had a complex 'history' and an already given community identity in Penyrheol, whereas in the Rhondda I had in comparison been history-less, known only as the son of my father and of the chapel. At the age of ten I thus found myself differently situated in Welsh time as well as in Welsh place.

My sense of being 'outsidered' by my own country first began in earnest, I suppose, when I entered Gowerton Grammar School only to find that (apart from the annual 'Eisteddfod' and Welsh lessons) it was largely a no-go area for Welsh speakers, although there were many such among my contemporaries. My first language was there destined to be kept firmly 'under the hatches', although (and I later discovered mine was a representative experience in this regard) many, if not most, of my teachers were themselves Welsh-speaking (as was the headmaster, come to that). It was during study for my GCE exams and then my A-levels that I first experienced a devotion, which later was to prove lifelong, to canonical 'English' literature (I have never believed it meaningless to make qualitative distinctions: on the contrary, I believe them to be as inevitable as they are culturally essential, however time-bound and contested such value judgements may prove to be). But it was at that time, too, that I discovered that to read some of these texts was also for me, in some ways, a 'foreign' experience, even though they could also offer me from time to time a fascinating mirror of my own cultural plight, suspended (both stimulatingly and disconcertingly as in some ways I sensed I was), between two potentially antagonistic linguistic cultures. It was in the character of 'Owen Glendower', from Shakespeare's *Henry IV, Part One*, that I found my most intriguing twin. On the one hand, I was already capable of dimly sensing (and personally resenting) the send-up of him by Shakespeare as an in-effectual hot-air romantic, a bardic 'wizard' as self-aggrandising as he is substantially impotent:

> GLENDOWER.   I can call spirits from the vasty deep.
> HOTSPUR.   Why, so can I, or so can any man;
> But will they come when you do call for them? (*Henry IV, Part One*, III.i)

And yet, this Glendower is treated by no means unsympathetically, responding as he evidently is to the provocatively superior airs of a Hotspur who repeatedly taunts him for speaking a base and barbarous tongue. Above all, I felt that Shakespeare had understood and voiced one of my deepest feelings when he had his Welsh-speaking Glendower haughtily (and indeed movingly) protest:

> I can speak English, lord, as well as you;
> For I was train'd up in the English court;
> Where, being but young, I framed to the harp
> Many an English ditty lovely well
> And gave the tongue a helpful ornament[.]

And disarmingly even-handed as usual, Shakespeare also mollified me with his treatment of the meeting between Mortimer and his wife, Glendower's daughter, who speaks only Welsh ('O, I am ignorance itself in this'); for me, it demonstrated that tolerance for other tongues that Shakespeare himself no doubt had occasion to practise when lodging – by deliberate choice – amongst foreigners while working at the Globe.[9] Spoken, as it very probably was, by members of his Globe company, Welsh was not only for Shakespeare the ancient, aboriginal language of Britain, it was also a contemporary tongue, one of the many languages spoken by the large immigrant community of London. Moreover, as a prominent signifier of conspicuous 'regional' difference within Britain, Welsh was no doubt recognised by Shakespeare as a marker of the rural 'provincialism' that, for all his metropolitan success, remained an indelible feature of his own character. My sensing of such matters, then, may have been an unconscious preparation for, or prefiguration of, my later interest in inserting Welsh into the context of an embryonically multi-lingual and multi-cultural Wales, and of reading the literatures of Wales against the background of various other literatures.

Of these, the one that most came to absorb my attention was the literary culture of the United States, and in eventually editing *Gweld Sêr: Cymru a Chanrif America* ('Seeing Stars: Wales and the American Century') I provided myself both with an opportunity to explore Welsh–American cultural relations and exchanges vicariously (a subject I had also previously addressed in a discrete chapter of *Corresponding Cultures*) and to outline, in an introductory essay, the various points of connection I had early come to feel, in rather personal and accordingly somewhat prejudiced terms, between the literatures of Wales and the States.

In that essay in *Gweld Sêr*, I playfully speculated that my fascination with things American might date back as far as my prenatal state, when two GIs ominously destined for the Normandy landings had been billeted on my parents a couple of months before I was born. More credibly – and persuasively, I hope – I concluded it more likely dated from the occasion, in my mid-teens, when my family belatedly acquired a television, just in time to witness that most thrillingly American of all decades, the 1960s. It provided us with the most appallingly convincing experience of Reality TV, in the form of the Cuban crisis, the assassination of the Kennedy brothers, the killing on-camera of Lee Harvey Oswald, the great Civil Rights marches, and the assassination of Martin Luther King, not to mention the exhilarating experience of the first moon landing and the early astonishing triumphs of the young Cassius Clay. My adult imagination is therefore very much a child of the American 1960s, and it was the small screen, with its *The Cabin in the Clearing*, its *Sergeant Bilko* and its *I Love Lucy*, that seduced my attention, and not the epic Hollywood Westerns of the day, or the outrageous gyrations of Bill Haley with his rocking 'Around the Clock', or the adolescent riots that seemed the invariable accompaniment to the screenings of that great heart-throb Elvis Presley in *Jailhouse Rock*.

Already by the time I entered college in the autumn of 1962, the America of the small screen had conditioned me to favour American culture, and it so seemed natural to follow an American Literature special option during my two years of specialist undergraduate study. While its foreignness was underscored for me by the slow, relaxed Californian drawl of my tutor, the eminent scholar George Dekker (who later migrated to Stanford via Essex), this new literary culture also seemed strangely familiar from the outset. It also seemed liberating and affirming of my own Welsh cultural identity. That was because I (mistakenly, of course) detected in the nineteenth- and twentieth-century writers we studied prominent features of my Wales. There was the open concern with identity politics, the anxiety of influence (in the form of a complex relation to traditional English literature), the unmistakeable signs of religious origins, the apparent social egalitarianism. It was the extravagant presence of the latter that first attracted me to the poetry of Walt Whitman, in whose work I was eventually to specialise, and when I came to publish my own experiments in translating some of Whitman's poems into Welsh I pointed out in my introduction that in rhythm they strongly echoed those of the Bible in ways that reminded me of some Welsh-language writing during the Nonconformist era.[10] That era was again brought to my mind when I encountered the mid-nineteenth-century New England of Hawthorne's writing, Bible-black as his works were (contrary, of course, to the sceptical world view of their author) with his society's preoccupation with sin, while I immediately recognised in Thoreau's cussedly principled individualism the influence of an American dissent that was cousin to that of my chapel Wales. That Emerson's Transcendentalism originated in Calvinism, by way of an extreme reaction against it, was no surprise to me, accustomed as I was to the twentieth-century drift towards humane religious liberalism of some Nonconformist ministers in Wales.

And then there was the different literature of the American South. Granted the odious history of repellent Southern racism I nevertheless became fascinated with the literary productions of a defeated people. Realising that the New Criticism I was being taught in the form of Practical Criticism was very largely the strategic product of a South determined to emphasise the rich complexity of its inherited cultural sensibility contrasted with the crass simplifications of the industrialised, socially levelling, 'occupying power' of the North, I developed a Welsh interest in leading figures such as Allen Tate, Robert Penn Warren and Cleanth Brooks. Faulkner's great novels I found compelling, because they bore such remarkable testimony – not least in the tortuous passages and tormented inner structures of his seemingly endless sentences – to the past's tentacular grip on the Southern mind. That remorseless sense of the present being, as Bergson had put it, no more than the past gnawing into the future reminded me of the past-orientated fixations of some of the best Welsh-language writers. On the other hand, in the history-lite approach of the North to the present, I felt I detected similarities to Wales's 'new' literature in English.

In so many writers, North and South, I found examples of a Gothic style strikingly like that which seemed ubiquitous in anglophone Welsh writing, particularly of the inter-war period. For Caradoc Evans (or even Caradog Prichard if it came to that) see Erskine Caldwell or Flannery O'Connor – or of course the great Nathaniel Hawthorne and the even greater Herman Melville. Furthermore, there were the Realist writers from Dreiser and Norris through Upton Sinclair and James T. Farrell and the social protest writers like John Steinbeck, all of whom reminded me of the 'Anglo-Welsh' novelists of the inter-war years. There were the Native American writers – most particularly Sherman Alexie and N. Scott Momaday[11] – and of course the African American writers from the Harlem Renaissance onwards, all of whom spoke of conditions of disempowerment to which I, as a Welshman, could respond, although even then, in my most callow years, I never entirely lost sight of the vast gulf of difference between my immensely privileged situation and theirs.

And then, as I gradually matured in understanding, the literatures of the US seemed steadily to grow into an inalienable and invincible foreignness that at first I had barely been capable of acknowledging. Eventually, I was able to turn that to advantage, as when, in my first book-length study of Whitman, I paradoxically took the measure of his 'difference' by using my Wales-induced awareness of the profound inequalities, and attendant social tensions and conflicts, that could underlie apparent social cohesion and egalitarian solidarities, to bring out the fine cracks, fissures and fractures hidden in the smooth confident surface of Whitman's intoxicating assertions, and to demonstrate that these divisions were those specific to the mid-nineteenth-century America to which Whitman the apparent universalist was secretly in thrall.

But what proved to endure through all the phases of my understanding was that sense, so early awakened, of the liberating properties for me of an American culture that, unlike English culture, never gave me the impression it felt it had my measure as a Welshman. In American literature – as in America itself when eventually I came to visit it – I felt free to be who I was, confident that I would not be pigeonholed. My career as an 'Americanist' of sorts became a necessary complement and ballast to my career as a specialist in Wales's literary cultures, not least because it periodically freed me from the otherwise unbearable pressures of being confined to an endlessly fissiparous and wearyingly and wearingly conflicted Welshness.

In recent years I have seriously wondered how far in responding so immediately, viscerally, and with such a shock of personal recognition, to Glendower's touchingly proud protestation 'I can speak English, Lord, as well as you' – as self-defensive a protestation as it is self-assertive – I wasn't precociously recognising the voicing of a primary motivating force of my whole future professional career. Have I perhaps, in all my subsequent teaching and writing, essentially been driven by an overwhelming need to demonstrate to my cultural over-lords a degree of mastery of English and its literatures? It is a need I came to sense in so many 'Anglo-Welsh' writers, including some of those – such as Dylan Thomas – who knew no Welsh; and in their case – as perhaps in mine – it frequently took the form either of a flamboyantly exhibitionist English, as instanced for example in the writings of Dylan Thomas or Glyn Jones, or of a stylishly hypercorrect English, as found in the work of Gwyn Jones. Such writings are the telltale signs of a subaltern 'display' culture.

I was certainly aware, as a callow undergraduate student made to feel uneasy by some of my teachers at my linguistic difference and provincial cultural 'oddness', of a quiet (and unconfident) wish to equal – if not to better – them at their own game. And it was at university, too, that I discovered with delight that no less an author than Joyce was an authority on the vexed issue of an 'acquired' language:

[Stephen Dedalus] thought: The language in which we are speaking is his before it is mine . . . I cannot speak or write these words without unrest of spirit. His language, so familiar and so foreign, will always be for me an acquired speech. I have not made or accepted its words. My voice holds them at bay. My soul frets in the shadow of his language.[12]

When I listen to Dylan Thomas booming his own poetry in that strange, compelling, synthetic, 'cut-glass accent' of his, it is that phrase of Joyce's that comes to mind – 'My voice holds them at bay' – even though I readily concede that Thomas himself never did feel his soul 'fretting in the shadow' of an 'acquired language'. To begin by acknowledging both of these perceptions may yet, it seems to me, prove a fruitful way of preparing oneself to consider much 'Anglo-Welsh' writing. And, obviously, in responding to textual promptings such as this I was unknowingly demonstrating an instinctive affinity with what later came to be known as 'post-colonial literature', and preparing myself to understand the literatures of Wales as offering me – in however complex, equivocal and controversial a sense – ample and fascinating instances of the post-colonial condition.[13]

I was early sensitised, then, by my experience of reading English texts that deepened my sense of 'otherness' as a Welsh reader, to the fact that all literary works unavoidably have a social, cultural and political dimension – although only later did I progress to a much more sophisticated and accurate understanding of how, being so deeply 'inscribed' in literary texts, this dimension influentially informed the structure of the works as well as manifesting itself in their content. And this early education in the politics of literature primed me, I believe, not only for my later studies in the literatures of Wales – literatures that, owing to the long subordinated nature of the Welsh experience, have always been particularly rich in their political implications – but also for my studies of American poetry, and most particularly of the work of America's 'national' poet, Walt Whitman. Hence my insistence, in the opening pages of both of my book-length Whitman studies – no doubt to the continuing bafflement of American readers – on the distinctively Welsh provenance and character of my approaches to his poetry.[14]

My early education in literature also proved foundational in one final important respect. It made me aware of how culturally determined and circumscribed was a reader's response to such texts. This was brought home to me when, having been so excited in sixth form by reading the great Welsh-language novels of Daniel Owen, I frustratedly came to realise, as an undergraduate, that to compare – in a way that seemed so obvious and potentially fruitful to me – Owen with his near-contemporary (and, indeed, literary master) Charles Dickens would be a futile exercise, as my monoglot English teachers would be incapable of understanding the comparison, even if they didn't dismiss it with the amused and tolerant condescension they usually seemed to reserve for things Welsh. Determined therefore as I later became to treat the two literatures of Wales as the discursive products and textual manifestations of a single, partly bicultural, nation, I understood from the beginning that I would be faced with the challenge of contextualising my discussions of Welsh-language texts in a manner that would make my treatment of them both comprehensible and illuminating for my English-language readers.

Such self-indulgent recollections are offered only as preliminary indications of the formative influence of my early personal circumstances on the core structure of my subsequent thinking and writing about Wales, but to continue in like vein would be tedious. It is high time for attention to return to influential formative circumstances of a more general and somewhat more objective kind.

* * *

While a concern to 'pluralise' Wales has remained constant throughout my publishing career, the politico-cultural conditions under which my researches have been conducted have changed dramatically during this period. This is so obviously the case at the level of, say, the development of Wales towards its own national assembly, that it scarcely needs detailed recording. Not so, however, the changes that have taken place at the subordinate level that most immediately affected me, that is at the level of the higher education system of which my work has obviously been the product. And what in particular, I think, might usefully be recorded at this reflective juncture is the seismic shift that has occurred over the last thirty and more years in attitudes from within the academy, as from without, towards the anglophone literary culture of Wales, a shift I welcome because in the Welsh context it represents a shift away from a macrocosmopolitan to a microcosmopolitan approach to literary studies. Such indulgent recollection is, no doubt, a sign that I have now reached the age when, as Goethe put it, a person becomes historical to himself, and 'his fellow human beings become historical to him'.

Over fifty years ago, when I embarked as an undergraduate upon the study of 'English Literature' at University College, Swansea, the body of creative writing produced in English by Wales was known as 'Anglo-Welsh Literature' – a queasy term that perfectly captured the unease felt by Welsh society and the academic community alike as to the character, status and indeed the calibre, of this writing. Grudging respect for Welsh-language literature as the prior and primary voice of historical nationhood, an anxiety (heightened during the turbulent 1960s) not to encourage 'nationalist' sentiment or to dilute British solidarities, and a characteristically provincial unwillingness to believe that Wales could have produced any anglophone writers worthy of serious attention, ensured that society at large scarcely registered the presence of an 'Anglo-Welsh' literature. And such an outlook was fully endorsed by an academic community the confirmed Anglophilia of whose departments of English was significantly amplified by the passionate commitment of key staff members to those imposing cultural values so influentially enshrined in the formidable F. R. Leavis's writings on the Great Tradition of the English novel. English departments across the university sector in Wales were thus proudly wedded to what they deemed to be an enlightened macrocosmopolitan outlook – Leavis even spent a missionary year in the provinces at the University College of North Wales, Bangor, in 1969. Operating in such an environment, I quickly learnt to slight Henry Vaughan's bilingual roots in the Usk valley in favour of treating him as a great European Baroque exponent of English metaphysical poetry, to deplore the gauche provincial garrulity that disqualified Dylan Thomas from serious attention, and to find in Raymond Williams's early work clear evidence of calibre sufficient to make him Leavis's revisionist successor as champion on the world stage of an English cultural nationalism.

Yet, at the same time, I began slowly to intuit a number of things. First, my involvement in the study of American literature made me gradually aware that Leavisite anglocentrism was, in fact, the product in part of post-imperial crisis. All of the fear and hostile resentment of an England fatally weakened by the Second World War was concentrated in Leavis's impassioned anti-Americanism, and insofar as Wales deferentially persisted in identifying with his ostensibly literary evaluations it was also blinding itself to those aspects of its own historical situation that were illuminated much more fully by American than by English literature.[15] Secondly, I began to intuit that some of the Welsh scholars who taught me were, in fact, living a kind of double intellectual life, shyly moonlighting as students (and even as *producers*) of 'Anglo-Welsh literature'. For instance, the lovable Cecil Price (to whom I am personally indebted beyond measure) capitalised on his eminence as a Sheridan scholar of world renown to quietly research the history of the English theatre in Wales, resulting in a pioneering production he was always inclined to dismiss as a whimsical piece of self-indulgence and whose 'real' academic value he was always anxious to disclaim.[16]

Alerted by such an example of 'alternative', 'extra-curricular' scholarly practice I began to reflect on further intriguing evidence of like 'underground' activity. One of Cecil Price's closest friends in academe, I realised, was the flamboyant Gwyn Jones, notoriously authoritarian Professor of English at the University College of Wales, Aberystwyth (and later at University College, Cardiff, where he resisted every suggestion that he lecture on Dylan Thomas, whom he had known, even to the student English Society). A renowned international authority on Icelandic saga, and a stickler for 'Oxbridge' standards of traditional literary scholarship, he had for decades enjoyed a second career as gifted 'Anglo-Welsh' writer and mentor of anglophone writing talent in Wales, not least through establishing and editing the *Welsh Review* during the 1940s. In choosing the liminal zone between creative writing and academic scholarship as his preferred terrain for exploring and practising Anglo-Welshness, Jones was the forerunner of several other key investigators of Anglo-Welsh literature who likewise worked 'off-piste'. These included the two poets and scholar-teachers Raymond Garlick and Roland Mathias, who anchored their own invaluable individual initiatives to the indispensable journal the *Anglo-Welsh Review* that they in effect jointly developed from its tentative beginning as *Dock Leaves* into the major organ of record of a cautiously developing 'Anglo-Welsh studies'. Their strikingly gifted younger contemporary Tony Conran likewise embarked on his career as one of Wales's most distinguished poet-critics outside the walls of the university, despite being appointed tutor in English at the University College of North Wales, Bangor.

Graduating in English from Swansea in 1965 I still had only the very dimmest sense of such formative developments, but it became clear enough over the next decade or more that I was living through a revolution in Welsh cultural history that was being powered by major social, economic and political transformations. Some of these were global in origin as in implication – the final dismemberment of Empire, the collapse of British industrial civilisation, the wave of grass-roots protest movements from the US to Europe, the irresistible rise of popular culture and crisis of 'high culture', the dramatic ethnic diversification of the UK population. Others were local, but often featured the transformation of global trends into Welsh terms: the Tryweryn protests and campaigns of Cymdeithas yr Iaith Gymraeg, the jolt given to the hegemonic British state in Wales by the rise of Plaid Cymru, the violently divisive issue of the Investiture, the evidently terminal decline of industrial south Wales. These and other major fractures to the long-established order led to radical cultural realignments involving, for example, the emergence of a common front between Welsh-language and English-language writers and to conditions seriously favourable, for the very first time in Welsh history, to the development of a bicultural identity. Two publishing events of the mid-1960s helped reinforce this seminal development: *Poetry Wales* was founded in 1965 by Meic Stephens to provide young Welsh anglophone poets with an opportunity to see their work in print, and in 1967 Tony Conran published the *Penguin Book of Welsh Verse*, a revelatory anthology of Welsh poetry from the sixth century to the twentieth in English translation.

The distinctively Welsh version of a 1960s 'counter-culture' was formidably reinforced with the formation by the UK government, in 1967, of an Arts Council for Wales served by a number of discrete art-form committees, of which one of the most financially powerful and culturally influential was the Literature Committee (which I later came to chair). Its director, for almost a quarter of a century, was Meic Stephens, a young poet who proved to be a visionary (if controversial) administrator of inexhaustible determination and energy and insofar as any one person can be credited with having transformed what had been the marginalised cultural phenomenon of 'Anglo-Welsh Literature' into the present-day book industry of 'Welsh Writing in English', it is undoubtedly he. Most of his efforts understandably went on supporting writers and creating a rudimentary publishing infrastructure that respected professional standards in a Wales whose authors had hitherto had to look to London (or occasionally to Dublin) for publication outlets. But Stephens had an acute sense of historical perspective and a sometime-teacher's awareness of the role of the educational sector in fashioning lifelong habits of reading. Consequently, he enabled the establishment of the first bona fide

publisher of Welsh anglophone literature (Poetry Wales Press, subsequently Seren Books), and commissioned and launched an impressive
range of critical and scholarly publications, from the pioneering
Writers of Wales series of monographs to the magisterial *Oxford
Companion to the Literature of Wales* that he himself so consummately
edited. It would not be entirely disproportionate to describe these
initiatives as paradigm-shifting in the context of Wales's apprehension
of its own literary tradition and cultural profile. And the rise in Welsh
academia of a cohort of scholars committed to exploring the anglophone literary culture of Wales would scarcely have been possible
without the enticing preliminary mapping of the field that had been
undertaken under the auspices of the Welsh Arts Council.

In his work, Stephens benefited from earlier initiatives by lone
individuals such as Bryn Griffiths and by Sally Roberts Jones, one
of the key figures in the creation of an English-language section of
Yr Academi Gymreig (The Welsh Academy), the first institution to
appreciate the need to bring significant English-language texts from
the Welsh past back into print, thus anticipating by almost half a
century the flagship *Library of Wales* series launched in 2005 by
the Welsh Government. In the absence of any university literature
specialists competent to edit such texts, the Academi turned to Dai
Smith,[17] a specialist in coalfield culture and lavishly talented young
member of the school of Left-leaning Welsh historians whose emergence during the post-war period had so radically extended and
enriched understanding of the social, political and economic past
of modern Wales. And given the particular interest of many of those
historians in the dramatic history of the South Wales coalfield, attention naturally tended to be concentrated on writers from this richly
congested area.

The 1960s also saw the establishing of courses, and indeed of
departments, of 'American studies' in British universities, a development openly supported by the American Embassy in London, the
newly established Institute for United States Studies at the University
of London (whose founding director was an Aberystwyth-educated
Welshman, Howell Daniels), and covertly by the CIA. As an undergraduate, I myself had profited from such an initiative and subsequent
to my appointment to the staff at Swansea I embarked on a career
that was to result in my establishing my international credentials as
a Whitman scholar and spending two periods as Visiting Professor at
Harvard University. It was at this time that I became fast friends with

one of the founding figures of the great *Library of America* series, the distinguished Americanist Dan Aaron, and it was conversations with him that led later to my recommending to the Welsh Assembly Government that it seriously consider funding a parallel series of classic reprints in Wales to be called *The Library of Wales*. In keeping with several of my contemporaries in Wales I was to find that an acknowledged 'global' status as a 'mainstream' scholar, confirmed by my election as Fellow of the prestigious British Academy, was to provide me with indispensable cover within academe as I persisted in venturing on an otherwise risky maverick second career as a scholar of Welsh Writing in English.

Exactly how disadvantageous such a career might otherwise have proved was brought home dramatically when I very belatedly applied for a Personal Chair. The interview was pleasant enough, apart from aggressive questioning by one Valleys-boy turned 'Oggsford man' (as *The Great Gatsby* acidly puts it) who insisted on suggesting that my record of extensive publication on the literatures of Wales made mine a mere provincial reputation, unworthy of recognition by promotion to his own rank of Professor. It was, I subsequently learnt, only an exceedingly flattering letter of support from Helen Vendler, one of the greatest literary critics not only of Harvard but of the whole of the US, that reduced him eventually to silence.

The embracing of 'American studies' by British universities opened the doors of erstwhile conservative departments of English to the study of literatures in English whose provenance was not England. This later led to a distinction being drawn between 'English literature' and 'english literature', the former being the literature of England itself, the latter being the term coined to describe the literatures in English that had proliferated across the globe in the wake of the decolonisation movements of the post-war period. Such a distinction was in due course to help legitimise, and indeed to 'normalise', the 'english' literature of Wales, and to make it more visible both to the Welsh themselves and to outsiders.

Following on from the craze for things American, the 1970s saw the growth, across the UK higher education system, of 'Commonwealth studies'. The precursor of what later became known as 'postcolonial studies', it provided Ned Thomas, newly appointed as lecturer in the Department of English at University College, Aberystwyth, with an opportunity to smuggle specimens of the anglophone writing of Wales (alongside translations from Welsh-language literature) into a course of study of a kind grudgingly accepted at the time by British universities as legitimate. In so doing, he was capitalising on his impeccable reputation as an internationalist. Multilingual, and a confirmed Europhile with experience of working as an academic on the Continent, he had latterly been the editor of the Russian-language periodical sponsored by the British government as a propaganda tool during the Cold War.[18] Such was the state of cultural affairs in the Wales of the early 1970s, however, that Ned Thomas discovered the Welsh anglophone texts he wanted to include in his Commonwealth literature course were no longer in print. He therefore had to xerox passages from library copies in order to compile booklets for the use of his students. And in Jeremy Hooker, a fine poet and exceptional critic, Thomas found a young colleague who shared his own admiration for the neglected writers of Wales.

Other individuals ventured on similarly innovative ventures elsewhere. At Trinity College, Carmarthen, Raymond Garlick, along with a few colleagues, took advantage of the somewhat more intellectually permissive Training College culture to insert 'Anglo-Welsh' elements into the syllabus, while at St David's University College, Lampeter, Belinda Humfrey extended her core interest in the work of the Powys brothers into a wider preoccupation with selected aspects of the anglophone literary tradition of Wales and was one of the first to add examples from it to the academic syllabus.[19]

It was not until the mid-1980s, however, that literature scholars across the HE sector in Wales set in train a more ambitious programme of interlinked developments resulting from an informal meeting of young academics at University College, Swansea in 1984.[19] The meeting had been convened by me largely at the instigation of John Pikoulis of University College Cardiff's Department of Extra-Mural Studies, its primary purpose being to bring together a small group of young scholars with a view to exploring the possibility of creating some kind of informal professional alliance based on shared interests in the English-language literature of Wales. This resulted in the formation of a 'self-help' organisation that christened itself 'The University of Wales Association for the Study of Welsh Writing in English' (AWWE) of which I served as Secretary.[21] Starved though it was of any financial support and lacking any formal institutional validation, the fledgling association – consisting both of intramural and extramural university staff from across the HE sector in Wales,[22] and consciously appealing as much to a lay as to an academic constituency – nevertheless soon

arranged for a conference to be held annually at the University of
Wales's centre at Gregynog, near Newtown,[23] and entered boldly into
an informal agreement with two presses – the University of Wales
Press and Seren Books – with a view to establishing three series of
publications: one (which I edited) would feature significant creative
texts carefully selected and edited with an eye to the schools market;
another would consist of authoritative scholarly editions of the work
of major authors; and the third would take the form of biographical
and critical studies. It was this major tripartite publishing initiative
instigated by AWWE that was, in due course, to help enable the
prestigious *Library of Wales* project and to pave the way for such
valuable series as *Writing Wales in English* and *Gender Studies in
Wales*.

   In the end, upwards of two dozen books bearing the AWWE imprint
appeared from a number of presses, an impressive body of work to
have been accomplished by what was, in fact, a tiny stage-army of
scholars – no sooner had a scholar exited one side of the stage proudly
bearing a volume than s/he reappeared perforce on the other side of
the stage equipped with a new publication. The first comprehensive
history of Welsh Writing in English, published in 2003, was the cumu-
lative product of all this scholarship and should have been widely
recognised and welcomed in Wales and beyond as a landmark volume.[24]
That it was not was no doubt indicative of the residue of ignorance
– and indeed apathy – that continued to exist not only within the Welsh
academy but also in Welsh cultural circles in general and beyond.

   However, hopeful signs of an incipient change in the intellectual
climate began to appear at the turn of the millennium, most notably
in the form of the recognition for the first time by the UK Research
Assessment Exercise of Welsh Writing in English as a legitimate field
of scholarly activity, and the commissioning by the Welsh Assembly
Government of a review of its programme of provision for the anglophone culture of Wales. This resulted in the award in 2004 of a sum
of a quarter of a million pounds to the Welsh Books Council to
administer an extensive programme of grant-support for the English-
language book industry in Wales. Combined with the smaller sum for
the grant support of English-language literature that had been transferred from the Welsh Arts Council the previous year, this government
investment enabled the Books Council, under my Chairmanship, to
embark on an ambitious, multi-faceted funding scheme that would
totally change the Welsh literary landscape.

From its inception, AWWE had been concerned to introduce and manage a consciousness-raising campaign to increase awareness of Welsh Writing in English both at home and abroad. School visits were organised, with an eye as much to the educating of teachers as of pupils, and eventually Masters courses began to be developed at several university colleges, with the intention of attracting not only postgraduate students but also teachers keen to take advantage of INSET (in-service training) opportunities. Welsh Writing in English began to be recognised, too, at undergraduate level, and later still, postgraduate research was encouraged. A final development was the emergence of specialist centres of advanced research such as CREW (the Centre for Research into the English Literature and Language of Wales) at Swansea (home to both the *Encyclopaedia of Wales* project and *BWLET (Bibliography of Welsh-Language Literature in English Translation)*), to whose growth my late friend and colleague James A. Davies made such a notable contribution; and the R. S. Thomas Centre (Bangor) that has developed into the world's major Thomas archive. The success of this programme of interlinked initiatives in developing a new generation of scholars may partly be gauged by statistics that show that, up to the time of writing, more than sixty doctoral dissertations on Welsh Writing in English have been produced over the last decade or so by the HE sector in Wales.

Particularly worthy of emphasis, perhaps, is the fact that all these developments were the result of ready, friendly, mutually supportive collaboration between colleagues across all of Wales's university system, and that at a time when official UK government policy was to encourage ruthless competition between individuals, disciplines and institutions. But there was one sad, and fateful, occasion, when institutional selfishness won out. When, a decade or so ago, first I, and then (in collaboration with me) Kirsti Bohata, very much with the enthusiastic support of colleagues right across the sector, succeeded in putting together a highly detailed proposal for the establishment of an inter-university, Wales-wide, National Research Institute for the study of Welsh Writing in English – a proposal actually prepared in response to a recommendation by the then Education Minister, Jane Davidson – it was scuppered by the refusal of several key institutions to support it, although it would have brought significant sums of research money (from the Welsh Government's substantial fund to reconfigure HE in Wales) into their respective coffers. Theirs was, I continue to feel, a negative decision of historic significance.

Very much with an eye to internationalisation, AWWE arranged during the 1990s for piratical groups of raiding scholars to descend on international conferences from France, Germany, Luxembourg and Slovakia to the US and Canada, and to deliver a salvo of papers, while tentative working alliances were established with cognate organisations in Scotland and Ireland. Among the long-term consequences of these and other missionary endeavours was the gradual piecemeal establishment of leading figures from AWWE in influential roles within the academic and cultural sectors in Wales, a development that facilitated the 'normalising' and 'mainstreaming' of what had begun as very much a suspect programme of peripheral studies. And, of course, the training, over some three decades, of several cohorts of talented young scholars meant that Wales was provided for the first time with the means of developing a spectrum of approaches to its anglophone literary culture consonant with the exciting diversification of critical discourses and analytical paradigms that characterised contemporary literary studies worldwide. Crucial to this latter development was the establishment (1995) by AWWE of a specialist journal – the *Yearbook for Welsh Writing in English*[25] – that, under the impeccable stewardship of its founding editor, Tony Brown, established new standards for literary and cultural criticism in Wales.

The *Yearbook* was, in a way, a companion to the *New Welsh Review*, the literary periodical the Association had co-founded a few years earlier in 1988 (in partnership with the English-language section of Yr Academi Gymreig) under the scrupulous editorship of Belinda Humfrey. As, with the passage of time, that periodical gradually inclined more towards creative writing than critical discussion, Association members began to feel the need for a new, scholarly, publication. The launch of the *Yearbook* satisfied that need and over the next twenty years the journal went on to contribute very substantially to the professionalisation of the study of Welsh Writing in English and to the related development of a cadre of academic specialists well versed in contemporary critical discourses.

Under the auspices – in the most relaxed and hospitable of senses – of an AWWE that has by now matured into a multigenerational fellowship of mutually supportive scholars, the professional study of Wales's anglophone literary culture has been steadily and quietly transformed. Among the most spectacular of the consequences have probably been the revelatory uncovering of a substantial body of writing by Welsh women, indicative explorations of Wales's bicultural past and present, and the increasingly confident examination of Welsh writing in a global perspective. Not that there isn't far more work yet to be done. Indeed, the study of Welsh Writing in English remains very much at an inaugural stage. Even before one allows for the certainty that the rising generation of young scholars will determine its own unguessable priorities and will set its own distinctive agenda for research, there are so many enticing subjects and resources already staring today's salaried academics in the face – for instance, the National Library of Wales's extensive and valuable holdings of authors' manuscript collections remain virtually unexplored, as does the Library's rich archive of radio features, scripts, plays and poems by Wales's anglophone writers of yesterday; the transformative contribution to literature made by key institutions such as the Welsh Arts Council and the Welsh Books Council has yet to be properly registered, let alone properly evaluated; there has been no sustained attempt made to determine Wales's place in the cultural reconfiguration of the 'British Isles' as an 'Anglo-Celtic Archipelago'; nor has the process of disentangling the complex implications of the traditional embeddedness of Welsh Writing in English in an Anglocentric 'British' literary tradition even begun as yet.

That there is a deficit of like magnitude when it comes to the institutionalisation of this important area of study becomes glaringly apparent the minute one begins to consider the situation in Ireland and Scotland, neighbouring countries that officially recognise their respective literary traditions as a global asset and ensure that the study of native literatures at both school and university level is not only encouraged but actively facilitated and financially supported. In stark contrast, neither the Higher Education Funding Council for Wales nor the Welsh HE sector is in any way expected, let alone obliged, to safeguard and develop the academic study of an anglophone literary culture that contributes so seminally to the national profile of present-day Wales, while the challenge of 'normalising' the study of Welsh Writing in English in the schools of Wales has yet to be properly confronted and fully met.

And then, there is the crucial issue of the future of the University of Wales Press, the nation's sole academic publisher, without whose encouragement and support the revelatory cultural scholarship of the last thirty years would not have been possible. Publication, after all, not only remains a vital means of disseminating research, it is also a vital stimulus to research. Cynically deserted by the academic institutions that should be cherishing it for its distinguished past record and eager to exploit its potential, and casually abandoned by scholars intent on their own short-term interests rather than the wider, long-term cultural good, the Press currently faces a struggle to survive. It is a daunting and dismaying prospect.

* * *

Refracted through the prism of the body of research enabled by AWWE (and almost exclusively published by UWP) over the last three decades, the anglophone literary culture of Wales has by degrees revealed the full spectrum of its colours of saying. And it is that valuable ongoing process of intra-cultural diversification that has provided context, precedent and incentive for the sample essays that are collected in this volume. In miniature form, they mirror the multivalent readings of the culture that have characterised the wide-ranging scholarship developed under the auspices of AWWE. Thus, hopefully, they instance, albeit within a narrowly limited compass, the microcosmopolitan character of a small country.

Notes

1   Jan Morris, *Wales: Epic Views of a Small Country* (Oxford: Oxford University Press, 1984).
2   Michael Cronin, 'Global Questions and Local Visions: A Microcosmopolitan Perspective', in Alyce von Rothkirch and Daniel Williams (eds), *Beyond the Difference: Welsh Literature in Comparative Contexts* (Cardiff: University of Wales Press, 2004), pp. 186–202.
3   M. Wynn Thomas, *Internal Difference: Literature in Twentieth-Century Wales* (Cardiff: University of Wales Press, 1992).
4   M. Wynn Thomas, *Corresponding Cultures: The Two Literatures of Wales* (Cardiff: University of Wales Press, 1999); M. Wynn Thomas (ed.), *DiFfinio Dwy Lenyddiaeth Cymru* (Caerdydd: Gwasg Prifysgol Cymru, 1995).
5   M. Wynn Thomas, 'Ewtopia: cyfandir dychymyg y Cymry', in Geraint H. Jenkins (ed.), *Cymru a'r Cymry 2000: Wales and the Welsh 2000* (Aberystwyth: Centre for Advanced Welsh and Celtic Studies, 2001), pp. 99–118.
6   M. Wynn Thomas, *In the Shadow of the Pulpit: Literature and Nonconformist Wales* (Cardiff: University of Wales Press, 2010).
7   M. Wynn Thomas, *The Nations of Wales, 1890–1914* (Cardiff: University of Wales Press, 2016).
8   There are ten volumes in this valuable series in all. See particularly my introductory essay to Hywel Teifi Edwards (ed.), *Yn gymysg oll i gyd* (Llandysul: Gwasg Gomer, 2003).

[9]   See Charles Nicholl's fascinating study *The Lodger* (London: Penguin, 2008).

[10] M. Wynn Thomas (trans.), *Dail Glaswellt, Walt Whitman* (Llandysul: Gwasg Gomer, on behalf of Yr Academi Gymreig, 1995).

[11] Momaday's *House Made of Dawn* must be one of the greatest American novels of the twentieth century.

[12] James Joyce, *A Portrait of the Artist as a Young Man* (London: Penguin, 2000), 2005.

[13] In my judgement, the best study by some distance on this subject is that by Kirsti Bohata, *Postcolonialism Revisited* (Cardiff: University of Wales Press, 2004), based on a doctoral thesis completed under my supervision.

[14] M. Wynn Thomas, *The Lunar Light of Whitman's Poetry* (Cambridge, MA: Harvard University Press, 1987); M. Wynn Thomas, *Transatlantic Connections: Whitman U.S., Whitman U.K.* (Iowa City: University of Iowa Press, 2005). The latter devotes a chapter to the reception of Whitman's poetry in Wales.

[15] See 'America: Cân fy Hunan', in M. Wynn Thomas (ed.), *Gweld Sêr: Cymru a Chanrif America* (Caerdydd: Gwasg Prifysgol Cymru, 2001), pp. 1–29. See also the Preface to M. Wynn Thomas, *Transatlantic Connections: Whitman U.S./ Whitman U.K.*

[16] Price was, however, one of the first 'English' academics in Wales to supervise doctoral work on 'Anglo-Welsh' authors, including the American Kent Thompson's pioneering study in the mid-1960s of Dylan Thomas's Swansea, and Sandra Anstey's groundbreaking examination of R. S. Thomas's poetry and prose in the mid-1970s. And, also at Swansea, Désirée Hirst was an early enthusiastic champion of the 'Anglo-Welsh' credentials of David Jones and an admirer of Emyr Humphreys. At Cardiff, Terence Hawkes published occasionally on Anglo-Welsh writing, while R. George Thomas produced some perceptive essays on R. S. Thomas, and also specialised in the poetry of Edward Thomas.

[17] Coincidentally, Dai Smith was later to become Editor of the *Library of Wales* series.

[18] Ned Thomas, *Bydoedd: Cofiant Cyfnod* (Tal-y-bont: Y Lolfa, 2010).

[19] As late as 1986, the study of Welsh Writing in English across the HE sector was limited to the following: 'one undergraduate course at Aberystwyth and occasional postgraduate theses; no undergraduate courses at Bangor, though with the occasional MA thesis; no teaching in the field at the Department of English at Cardiff, some in Extramural teaching; at Lampeter, which under the guidance of Belinda Humfrey was very much a path-finder in the field, there was some provision at both undergraduate and MA level; at Swansea there was some teaching of Welsh Writing in English in the context of modern literature, a (new) special author course on Dylan Thomas and a recently introduced MA scheme.' Information drawn from the History of the Association compiled by Professor Tony Brown for the AWWE website.

[20] I am deeply indebted to my friend Professor Tony Brown for sharing his 'A Short History' of AWWE with me, and for his advice in the writing of this Preface.

[21] At that time, there was but the one, federal, university in Wales. As a new, plural, HE sector began to be developed, the Association renamed itself 'The Universities of Wales Association for the Study of Welsh Writing in English', which was later shortened (1996) to 'The Association for Welsh Writing in English'.

[22] Notable figures in this connection were Tom Thomas, English Tutor in the Extra-Mural Department at University College, Swansea and Wyndham Griffiths, English Tutor in the Extra-Mural Department at University College, Swansea. The latter became an active member of the Association and, along with his close friend and colleague Tom, organised a number of internationally successful Dylan Thomas Conferences at Swansea during the mid-1970s. One of the young students who attended these conferences was Mark Abley, who went on to considerable fame as a writer in his native Canada.

[23] The first conference was held in 1986.

[24] M. Wynn Thomas (ed.), *Welsh Writing in English* (Cardiff: University of Wales Press, 2003).

[25] This was rebranded under subsequent editors, first as *Almanac* and then (and currently) as the *International Journal for Welsh Writing in English*.

1

THE SCARLET WOMAN: LYNETTE ROBERTS

Lynette Roberts and Keidrych Rhys were married in Llansteffan on 4 October 1939. The very same month her poem 'To Keidrych Rhys' was published in *Wales*, the brash harlequinade of a literary journal established and edited (up to this particular number) by Rhys, her colourful, buccaneering, incorrigibly errant new husband. 'I have seen,' she there declared with a bardic claim to omnipresence that later, no doubt, she would have recognised made her unconscious kin to the ancient Taliesin, legendary poet-prophet of her adopted country,[1]

> light birds sailing
> A ploughed field in wine
> Whose ribs expose grave treasures
> Inca's gilt-edged mine; . . .
> I have seen, the mountain of pumas
> Harbour a blue-white horse.
> The tinsel-rain on dogs coat
> Zebra shoes at night.[2]

It reads like an ecstatic epithalamium, while its title, 'To Keidrych Rhys', seems also to turn it into a gift-giving ritual: a bride's ceremonial public display of her lavish dowry. That dowry, as the poem makes clear, is all the exotica of her 'foreign' imagination. And it is this largesse, in all its richness, that is again flaunted in the 'Poem' she published in the next (Winter) issue of *Wales*:

For my house is clothed in Scarlet.
Scarlet my household, Scarlet my mind, spiced herbed and cherished,
     all alcoves wine
Laughter in corners, winks on air chasing shadows on ceiling bruins in
     lair.
Plush lacquered incense, open flowers on wall, frothed milk bread and
     honey to overcome falls
So come myth children, no longer fear, the winter is impotent under
     my care
For my house is clothed in Scarlet.[3]

Roberts had already lived an extraordinary life, peripatetic, adventurous
and not just international but intercontinental. From the beginning,
the solid privileges and comforts that were hers thanks to her Welsh
Australian father's career as manager (and later director) of Argentina's
Western Railways had been offset by his rather louche, freewheeling
personal conduct.[4] A family life supportive enough but rather rickety
and improvisatory had been permanently destabilised by the early
death of her mother. Thus partly, perhaps, in self-defence, Roberts
early developed a restless, daring, unconventional spirit of her own.
Resilience and adaptability had been hard-wired into her. As a girl,
she'd survived sleazy boarding houses; as a young woman in Buenos
Aires, she'd acted as her father's companion on formal occasions while
also holding her own 'soirées' for artists and intellectuals; in London,
she'd dabbled in bohemia yet acquired diplomas for interior decoration,
completed Constance Spry courses in flower arranging, and run her
own florist business.

     There is therefore, in retrospect, something rather poignant about
this defiant poem by a gutsy autumn bride about to start her married
life at the outbreak of war in a damp, cold, bleakly windy corner of
rural Wales, in a tiny stone cottage with an earthen floor. At least she
had her 'myth children' to comfort her and to nourish her imagination,
and from these she was to draw some of her solace in the challenging
years ahead. But at times it was hard. 'I feel chequered with energy',
she noted in her journal in the spring of 1940: 'Full of positive red
squares and black negative ones. What shall I do?' (*DLR*, 8). And
later that March, she recorded, 'The wind was cold. I drew my scarlet
cape around me and walked leisurely, as village people do' (*DLR*, 9).
It was an early attempt to adapt herself to her locality; to adopt its
normalities (that leisurely walk) for camouflage, but without entirely

repressing her creative energies – that defiantly scarlet cape which she took to wearing on all her walks became a blazon of her quietly scandalous internal difference, as did the 'scarlet letter' of Hester Prynne in Nathaniel Hawthorne's celebrated novel. The poetry of the next few years was to show her devising strikingly original strategies of adaptation that would guarantee the creative survival of her singular identity.

In the same, October, issue of *Wales* that saw the publication of his new wife's 'study in scarlet', Keidrych Rhys published a poem of his own, 'The Van Pool, Tichrig'. Which 'Van' he had in mind isn't entirely clear – *fan* (*ban* in its original, un-mutated, form) being simply the Welsh for 'peak'. A 'peak' is *y fan* ('f' in Welsh being the 'v' sound in English), and the Brecon Beacons peaks that loom over Keidrych Rhys's native district of the Ceidrych valley are known in Welsh as *Bannau* (plural of *ban*) Brycheiniog – the Breconshire peaks. But there is one *b/fan* adjacent to the localities identified in Rhys's poem that stands out in popular imagination as in cultural memory, along with the pool at its base. The latter is known as Llyn y Fan Fach ('the lake of the small peak', a neighbouring peak being named Y Fan Fawr ['the great peak']). Attached to the spot is a well-known and greatly loved legend; that of the Lady of the Lake. She it is who lived under the pool's waters until she was wooed ashore by the entrancing rhymes of a young shepherd, whom she duly agreed to marry. Together they had several sons, but she had warned her human husband at the outset of the strange unbreakable conditions on which their unlikely alliance was based, and when, somewhat unthinkingly, he broke each of these in turn over a period of years, she sadly gathered about her all the cattle she had brought out of her native depths as dowry and departed back to the waters from which she had briefly emerged.

Whether Rhys, who wrote several poems about the 'Van pool', actually had that specific lake and its legend in mind is immaterial. What is significant is that Lynette Roberts was to become enchanted by it. Noting this, critics and commentators have, unfortunately, been led so suppose that 'Hal-e-bant, Fan Fach', in the poem 'Plasnewydd', is an allusion to the tale. It is not. 'Fan' (abridgement of 'Fanny') was a very common name for a Welsh sheepdog, and in her Carmarthen-shire diary Roberts specifically mentions that her great friend and neighbour, Rosie Davies, had two sheepdogs, 'Fan and Tips' (*DLR*, 64). The phrase in the poem is therefore a record of the everyday instruction to a sheepdog, Fan (*fach*, 'little', being simply here a form of endearment akin to 'dear'), to *hal e bant*, 'send [or shoo] him [cow, sheep or naughty cat, *"pussy drwg"*] away.' After all, for the incomer Roberts the mundane minutiae of Llanybri constituted a new exotica.

No, the significance of the Llyn y Fan legend probably went much deeper with Roberts than that. Could she have failed to recognise key aspects of herself in the tragic, seductive figure of that fey, faery lady? In that denizen of a strange, alien, beguiling world? Didn't that instinctive early gesture of presenting herself to her husband and his world at the very moment of her marriage as a 'scarlet woman', a visitor from a distant, foreign, scandalously opulent world, come to rhyme eerily in her ears with the story of the ill-fated Lady? Might it therefore not prove prophetic of a similar fate for herself? And might not her poetry bear witness to her predicament? What follows is a reflection on precisely such possibilities.

* * *

The poem with which Lynette Roberts announced her mature arrival as 'Welsh' poet to the world could scarcely have been more different than 'To Keidrych Rhys'. Her first collection, *Poems* (1944), opens with 'Poem from Llanybri', a title that designedly and deservedly represents Roberts as grounded in her adopted village. In it, she – who had lived in the village for less than two years – confidently presents herself as an insider, a native well versed in local customs and thoroughly (even nonchalantly) au fait with the patois; indeed as someone already 'authorised' to act as the confident voice of her community and to speak on its behalf. Hers is an impressive impersonation – for such it surely is – of cultural authority. But fully to appreciate its performative aspects and to value its complex, hard-earned, achievement one needs to acquaint oneself with writings by Roberts of an entirely different kind and place: those related to her earliest years in Argentina. It is, after all, no coincidence that the collection that opens with 'Poem from Llanybri' draws to a conclusion with a suite of poems about South America, before ending with a return to Cwmcelyn. As she noted in July 1941, 'I have a backward glance at the Argentine[,] my father and Mechita [where she was born]. I start a series of poems which were written here in Tygwyn but they are a South American group' (*DLR*, 218).

'Here are cucumbers in flower, tomatoes and sweet-corn,' she noted in her journal on 13 July 1941, 'but in my home – the South American home – we have bee-like humming-birds, flamingos wandering in the paddock, white peacocks, and the sun's resilient rays' (*DLR*, 37). No doubt sensitised anew by such nostalgic recollection, her eye was caught just two days later by the scarlet that seemed always to take her back in imagination to Argentina, prompting her to plan a 'Poem on Moorhen and its scarlet garters' (*DLR*, 8).[5] She had nevertheless settled into her Welsh village with impressive resolution, had already grown to love aspects of life there, had started to master, through hard physical labour, some of the important skills and crafts of subsistence country living, and had begun to investigate her physical surroundings with a formidably 'scientific' analytic and forensic thoroughness even while appreciating its aesthetic and compositional aspects, brilliantly registering its characteristic forms, colours and textures with an artist's subtlety and sensitivity.

With the passing of time, she obviously came to feel real solidarity with the locals, and in particular to value the 'sisterhood' of women, strengthened by wartime conditions when, as she discovered through her own experience, they were left to survive traumas, from childbirth to bombing, while struggling to keep body and soul together not only for themselves but for their whole families. It was this practical experience of tough woman-power that led her, on VJ day, to declare angrily that 'War will continue until women become freed from slavery . . . it will exist until they become no longer the slaves of men but their leaders towards a preservation of life' (*DLR*, 69). And her campaigning identification with her subjugated gender, implicit in many of the poems in her 1944 collection, strengthened her inclination to identify with the Welsh as a subjugated people (*DLR*, 69). Her poetry was designed to promote liberation on both fronts.

Yet the value of Llanybri lay for her in its abiding, irreducible 'foreignness'. To the last, she remained what sociologists would label 'a participating observer'. To the very end she had to work hard to 'read' the locality– indeed omnivorous reading became an indispensable means, alongside constantly heightened observation, of gaining a clarity of understanding. And clarity was, for her, not just a passion but a consuming craving. She demanded of herself exactness of verbal and perceptual definition – her writing was underpinned by an obsession with classification and categorisation that led to her autodidact's love-affair with all the 'ologies' – anthropology, mythology, etymology, entomology, geology, mineralogy, ornithology, lepidopterology and several more. Her appetite for clarity understandably made her impatient of the vague 'Celtic Twilight' maunderings of Ernest Rhys, that irrepressible veteran of the 1890s (as well as unlikely friend of Whitman, Yeats and Pound) who turned up on her doorstep like a cheerful, irresponsible tramp.[6]

Her taste for dispassionate precision was no doubt in part inherited from her engineer father – she inclined to treat poems not as organic secretions but as complex functional assemblages, rather as he must have viewed railways. But it may also have owed something to her early exposure to the clarity of Argentinian light, particularly in the region of the Andes. She commented with characteristic exactitude on the contrasting light of Wales, when mist and soft rain suddenly lifted and creatures, things and objects, caught in a 'magnesium light', stood out as if elementalised, washed clean of all superfluities:

> The rain, the continual downpour of rain, may also compensate us indirectly, by giving us that pure day which precedes it . . . During those intervals the rain water is reflected back to us through a magnetic prism of light . . . Here, then, in Wales, we frequently get three concentrations of light, where normally most countries only have two. This third eye, or shaft of light, gives us the same privilege as many of our scattered islands hold, which are devoted to the Saints. That light magnifies, radiates truth, and cleanses our dusty spirits. (*DLR*, 130)

She also valued the way the slow tempo and leisurely rhythm of life in a rural community enhanced awareness of every detail of ordinary living (*DLR*, 64). And then there was the contrast with the 'rich, mellow tones of English farmhouses', that meant she, like other English visitors, felt 'estranged and left singularly apart' (*DLR*, 128). She even felt that, in its clear-cut geometrical forms and simple colours, the village of Llanybri resembled a Cubist painting: 'the sharp outline of the whitewashed farms and houses as they stand against the skyline; the way in which the walls project geometrical planes of light that resemble the still life-life models of squares and cubes' (*DLR*, 127).

Like Hopkins, Roberts revered the sacred quiddity and inscape of bird, stone, leaf and flower, and, again like him, she came to believe that the strict-metre poetry of traditional Welsh *barddas* was perfectly consonant in its 'hardness' and disciplined exactitudes of sound and metre with the society and landscape to which it was truly 'native'.

She came to view traditional Welsh rural crafts and architecture in the same 'light'. There was percipience in her early comment that the poetic form of the Welsh *englyn* – which she proceeded to approximate in English – was 'itself like the village, like a piece of quartz' (*DLR*, 5).

The foreignness of Llanybri was, then, indispensable to her creativity. While empathising strongly with a village community in which 'every home [is] a separate unit of the nation's culture' (130), she was aware of the secretiveness and peasant tricksiness of her neighbours. 'The continual subjugation of the Welsh by conquerors has made them distrustful of strangers', she noted sympathetically: 'They have grown accustomed to using their wits' (*DLR*, 69). Even as the village genuinely became a deeply loved home, it was not entirely 'my home', which was still 'the South American home'. In the summer of 1941 she could still feel 'lonely and homesick for the Argentine' (*DLR*, 37), recalling the pampas, the Incas' mountain grave, her railway-engineer father, the great River Plate region, the convent where she was educated, and Mechita where she was born. 'I had the strong desire', she frankly admitted, 'to leave the village and go to South America.' A year earlier, she had confessed to feeling 'cramped and barred from life', 'tired of reading *The Western Mail* every day. The only news from the outside world. I'm tired of reading the poems of puny poets and want to do something. Something. I don't know what' (*DLR*, 9). The fall of France in the summer of 1940 had prompted a revealingly impassioned response:

> I felt like running off to France and selling my British status. And I could do this, since I held an Argentinean Passport and could demand protection from the Argentine Embassy. If it were not for the understanding and knowledge of most of the people here in Llanybri, there and everywhere, I would REBEL and mightily. The villagers are superb in thought and action, and strangely enough there is considerable unity in their thoughts and approach to the war. They are far more intelligent and efficient than most of the ways and means of Parliament. (*DLR*, 17)

A prison Llanybri could seem at times for her spirit –some of the locals even briefly suspected her of spying – even as it was becoming a refuge and a place of sanity in a mad world, and a catalyst of creativity. Even in Llanybri, the New World was ever present at the deepest levels of her being, although it was not until war's end that she explicitly began to address the formative significance of her native South America in her writings.

* * *

Her sensuous memories of Argentina retained an almost hallucinatory intensity for Roberts ('Memory widens your senses', she was later suggestively to write of her New World recollections), partly perhaps because her periods of living there were ephemerally brief and partly because they marked emotionally charged experiences in her family life. Her heightened powers of sensuous attention and recall were in any case always the most stunningly impressive aspect of both her personal life and her creative imagination. 'One of my earliest memories', she wrote in her bewitching radio talk on the origins of her South American poems, 'was to wander out of the gate and stare at the South American pampas.' 'The New World', she hauntingly admitted, 'with its strange subtlety absorbed me with its vivid impressions, the spinning windmills irrigating the *quintas*, and as the corrugated containers filled with water, I bathed in them within shadow of the peach trees' (*DLR*, 107).

But these impressions were not simply filed away in memory to be retrieved as nostalgia, they actively informed her responses even to Llanybri, eventually finding issue in her creative work. The suite of powerful poems included in her 1944 collection offer overt evidence of this. But more intriguing, if less arresting, are the examples available in the same collection, as in her journal, of more covert forms of indebtedness to her South American past. Later, in her radio talk, she was to place on public record her indignation at what was happening to the traditional life style of the 'peasants/peons' of her native land.

> The small *pueta* where people lived with their horses tethered to the wooden posts outside their shacks, their songs, knife-fights, guitars, the dark shadows of the peons cast as they gamble behind clouds of dust as the horse race took place. These were and still are at the root culture of the Argentine soil. So when the thatched roofs were torn down and corrugated roofs placed in their stead and values were placed on the wrong issues, I rebelled and wrote to establish belief in these people in my poem called 'The New World'. (*DLR*, 108)

That poem, published in her 1944 collection, opens by evoking the original life of the peons, before they were forced first to flee 'unwanted further on into the land'. There, where 'Spiders lifted the lids of their homes and slammed them back' – the detail is taken directly from her own earliest memories of the dusty end-of-the-line township of Mechita where she was born – 'they strove, the harder not to be seen'. But to no avail. Modernity, in the form of a rapacious capitalism, caught ruthlessly up with them:

> Lost now. No sound or care can revive their ways:
> La Plata gambles on their courage, spends too flippantly,
> Mocks beauty from the shading tree, mounts a corrugated roof
> over their cultured hut. (*CP*, 29)

The anger in these lines was magnified when her uncomprehending London editor asked her to alter the phrase about the corrugated roof, because

> it was so ugly. He did not see that that was the purpose of the whole poem. The *estancias* were being sold or mortgaged and the money drifted into the Casinos at La Plata. The peon or gaucho and the land were left in despair. (*DLR*, 109)

In 1872 the gaucho's colourful, violent style of living had been famously glorified by José Hernandez in *Martín Fierro* (1872/1879), the 'national epic' that came to be regarded as epitomising 'the root culture of the Argentinean soil'. And Roberts's memories of both gauchos and peons were themselves clearly rooted, as her radio talk shows, in a very small child's frustration at having been debarred from knowing more about their tantalisingly close but mysteriously 'other', seemingly 'authentic' and 'indigenous' world.

In fact, as we can now see, her 'instinctive' sense of that world's 'otherness' had a cultural provenance. She grew up within the extensive immigrant, settler, community of an 'Anglo'[7] professional class and was thus very largely isolated not only from the indigenous cultures but from the dominant Hispanic culture of the country. Her response to the countryside, even, was mediated by the works of enormously influential 'Anglo-Argentinian' writers like W. H. Hudson, to whose books Hispanic as well as British children were routinely introduced at school. In this respect, her positioning within Argentina was, like her situation in Llanybri, largely that of a participating outsider.[8] And the Eurocentricity of her outlook is everywhere marked.

It had, of course, been a common practice of European artists and intellectuals for two centuries to attribute sterling, precious, even redemptive qualities to a 'peasant' existence, valued for its supposed 'authenticities'.[9] But in Roberts's case such an ideology had a distinctive individual relevance and a corresponding intensity that made it a valuable creative asset. As we shall see, her sympathy with the dispossessed peons and gauchos fed into her gradual awareness that the Welsh – particularly the 'peasant' Welsh-speakers of Llanybri and the rest of rural Wales – were a long-subjugated people, their traditions variously threatened by mummification, barbaric modernisation and obliteration.[10] Her empathy with their plight also fed into her poetics, central to which was the attempt at a sympathetic melding of old and new.

But it was not only the peons and gauchos of Argentina with whom she imaginatively identified. An interest in the native peoples is manifest in an interesting poem she wrote for radio about a notable incident in the early history of the Welsh colony in Patagonia. In 1863, eighteen years after the first landing in Puerto Madryn, four young men from what was still at that point an exclusively coastal settlement ventured prospecting along the Chubut river. Two of them penetrated inland some four hundred miles, as far as the Andean foothills, where a couple of Araucanians (members of the indigenous ethno-cultural group nowadays known as the Mapuche) alarmed them with an invitation to visit their encampment. Rapidly retracing their steps, they had almost reached the safety of the settled region when they were ambushed. One of them was killed, but the other, John Evans, managed a Douglas Fairbanks escape by frantically spurring his horse into a prodigious leap across a canyon and then making his solitary way back through desert storms to the colony. Glyn Williams, a modern authority on the Welsh in Patagonia, has set the incident in context:

> This was the first sign of hostility by the native people against any member of the Welsh Colony in eighteen years of contact. There had been several occasions when they had expressed dissatisfaction with the Welsh occupance of their territory, but the evidence suggests that any threat of hostility by one of the groups against the Colony resulted in discussion by one of the other groups. The probable reason for this lies in the cruel genocidal campaign carried on against the native people

independently by both the Argentine and Chilean armies between 1879 and 1885. It has been suggested that the Indians were a group of Northern Araucans who were driven south by the military and took the opportunity of strengthening the Argentinian harassment.[11]

It was to this episode, relayed to her by Cadvan Hughes, the son-in-law of John Evans, that Roberts turned when, at the end of the war, she began to consider ways in which she might put her childhood experiences in Argentina to creative advantage. Rejecting as too hackneyed the idea of a book of memoirs, she resolved instead to write a ballad about the Patagonian story, but 'in it of course [to use] many of my own memories, as a background, or reconstruction of the event' (*CP*, 112). She itemised some of the sensuous recollections of the pampas she particularly wanted to record:

> The quality of the thistles which they used for fuel and making rennet, their hollowness and crack, seeing iguanas as they flashed past from before the horses' hoofs, the legends, the racoon that I found on my dressing table, and who later was found curled up in sleep on my bed, the nutrias in hundreds, and flight, colour and song of the myriad birds, these I wanted to recreate. (*CP*, 112–13)[12]

As for the ballad form for which she opted, she undoubtedly appreciated its origins as a 'peasant', 'folk' form and its long history of local storytelling. But, given her enthusiasm at this time for the old 'Welsh penillion' (simple stanzas of folk experience and wisdom to be sung to harp accompaniment) she may also have felt the ballad provided a rough but acceptable English cultural equivalent. 'I still have an ardent PASSION for *penillion*,' she wrote to Graves in 1947, 'I want to write *penillion* . . . I believe it is the most authentic and most wholesome material from which to build up any rural poetry. It is never sentimental in its original state' (*DLR*, 185).[13] And, since the poem makes explicit mention of Hernandez's *Martín Fierro* ('O ghost of Martín Fierro save us' [*CP*, 122]), it is further possible she may have felt the ballad form had a 'folk' pedigree and popular authority corresponding to the *payados* of the '*gauchesco*'.[14] Indeed, the most adept because best adapted of the four Welsh adventurers whose story she tells is specifically commended for having learnt gaucho skills: 'He looked the gaucho in "wide awake" hat, / And lived that life as a guide' (*CP*, 119). In her autobiography, she specifically associated her ballad with the gaucho figure. Noting that a friend had sent her a record of native music for use in the radio broadcast of 'El Dorado', she added, 'He also sent a very large book of national Gaucho implements which has been very useful' (*DLP*, 203). Given this mixture of sources, then, she may have viewed her ballad as a fruitful cultural hybrid; a mix of Welsh, English and Argentinian cultural forms; a creative blend of Old World and New.

That the poem connected Lynette Roberts to her earliest childhood in a particularly intimate way is underlined by its concluding with an old Spanish lullaby 'which my mother in Mechita sang to me' (*CP*, 113). She likewise identified strongly with the first Welsh settlers of Patagonia – although her personal wish to 'identify' as Welsh (if only partially) was a recent phenomenon, the product of her stay in Llanybri. It was evidently important for her to establish that the friendly relations the Welsh enjoyed with the native tribes marked them apart from the Spanish, and for that matter the English. The band that attacked the four Welsh prospectors are clearly identified as a maverick group of avengers, outraged by the wholesale slaughter of natives by General Julio Argentino Roca and his forces during the infamous genocidal 'Conquest of the Desert'. In pointed contrast, Roberts gives pride of place to one of the colonists' key 'myths of origin', as related by Davies:

> 'Not long ago when we lived in caves,
> And Indians stood bare . . .
> From nowhere . . . My father spoke:
> The Chief stood back with care.
>
> Suddenly the Indian's wife bent down,
> And with thorn and thread as sinew,
> Without a word Father's trousers tacked
> And repaired the tear as new.' (CP, 121)

The Patagonian equivalent of the Pocahontas story, this episode serves much the same purpose: it suggests that in welcoming the Welsh, the native tribes implicitly bestowed a blessing on their invasion of the land. And in highlighting this 'myth',[15] it is as if Roberts is claiming that same blessing for herself, in the name of the 'Welshness' she supposedly shared with those first settlers. Hers, thus, becomes an authentic, primal relation to the land, 'innocent' of the stigma of violent misappropriation that marks the relationship to it of colonists like the Anglos and the Hispanics. In this way, the Welsh connection helped assuage the guilt she felt at the possibility of having been, if only by virtue of the white skin that bespoke her Europeanness, complicit in the seizure of the land from its original populations. Had she not read as a girl 'that the Incas if they shot a white man buried him upside down' (*DLR*, 195)?

Not that Roberts's interest in Patagonia was entirely nostalgic. On the contrary. She concluded her radio broadcast on the Welsh connection with an impassioned plea for contemporary Wales to pay attention to what had been achieved in the face of substantial odds in 'Y Wladfa', because there was so much to learn from the courage, adventure, resources and enterprise of the early settlers. Broadcast in 1945, her comments therefore applied in part to the immediate post-war period. But by then her six-year stay in Llanybri had made her aware of a far older, indeed seemingly chronic, malaise of the Welsh psyche, a lack of self-confidence that was the consequence of 'continual subjugation . . . by conquerors', as she perceptively put it in a diary entry that same year (*DLR*, 69). As a result, she remarked in her broadcast, 'Wales seems oppressed partly through her own misdirection, and partly through outside jurisdiction' (*DLR*, 133). A concentration on Welsh Patagonia 'would help to extend [the country's] vision, which at the moment, through suffering, has become too parochial. An exchange, I believe, on all matters, such as agriculture, political and cultural, would stimulate and help both countries to develop.'

This (liberating) concern to bring out the international dimensions and connections of Welsh life both past and present finds interesting creative issue in Roberts's poetry. The grandiose pseudo-scholarship paraded by Robert Graves as he constructed his own ingenious personal poetic mythography in a series of articles that culminated in *The White Goddess* appealed greatly to her, as the sustained correspondence between Graves and herself confirms. His fanciful narrative seemed to 'prove' that ancient Wales had been firmly linked in to a mythic pathway that had extended along the seaways and trade routes all the way through the Mediterranean to the Aegean and onwards to India, the source of all Indo-European cultures. Ancient Welsh legend and poetry everywhere bore covert testimony, he claimed, to this esoteric international 'songline', in which was encoded the primal secret religion of the 'White Goddess', whose priests were the Druids and whose initiates were the bards.

Roberts's poem 'The Circle of C' is one in which she connects herself as Llanybri poet to this supposed tradition, since her consciously 'bardic' imagination, having been initiated into Graves's secret lore, perceives the 'C' of 'Cwmcelyn' (and of 'cinder' and 'curlew', both words that play a key role in the poem) to be a letter from the sacred 'tree alphabet' of the Celts.[16] Cwmcelyn Bay thus reveals its hidden Druidic aspects to her. Accordingly, she assumes the role of a devotee and petitions the powers instinct in the sacred landscape to grant her prophetic insight so that she might foresee the fate of her lover (Keidrych Rhys, then away on war duty guarding the east coast of England). The Delphic answer she receives is, of course, full of dark foreboding and delivered against the background of the baying of the 'Dogs of Annwn' (the Celtic underworld). The 'C' of the title seems also to refer to the belief she shared with Graves that the travels of the magical 'White Cow' (emblem and emissary, so to speak, of the White Goddess) traced a 'circular route' (168). And her belief in the sacred significance of the letter surfaces again when, in her essay on 'Village Dialect', she mentions 'a reference by Giraldus to the circular dance of the Welsh and this is from his *Itinerarium Kambriae*, 1188 AD' (120).

The estuarine situation of Llanybri, which features so prominently not only in 'Cwmcelyn' but in her major poem 'Gods with Stainless Ears', fitted in perfectly with Graves's theories, since the myths that were the carriers of the White Goddess religion travelled along the ancient sea routes. Roberts homed in on *Finnegans Wake* because it made mention of the 'Celtic' link between the Liffey and the Towy: 'Joyce . . . linked up the close mythology and dialect between the peoples of Eire and Wales – the Liffey – "Towy too"' (*DLR*, 119). All this accorded well with Lynette Roberts's own deep respect for the sea, dating from her early experiences of ten transatlantic journeys between Britain and South America. 'For the British born in the Argentine', she wrote, 'there are many voyages', and in 'Seagulls' she captured the nexus of experiences that was, for her, the essence of these trips. Describing a typical stopover en route at a port in the Canaries, the poem artfully encapsulates the ambivalences of feeling about land and sea. While the former offers the stability of ties, those ties take the form of the greedy locals who come alongside in their rowing boats only to fleece the voyagers by selling them shoddy 'bargains'. As for the sea, that is wistfully associated with the 'seagulls' easy glide' but also viewed queasily as 'an ocean of uncertainty'(*CP*,17).

Elsewhere, as if seeking for a magical sea route that would connect
Argentina to Llanybri through a transatlantic extension of the White
Goddess trail, she makes an interesting suggestion in a letter to Graves
about the possible meaning of a phrase from a famous boast by the
legendary poet, magician, priest and shape-changer Taliesin:

> What puzzles me is what does he mean by I was born 'Under the region
> of the summer stars'. As the legend carries the tale in various versions
> that he was shipwrecked & found in a coracle, or like Moses cradled in
> reeds, I have often wondered if it may have meant under the Southern
> Hemisphere or tropical stars. (*DLR*, 173)

Partly motivated by stories like this, Roberts thoroughly researched
the history of the Welsh coracle. Fascinated by its continuing use in
the Llanybri vicinity during her period there, she campaigned strongly
for the modest 'industry' it served to be publicly supported. She also
wanted it to take advantage of modern synthetic textiles and for
coracles to be 'machine-sprayed with ICI plastics' (*DLR*, 136). But
at the same time her passion for the coracle was steeped in her poet's
sensitivity to the numinous aura by which the little 'primitive' craft
had, over many centuries if not millennia, come to be invisibly haloed:
'The coracle men working on the rivers, the play of magic, ritual,
superstition, prophets of the sky and foretellers of the ocean bed,
these attributes remained a force in their trade, both for their gain
and their protection' (*DLR*, 69).

Her deep wish to connect Argentina to the Celtic world of ancient
Wales is again manifest in her Patagonian ballad 'El Dorado', when
Parry, one of the four young Welsh adventurers, imagines he sees a
'Welsh' horse in the wild herd that descends on them, almost trampling
them underfoot as it sweeps madly past:

> And that white
> Horse with the black mane
> Ears, fetlock, muzzle and tail,
> Is surely a Dynevor strain.

The white cattle (with red ears) of Dynevor Park, Llandeilo, are
reputed to date back to the ninth century and the period of Rhodri
Fawr. Associated with them are various legends, such as their use in
Druidic sacrificial rituals, and the special protection accorded the

breed in the tenth-century Laws of Hywel Dda – supposedly confirming
the sacred status the cattle had enjoyed in Celtic culture, as evidenced
by mentions in old Irish saga. Lynette Roberts's letters to Graves
include meditations on the significance of white creatures in Celtic
legend and literature, particularly when combined with red (or russet)
ears, as in the story of Pwyll, Pendefig Dyfed in the *Mabinogion* (*DLR*,
168).

* * *

Lynette Roberts, then, partly 'read' Llanybri through Argentina, just
as she came retrospectively to 'read' Argentina (for example the
settlement of Patagonia) partly through Llanybri. Hers was a hybrid
imagination – no wonder she was so taken with the universal village
practice of making *pele* (Welsh for 'balls') for burning on the fire. A
mixture of coal dust, clay and water (Roberts provides the 'recipe' in
great detail [*DLR*, 7]) the *pele* seemed to her perfect for burning in a
homely hearth. And she was similarly attracted to the mixed, or hybrid,
in her own poetics. A simple, striking example of her ambition to fuse
the New World with the Old is provided by one of her early poems,
'Rhode Island Red'. Not only does the very breed of the chicken
advertise its (North) American origins, in using the phrase 'Song of
joy I sing' to render the crowing of the cockerel, Roberts deliberately
invokes the Poet Laureate of both North and South America, Walt
Whitman. But rather than use a 'New World' poetic form, Roberts
turned to what she (wrongly) thought of as an English equivalent to
the Welsh englyn, a form she admired for its brevity, pithiness and
intricate system of internal alliteration and assonance.

One of the deepest of the interests that were consonant with her
hybrid imagination – the question of how paradoxically to respect
traditional cultures by modernising them, thus changing in order to
'conserve' – seems to have been born of her childhood anger at the
way the traditional life of the peons was being crassly disfigured and
thus effectively erased through the *wrong* kind of modernisation,
inflicted on them as the River Plate conurbation rapidly expanded.
But her anger was brought into sharp focus by her Llanybri experience,
because within months of settling in the village it became clear to her
she was confronting an unacknowledged crisis: 'the imposition of a
bourgeois and shallow town culture forced on their wholesome ways.
That is why I have such an interest in the village of Llanybri. I see

that in the future it will be forced to change for the worse' (*DLR*, 17). This remained her unwavering opinion throughout the years she lived and worked there, and still vibrating through her (increasingly nuanced and sophisticated) concerns may be felt the anger of the child recoiling from the horror of what the River Plate was doing to the peons. Also from the very beginning, she was very clear that protecting Llanybri did *not* mean fighting to preserve the status quo of the 'traditional'. Adaptation to the modern was not only inevitable it was highly desirable. But first it was necessary to identify and evaluate that which was distinctive and invaluable about not only the village but the whole locality and culture of which it was a part. The thoroughness and industry with which Roberts applied herself to the task of educating herself in this matter, even while raising three children virtually alone in a tiny cottage with minimum facilities, is as humbling as it is impressive. She had no water on tap and lived off the produce of back-breaking labour in her small, simple kitchen garden. That hers were the researches of an undirected autodidact and led her to rely on nineteenth-, and even eighteenth-, century sources that were unreliable when not wildly wayward was not her fault. And in any case such sources may have in some ways served her very well, since what a poet needs in order to assemble enabling fictions and effective operating systems is very different from the aims and purposes of a scholar.

Not only did she familiarise herself with the traditional architecture, crafts, dialect and literary culture of Llanybri and its environs, she also studied its natural habitat, becoming versed in local flora, bird, butterfly and animal life. And she went much further, exploring anthropology in order to understand the prehistory of human settlement in Wales, and further seeking to map the village and its environs in deep time by understanding its geology and mineralogy. In an aside to Robert Graves that throws interesting light on 'Gods with Stainless Ears' and highlights the committed hybridity of her imagination she comments 'Today [1944] we need myth more than ever: *but not blindly,* only in relation to its scientific handling: in relation to today. You will help us here – just as David Jones is helping us with his paintings'[17] (*DLR*, 169). And in a crucial passage from her Carmarthenshire diary she makes clear her wish to produce, through a creative fusion of different forms of knowledge, a psychically healing, holistic, re-integrative vision of the world:

The entomologists may learn the names of hundreds of insects entirely through their study of larva breeding and imago feeding. The ornithologist may notice the shape and leaf of trees; and when studying water birds in particular, the names of shells cast on the shores, the small fish rippling on the water-scales of the tide. And so, whether we are conscious of it or not, the intense and penetrating study of any of these branches in the field of a naturalist will in the end grow, until it covers an area of the whole field. Sky, plant, tree, animal and soil strata included. And in this way a natural conclusion and unity is reached, which politics, industrial problems and scientific research cannot achieve. (*DLR*, 62–3)

'Gods with Stainless Ears' can perhaps be read as a war requiem for the death, by grotesque distortion, of some such aspirational vision as this; as a terrible miscarriage of her lovingly conceived hybrid imagination. In a letter to Graves she explained she'd 'purposely set out . . . to use words in relation to today – both with regard to sound (i.e. discords ugly grating words) & meaning' (*DLR*, 181).[18]

The following single brilliant detail, not from the poem but from a prose fragment vividly describing the terrible 1941 raids on Swansea as seen from Llanybri, must suffice to illustrate the process at work:

A collyrium sky, chemically washed $Cu.DH_2$. A blasting flash impels Swansea to riot! Higher, absurdly higher, the sulphuric clouds roll with their stench of ore, we breathe naphthalene air, the pillars of smoke writhe, and the astringent sky lies pale at her sides . . . Alarmed, we stand puce beneath another flare, our blood distilled, cylindricals of glass. The raiders scatter, then return and form a piratic ring within our shores. High explosives splash up, blue, white, and green. We know all copper compounds are poisonous, we know also where they are. (*DLR*, 103)

The active interest Roberts had developed in mineralogy as part of her holistic surveying of Llanybri and its peninsula heightened her awareness that, for more than a century, Swansea had been one of the world's greatest metallurgical centres, and consequently dubbed 'Copperopolis'. The poisonous fumes emanating from the maze of great works had already blighted the landscape of the lower Tawe valley by the time a new petrochemical plant at Llandarcy was added to the deadly mix, and it's this new component that Roberts probably had in mind when referring to naphthalene (an organic compound with the formula $C_{10}H_8$) produced by the petroleum-refining process. Specific reference is twice made ($Cu.DH_2$, copper compounds) to the copper industry for which the town was most famous. Particularly powerful is the envisaging of a malign 'collyrium' (normally a harmless eye-wash) that consists of a 'chemically washed' copper. The metallurgical theme is continued through reference to the blue crystal cyanite – an aluminium silicate. And of course following the three-night Blitz of 1941 the area is smothered in the poisonous clouds of sulphur dioxide released. A response to the violent disintegration of a whole landscape, the whole passage is therefore a darkly parodic version of the holistic, integrative vision Roberts was so hopeful her hybrid imagination might achieve in Llanybri.

One interesting question that will have to be postponed to some other occasion is how far hers was, in spite of all its good intentions, essentially a 'colonial' incomer's relationship with the village. As has already been noted, hers had after all been a 'settler' consciousness, virtually from her birth. One prominent aspect of Roberts's otherwise conscientiously thorough self-education in the cultural mores of Llanybri was her seeming lack of interest in even attempting to learn Welsh at a time when most of the villagers struggled with English as a decidedly 'second' language. But that Roberts came to value what she somewhat perversely, and perhaps tellingly, persisted in calling the 'Kymric' language is unquestionable. She not only scolded the English for routinely excluding Welsh-language literature when purportedly surveying the history of literature in the British Isles,[19] but implicitly rebuked the Welsh themselves for needing to travel to distant Patagonia before they could muster up the courage to treat their language as vigorously living rather than moribund and dying. And she certainly made attempts to familiarise herself with Welsh-language poetry, from the very beginning of the great strict-metre tradition of *barddas* (in the process actively experimenting with the englyn form, for example [*CP*, 83]) to significant contemporary poets such as R. Williams Parry. And, acknowledging the work of W. J. Gruffydd, Dyfnallt and others in her notes to 'Gods with Stainless Ears', she adds that 'I have intentionally used Welsh quotations as this helps to give the conscious compact and culture of another nation' (*CP*, 76). Yet she seems not to have been particularly concerned to learn the Welsh language by which she was daily surrounded.

Instead, her passionate concern (fuelled by her memories of the River Plate peons) for the kind of innovation and adaptation that alone could ensure that what was valuable in 'tradition' was made meaningfully available to the present and, in suitably modified form, transmitted to the future, concentrated on a host of other signature cultural practices, customs, products and artefacts of her immediate locality. The dynamic figure leading the rural conservationist movement in the Wales of the period was the prominent ethnographer Dr Iorwerth Peate, at that time working towards establishing an open-air folk museum at St Fagans on the progressive Scandinavian model (*DLR*, 128).[20] While significantly influenced by his classic study of *The Welsh House* (1940), Roberts was concerned his conservationism might be misunderstood either to license the wrong kind of modernisation, or to promote resistance to every form of adaptation for contemporary use. She herself clearly and repeatedly argued for the courage to 'experiment and to build with the most up-to-date materials . . . provided it harmonises with the surrounding rural architecture' (*DLR*, 129). Hence her attack on the reactionary ruralism of the likes of 'Professors, who seem to live backwards anyway' (*DLR*, 51). 'Tradition can be evil', she insisted, 'when the root of its repetition is associated, as it is so much today, with FEAR' (*DLR*, 52). She wanted small-holdings to have fresh water on tap, electricity, spacious kitchens, dry walls and solid floors. The fruits of 'modern research and scientific knowledge' should be used for 'the good purpose of humanity', and not used – as in the bombing of Swansea – for evil, destructive ends.

Her 'Argentinian' instinct to associate creativity with hybridity and to understand tradition as harmonious change is thus apparent in her attitude towards both the practical affairs of rural life and her poetics. Indeed, by 1952 she was urging Welsh writers in both languages to find new forms of creative synthesis 'before the particularities of the Celtic imagination are once again submerged in an Anglicised culture' (*DLR*, 142). In retrospect, it can be seen that her own poetry had constituted exactly such an enterprise – the prefacing of the different sections of 'Gods with Stainless Ears' with epigraphs from Welsh-language poetry both old and new was calculated both to instance and to emblematise the kind of creative synthesis she already had in mind in the early 1940s.

'I grow [vegetables in wartime] for Llanybri, for Llanybri that I love and that has given me so much' (*DLR*, 21). Touchingly, Lynette Roberts was 'putting down roots' in the village as early as June 1940, just eight months after her arrival there. Yet she was fated ever to be as much 'scarlet woman' as 'native'. Significant aspects of her consciousness had, after all, been formed by Argentina. Her passion for 'deep time' and its human equivalent – Tradition – obviously owed much to an unconscious awareness that, although she herself was indeed 'native' to Argentina, her parents had only very recently migrated there, a late example of the great waves of European migration of peoples to the country during the nineteenth century. She had no claim on the 'aboriginal past', such as she came to feel in Llanybri. Likewise, her understanding of 'Tradition' as itself always, at any given point, 'hybrid' in character – the moment when the past meets the future and is modified by it – obviously owed much to her own peripatetic life, and the experience of searching for some meaningful form of continuity in the face of constant, restless change.

Her situation as 'Llanybri' poet is thus symbolically captured in an observation she recorded in her diary on 18 May 1942:

> I noticed a large splash of brilliant scarlet, a secretive flight from tree to tree until whatever it was hid deeper and thicker among the leaves. This sudden sensation of flight in colour disturbed me considerably . . . I had no idea what this could have been. It was so large. The Scarlet Cardinal in Buenos Aires, yes I had seen many of those, and flights of wild emerald green paraquets, but this vivid flash[?] (*DLR*, 44)

It turned out to be a great spotted woodpecker. Lynette Roberts's attachment to scarlet, always bringing with it memories of her South American 'home' – she entitled one of her most evocative poems about the vast plains of the pampas 'Blood and Scarlet Thorns' – had once more creatively sharpened her eye for her immediate surroundings in her new Welsh 'home' of Llanybri. 'While she was dying, in rural Wales', her daughter Angharad Rhys has movingly written, 'she kept reverting to Spanish – though not her first language it was the language of her childhood' (*CP*, x).

(To be published in Siriol McAvoy [ed.], *Locating Lynette Roberts* [Cardiff: University of Wales Press, forthcoming].)

Notes

[1] In her essay 'An Introduction to Village Dialect', she quotes one of Taliesin's famed boasts: 'I have been in the ark,/ With Noah and Alpha,/ I have seen the

destruction of Sodom and Gomorra,/ I was in Africa', etc. Patrick McGuinness (ed.), Lynette Roberts, *Diaries, Letters and Recollections* (Manchester: Carcanet, 2008), p. 108. Hereafter *DLR*.

2   First published in *Wales*, 10 (October 1939), 278–9. It is reprinted, but under the title 'Song of Praise', in Patrick McGuinness (ed.), Lynette Roberts, *Collected Poems* (Manchester: Carcanet, 2005), pp. 81–2, where it is mistakenly identified as first appearing in *The Welsh Review* in October 1939. Hereafter the *Collected Poems* will be cited as *CP*.

3   *Wales*, 11 (Winter 1939–40), 302. Reprinted in *CP*, p. 82.

4   From the very beginning of the construction of the extensive Argentinian rail network British engineers and shareholders had played a dominant role in its development. Rails, locomotives and rolling stock were likewise usually of British manufacture. And when the Western Railway Company was formed in 1855, its Vice-President, David Gowland, was a Briton. Roberts therefore grew up largely within an expatriate, 'Anglo' community.

5   Duly written, the poem was included in her first published collection, *Poems* (1944) (*CP*, 16). In it, she rejoiced that 'shocking the air/ With scarlet bill and garter' –the word 'shocking' is there surely charged with the village reception of the scarlet-caped Roberts herself – the water-bird could 'draw a wreath of joy/ From our pale receded hearts'.

6   At first she found the vivacity of the 'old, old, man' who had turned up unannounced 'bubbling over with joy', invigorating and entertaining (*DLR*, 12). But she quickly grew annoyed at 'the mock Celtic Twilight' era at the turn of the century of which he was by then the lone survivor, because 'he was still caught up in its aura when he met us, and, frankly, this nauseated me' (*DLR*, 13).

7   'Anglo', but by no means exclusively English. As well as representatives of all the nations of the British Isles, it also included 'colonials' such as Roberts's Cambro-Australian parents.

8   Although she, along with a friend, briefly held salons for writers, artists and intellectuals in Buenos Aires around 1930 – 'No English just Argentines were invited – philosophers, psychologists, journalists' (*DLR*, 202) – there is no evidence she was aware of the exciting new developments in contemporary Argentinian literature. At that time, *Modernismo* was being replaced by a new wave of writing perhaps most strikingly instanced in the work of the writers (who included the young Bórges) associated with the *Ultraísmo* movement. She makes clear her indebtedness to European (and specifically English) writers when writing of Patagonia in her essay on that region, where she singles out not only W. H. Hudson for praise but also A. F. Tschiffely's *This Way Southward* (*CP*, 130).

9   'If we do not listen to the rural wisdom of the common man we shall be a lost nation', she wrote in June, 1940. What was dangerous alike in capitalism, Socialism and Communism was the 'imposition of a bourgeois and shallow town culture [which] is forced on their wholesome ways. That is why I have such an interest in the village of Llanybri. I see that in future it will be forced

to change for the worse' (*DLR*, 17). In her further belief that 'the dignity and pride of the craftsmen and farm labourers should be permitted to prevail . . . I do not mean the retention of arty crafty work of the past', she was echoing, as she shortly discovered, the sentiments of respected Welsh ethnographers of the time such as Dr Iorwerth Peate (see below). She was also – as again slowly became clear to her – championing the cause of *y werin*, the reputedly devout and naturally cultured 'folk' of the rural, Welsh-speaking heartlands, whose way of life had come to be heavily idealised by such influential scholars as Sir O. M. Edwards. His classic *Cartrefi Cymru* ('The Homes/Hearths of Wales') became a huge popular success and contributed to the cult of the Welsh rural village, the ramifications of which are brilliantly analysed by Hywel Teifi Edwards in '"Y Pentre Gwyn" and "Manteg": from Blessed Plot to Hotspot' (in Alyce Rothkirch and Daniel Williams (eds), *Beyond the Difference: Welsh Literature in Comparative Perspectives* (Cardiff: University of Wales Press, 2014), pp. 8–20). Roberts's essays 'An Introduction to Village Dialect' and 'Simplicity of the Welsh Village' fit squarely into this cultural milieu.

[10] She believed the 'peasant' class to be an international phenomenon, and so easily set Llanybri in the context of her experiences elsewhere, including Argentina and Spain. Similarly, she believed this class of 'people of the soil' shared a vocabulary: 'in certain idioms there can be found relationships between peoples of the soil elsewhere; in Spain, Ireland, Italy, France, Iceland, Brittany' (*DLR*, 123).

[11] Glyn Williams, *The Desert and the Dream: A Study of Welsh Colonization in Chubut, 1865–1915* (Cardiff: University of Wales Press, 1975), p. 104; also Glyn Williams, *The Welsh in Patagonia: The State and the Ethnic Community* (Cardiff: University of Wales Press, 1991). There are several interesting differences of detail between the version of the episode recorded by Roberts and her informant and that offered by modern historians such as Williams.

[12] It would be interesting to compare Roberts's version of Patagonia with that of Eluned Morgan, a Welsh Patagonian born and raised in Gaiman, whose *Dringo'r Andes* (1904) is a classic account of her subsequent journey across the desert to the high mountains.

[13] In the notes to the *Collected Poems*, 'Penillion' are mistakenly described as a form of *barddas* (classic traditional strict-metre poetry). Around this time, the penillion were attracting much interest from such eminent Welsh-language writers and scholars as T. H. Parry-Williams, who produced an authoritative scholarly collection of them and wrote a poetry influenced by their colloquial rhythms and vocabulary. In addition, they fascinated 'Anglo-Welsh' poets such as Glyn Jones, who highly valued them as a 'people's poetry' and eventually translated a body of penillion into sprightly, rhyming English verse.

[14] *Gauchesco* (or 'gauchesque') writing, claiming to use the 'real' language of the gauchos themselves, flourished roughly between 1870 and 1920. It would therefore probably be very much 'in the air' when Roberts was a child.

[15] Recent scholarship has expressed considerable scepticism about such Welsh Patagonian claims to 'exceptionalism'. An underplayed history has been

uncovered of tensions between the native peoples and the Welsh settlers, and emphasis has been placed on the much wider history of colonisation of which the Patagonian venture was demonstrably a part. For instance, the extension of the Welsh settlement as far as the foothills of the Andes, that constituted the epic second phase of the venture, was a multinational enterprise financed by business interests in Buenos Aires. And this aspect of inland development is unconsciously prefigured in Roberts's ballad as, far from being innocent idealists, the four Welsh adventurers are hard-headed gold prospectors, whose values contrast strikingly with those of the natives on whose territories they trespass. Interestingly, Roberts's *Notes for an Autobiography* records an early personal experience of the difference between immigrant white and native Inca attitudes towards gold (*DLR*, 195).

[16] Graves was drawing upon the theories for the origins of Ogham outlined by R.A.S. Macalister in *The Secret Languages of Ireland* (Cambridge University Press, 1937). Macalister was later to revise his own theories which, while still predictably popular in neopagan and New Age circles, have not found support among later serious Celtic scholars. Both Graves and Roberts were also in thrall to the writings of that enthusiastic Druidophile, Edward 'Celtic' Davies (1756–1831).

[17] The affinities between Roberts's poetry and that of Jones remain to be explored thoroughly, as does her obvious respect for his work. She spent much of her time visiting T. S. Eliot in his Faber office in London recommending Jones's work to his attention and urging him to pay a visit to the recluse. (A deeply appreciative review of *In Parenthesis* by Vernon Watkins – 'unique writing' – had appeared in *Wales*, 5 [Summer 1938], 184.) Both Roberts and Jones shared a passion for reviewing and restructuring present experience in the light of 'deep time' and, in naming their son 'Prydein' (the old Welsh name for Britain – 'Prydain' in modern Welsh – favoured in medieval chronicles lamenting the loss of much of the Island to foreign invaders), Roberts and Rhys seem to have been signifying their own sympathy for Jones's vision of a modern post-imperial Britain that, no longer arrogantly Anglocentric, would be a genuine confederacy of all the peoples of the Island.

[18] Given Roberts's own admission that, in structure and texture, her long poem owed something to contemporary film, it might be interesting to compare 'Gods with Stainless Ears' to a classic groundbreaking documentary of the period, *Listening to Britain*. Directed for the Crown Film Unit by Humphrey Jennings and Stewart McAllister, and released in 1942, this is a highly atmospheric montage of the sounds and sights of Britain at war, without any linking voice-over commentary.

[19] '[T]here has been practically no acknowledgement of Welsh Literature in the past. This lack of recognition in the History of English [*sic*] Literature has yet to be adjusted' (*DLR*, 106). Such omission resulted, she added, in a 'tragic deformity'.

[20] For a highly informative account of Peate, his vision and his accomplishments, see Catrin Stevens, *Iorwerth C. Peate* (Cardiff: University of Wales Press, 1986).

2

MARGIAD EVANS AND EUDORA WELTY: A CONFLUENCE OF IMAGINATIONS

'I hate my writing and nearly everyone else's.'[1] Margiad Evans's bullish comment, recorded in a brief profile of her as a writer that appeared in Keidrych Rhys's rumbustious magazine *Wales* in the summer of 1938, shouldn't be taken too seriously. After all, she proceeded to claim that her only reason for writing was so as to be able to buy paintings and to enjoy country pursuits, an explanation that is unlikely to survive even brief enquiry. Her provocative statement is very much in keeping with the tone of Rhys's *Wales*, a self-consciously outrageous publication. Anxious to cultivate a cavalier image, it aimed to convey the ungovernable, irreverent spirit of a group of young Welsh Anglophone writers uncowed by their elders and indifferent to the metropolitan judgements of the English establishment. But the sharply discriminating reviews Evans occasionally contributed to periodicals of the period, such as *Wales* and the *Welsh Review*, confirm that hers was a fierce, demanding, and finely discriminating, literary intelligence.

There were, though, writers who readily survived even her most searching scrutiny. Kate Roberts was one such and another, according to Ceridwen Lloyd-Morgan, was the great writer from the Mississippi delta, Eudora Welty. In noting that the 'writers who earned [Evans's] unconditional praise were from outside the English metropolitan circle', Lloyd-Morgan identifies Welty as 'one of her great favourites'.[2] She particularly relished the 'power and fury' of the Southerner's prose, and Lloyd Morgan ventures to suggest that 'Welty may perhaps have had some influence on Margiad Evans's stories', noting possible 'stylistic affinities' between them and those by Welty collected in her 1943 collection *The Wide Net*.

Lloyd-Morgan's point is well made, but that term 'influence' is often much too glibly applied to relationships between writers without any awareness being shown of the complex, irreducibly nebulous and incorrigibly problematical character of the *kind* of relationship towards which the word vaguely gestures. Writers' notorious shyness of being cornered by such a term is no doubt partly due to their understandable wish to 'cover their tracks' – like skylarks, they prefer to take flight at a distance from their precious nests. But equally, like any reflective person, they understand how difficult it is to determine where, when and how any deep, unforeseen impulse of affinity originates. Who could possibly tell, as Wordsworth powerfully enquires in *The Prelude*, what portion of the river of one's mind comes from what source? After all, as Paul Klee otherwise imaged it, the relationship between a creative work and its 'sources' resembles that of a tree to its manifold, tangled roots: who would ever claim to be able to trace any given branch back to its origins in a single root?

Eudora Welty herself had forceful and subtle things to say about such matters. Commenting on the structure and texture of her own writings in her revealing memoir, *One Writer's Beginnings*, she thoughtfully observed:

> Each of us is moving; remembering, we discover; and most intensely do we experience this when our separate journeys converge. Our living experience at those meeting points is one of the charged dramatic fields of fiction.
>
> I'm prepared now to use the wonderful word *confluence*, which of itself exists as a reality and symbol in one. It is the only kind of symbol that for me as a writer has any weight, testifying to the pattern, one of the chief patterns, of human experience.[3]

Elsewhere in the same essay, she further glossed that term 'confluence', explaining that by it she had in mind

> a writer's own discovery of affinities. In writing, as in life, the connections of all sorts of relationship and kinds lie in wait of discovery, and give out their signals to the Geiger counter of the charged imagination, once it is drawn into the right field. (*OWB*, 99)

Furthermore, she insisted that such 'confluence' occurred only at those deeply solitary points when a mind paradoxically descried echoes of its own singular uniqueness in the mind of another, and was thereby quickened into new creation. 'What counts', she wrote of herself as a writer, 'is only what lies at the solitary core' (*OWB*, 101): only through the mysterious experience of confluence could such a core be penetrated and impregnated while somehow remaining virginal, pristine, inviolably itself.

In making such comments, Welty had in mind not only the kind of interconnective relationships within families and communities that she, as a writer, found herself exploring in her works, but also her analogous relationship with other authors, to whom she felt deeply indebted for enabling her own creative development. Two contemporaries whom she habitually called to mind in this context were William Faulkner and Virginia Woolf. And taking our cue from Welty's suggestive remarks, it would seem appropriate to consider Margiad Evans's interest in the Southerner's fiction under the rubric not of 'influence', but rather of 'confluence', as Welty interprets that term, because 'influence' is a concept that lends itself all too readily to the simplistic assumption that one writer passively absorbs what is 'learnt' from another, and is thus in danger of failing to take into account the shock of augmented self-recognition that is always a major aspect of a writer's unexpected, creatively responsive awakening to the work of a kindred spirit. Such, it seems to me, is the most interesting aspect of the relationship one perceives between the fiction of Evans and Welty.

* * *

In instancing what she means by Eudora Welty's 'influence' on Margiad Evans, Ceridwen Lloyd-Morgan points to a common concern with 'stories about working people in disadvantaged rural communities . . . told in a superb literary style' (*OY*, 4). But what I have termed 'confluence' operates at an altogether deeper and more radical level than that. It manifests itself in the singular manner in which both writers handle 'place' in their respective fictions. Both of them arrestingly, and indeed often disconcertingly, view human beings and their locales simply as different points on a single continuum: between them they constitute a single, highly distinctive, 'zone of consciousness' and it is this that both Welty and Evans recognize as constituting 'place'.

How instinctive this kind of vision was to Margiad Evans may be neatly illustrated by homing in on a small detail of a remark she made during the course of her otherwise routine review of *Old English Household Life*, an unremarkable study by Gertrude Jekyll and S. R. Jones. 'I have only to lift up my eyes to see one of the objects illustrated,' she observed, 'a white, earthenware horse who with us stands on the dresser, and is dusted every alternate Friday.'[4] This very peculiar choice of the word 'who', rather than the customary 'that' or 'which' used to denote an inanimate object, is a signature feature of Evans's strange, distinctive, style of vision and of narration. Such a disorienting, or rather re-orienting, use of 'who' prepares us to read the whole phrase – 'who with us stands on the dresser' – in a similarly unconventional way, understanding it now to be suggestive of the (earthenware!) horse's living, creaturely coexistence with its human 'owners': it is together and between them that ornament and people may be said to turn the house into a place of habitation. This offers us an insight into the peculiarity of Margiad Evans's 'places', where individuals repeatedly seem not so much alive to their world, or even alive in their world, but rather alive *with* their world, as their world, in its turn, seems alive with them.

Similar moments abound in Eudora Welty's classic 'autobiography of a writer', *One Writer's Beginnings*:

> In a children's art class, we sat in a ring on kindergarten chairs and drew three daffodils that had just been picked out of the yard; and while I was drawing, my sharpened yellow pencil and the cup of the yellow daffodil gave off whiffs just alike. That the pencil doing the drawing should give off the same smell as the flower it drew seemed part of the art lesson – as shouldn't it be? Children, like animals, use all their senses to discover the world. Then artists come along and discover it the same way, all over again. (*OWB*, 10)

Again, where others would distinguish between the inner world of human experience and the outer world of environment, Welty, like Evans, sees only a correspondence so intimate as to bind both together into a single complex, compound entity.

In such a context, it is not surprising to find her further noting that 'In my sensory education I include my physical awareness of the word' (*OWB*, 10). Elsewhere, in a review, she approvingly noted that 'the imprisonment of life in the word was as much a matter of the sense with Virginia Woolf as it was a concern of the intellect'.[5] 'Held in my mouth,' Welty recollected in *One Writer's Beginnings*, 'the moon became a word. It had the roundness of a Concord grape Grandpa took off his vine and gave me to suck out of its skin and swallow whole, in Ohio' (*OWB*, 10). A word here becomes an essential means of ingesting the world, and is thus central to the celebration of the communion of human beings with their intimate environment. And a similar aliveness to language is used to related effect in Margiad Evans's quirky writing. In 'Thomas Griffiths and Parson Pope', the old gardener 'smoked all the time. The wind, passing him, went away with the swirling blue breath of his pipe. The wind would jump suddenly down into the garden and shuffle the yellow ivy leaves out of the side-paths . . . The sky looked through one blue eye' (*OY*, 27). The human being and his environment form a single, undifferentiated, animated environment and language is a veritable incarnation of this peculiar experience of 'location'.

For both Evans and Welty, words are the synapses, or vital connect-ives, of the single, composite consciousness shared by people and the objects, creatures, natural forces and growing things of a unitary, inter-animated world. To read their fictions is to enter a realm not so much of cohabitation as of 'coexistentialism'.[6] The term was coined by Gaston Bachelard, the remarkable French phenomenologist who understood that 'the imagination is ceaselessly imagining and enriching itself with new images. It is this wealth of imagined being that I should like to explore' (*PS*, xxxvi). To that end he wrote the suggestively entitled *The Poetics of Space* (first published as *La poétique de l'espace* in 1958), declaring his concern to be with elaborating 'a phenomenology of the imagination' (*PS*, xviii). To study 'the onset of the image in an individual consciousness', he argued, 'can help us to restore the subjectivity of images and to measure their fullness, their strength and their transubjectivity' (*PS*, xix). Poetry was, for him, incomparably rich in such evidence, and a similar claim might usefully be made for the value of studying the compressed, 'poetic' short fictions of Eudora Welty and Margiad Evans.

While avoiding any sustained and systematic application of Bachelard's ideas, this essay will make occasional, adventitious use of his deeply suggestive insights. And it will do so not on the tacit assumption that these insights are somehow impartially authoritative but rather on the understanding that the climate of mind one en-counters in Bachelard's influential work is, in a sense, that of a particular era, approximately the first half of the twentieth century, during which the minds of Eudora Welty and Margiad Evans were also decisively shaped and they were unconsciously developing their deep, mentally formative assumptions. These two writers seem to me to have shared with Bachelard the legacy both of Symbolism and of Modernism, with their respective disclosures about the processes of consciousness, and to have operated, like him, on the same wavelength as such powerful thinkers of the period as Henri Bergson, Karl Jung and the originator of phenomenology, Edmund Husserl. But since the elective form of Welty and Evans was short fiction rather than Bachelard's poetry, to the love they shared with him for the mysterious potencies of symbol and image they added an excited addiction to story, tale, fable, legend, talk and myth. And whereas his subject was really the solitary soul – he rather effusively understood poetry to be 'a soul inaugurating a form' (*PS*, xxii) – their fascination was with the highly charged, dangerously electrified, web of 'community'.

* * *

Bachelard described his intention as being to conduct a 'topoanalysis', by which he meant 'the systematic psychological study of the sites of our intimate lives' (*PS*, 8). Central to his researches therefore was the figure of the house, because 'the house image would appear to have become the topography of our intimate being' (*PS*, xxxvi). Houses also figure prominently as psychic signifiers in the fiction of both Evans and Welty.[7] One notable instance is afforded by 'The Old Woman and the Wind', the short story that may surely be accounted one of Margiad Evans's most perfect accomplishments, beautifully shaped as it is to her compelling purpose and supercharged with several of her most intimate concerns. Through the vexed and varying relationship of the strange old hill-dweller Mrs Ashstone with the wind on the one hand and the villagers below on the other, Evans was able to explore the dialectical relationship between the wild and the domesticated, the contained and the boundless, between communal living and the solitary individual, and she herself no doubt oscillated between similar poles of her own, in her strange oddity of being a somewhat suspect female writer, semi-detached from the community around her and inclined to feel much closer kin to the natural world than to her immediate neighbours. Her ambivalent feelings about her imperious creative powers are mirrored in Mrs Ashstone's misgivings about her extraordinary relationship with the wind, and in the latter's allegedly 'witch-like' nature is suggested Evans's uneasy interest in the socially suspect powers of an unconventionally minded female artist of her time.

The story is brimful of perfectly functional examples of her perpetu-ally startling lyricism, faithful as the text is to the strange originality of her habitual angle of vision. Mrs Ashstone's house, like her very being, exists strictly in a dialectical relationship with the wind that is the presiding, defining presence of her life as it is the dominating presence in her environment. Its invisible plastic power is every-where palpably apparent, as in 'the flattened smoke coming down the chimney's neck in wisps like her own hair' (*OY*, 35). It even determines Mrs Ashstone's physical bearing, as 'her small, clutching hands' seemed always to be 'chasing the flying and broken things floating in the wind's wake' (*OY*, 36). From the vantage point of the village her remote upland house, distantly glimpsed 'where the greyness roamed the bracken', resembles 'a white pebble that a boy had flung out of the river' (*OY*, 38). But such an impression of impregnable solidity is contrary to the old widow's familiar experience of the house as an excitingly precarious, permeable dwelling-place, its porousness being the converse of the resolute solidity with which it stoically withstands 'the boulders of air the wind rolled against it' (*OY*, 38).

Bachelard writes at some length about poets' preoccupation with the relationship of house to storm. In evoking, as so frequently they do, the 'bestiary of the wind' (*PS*, 44), writers seem to him to focus figuratively on the destructive, animalistic side of the energies by which humans and universe are alike possessed. They turn the 'combatant house' (*PS*, 46) into a beleaguered fortress from which is exerted the 'counter-energy' of an individual's moral integrity. There is much of this in 'The Old Woman and the Wind', as the 'cruel rage and cruel envy'(*OY*, 37) Mrs Ashstone feels for the villagers below find expres-sion through her relationship with the wind. Indeed, in describing a tempest, Evans accidentally echoes Bachelard *avant la lettre* when she says that 'a beast roared in the chimney' (*OY*, 38). But Evans also puts the wind to very different figurative use, such as is again touched on by Bachelard when he considers the ways in which, through its dynamic relationship to wind and storm, a house can become expressive of the 'cosmic' positioning of humankind. 'The Old Woman and the Wind' is centrally concerned with this 'anthropo-cosmology' (*PS*, 470). Mrs Ashstone's cottage exists primarily as the site of a dialectical relationship evidenced in the alternation of the monstrous howl of the tempest and a correspondingly heightened, uncanny silence in

which quieter powers make their mysterious presence known: 'she
heard nothing except clock, kettle, and mouse. She felt that she lived
in these stirrings' (*OY*, 39). When Mrs Ashstone finally throws in her
lot with her exposed upland home, rather than opting to take the
enticingly offered key to one of the trim houses in the village, she
understands perfectly the reason for her choice:

> Down there I couldn't hardly tell whether I were glad or sorry. I couldn't
> seem to *hear*, and that's the reason as I don't want to change my ways
> now. I do like to hear even the mice in me cupboard, and the cockroaches,
> I'm that curious and learned. (*OY*, 43: emphasis in the original)

And implicit in her decision is the determination to be absolute mistress
of her own house rather than a mere 'home-keeper' for a husband,
as the village women seem primarily to be. When Evans observes that
Mrs Ashstone was so 'ignorant' and de-socialised that she'd forgotten
that the prefix 'Mrs' signified a woman's married status and now
supposed it instead to be a first name, like 'Annie', she is implying a
great deal. And when Mrs Ashstone claims a singular and unlikely
'learnedness' for herself at the end of the story, Margiad Evans fully
respects the apparently anomalous application of such a term. Such
superior 'learnedness' is the old woman's reward for her socially
perceived 'ignorance', her unregenerate, pagan independence.

Halfway through 'The Old Woman and the Wind', Captain Ifor,
a pillar of the local village community, teasingly asks the visiting
Mrs Ashstone whether she's 'down from [her] eyrie' (*OY*, 37). She is
baffled: 'what was an ar-ray, and what had it do with her hill?' Her
maverick intelligence, resolutely uncomprehending of village ways, is
as ever the strong solvent of established language, attuned as she is
to the alternative idiom of wind, and stone, and mice, and grass, and
rain. At the story's end, Captain Ifor repeats the word in his attempt
to tempt her away from her hill fastness: 'Get you down from that
eyrie of yours' (*OY*, 42). But in rejecting his proffered key Mrs Ashstone
also refuses to speak his language, and as the conclusion of the story
confirms, her instincts in this respect are true ones. Live in an 'eyrie'
she may, from the villagers' point of view, but through her strange
communion with her environment, her intimate relationship with the
secret consciousness of place, the old woman knows her house to be
'eerie' in quite another sense: an 'uncanny' place in which she is at
once safely at home and permanently 'unhoused', an unaccommodated

dweller, along with mouse and boulder and wind and grass, in the cosmos itself. In 'The Old Woman and the Wind' the house thus becomes, in Bachelard's terms, 'an instrument with which to confront the cosmos' (*PS*, 46). 'A house that is as dynamic as this', he writes elsewhere, 'allows the poet to inhabit the universe. Or, to put it differently, the universe comes to inhabit his house' (*PS*, 51).

* * *

'The house', Bachelard further remarks, 'shelters day-dreaming, the house protects the dreamer, the house allows one to dream in peace' (*PS*, 6). Such indeed proves to be the case in Eudora Welty's 'June Recital', the remarkable long story that appears in her consummate collection of interconnected tales, *The Golden Apples*.[8] All these stories are related, either directly or indirectly, to Morgana, a small Mississippi town named in part, as Welty repeatedly affirmed in interviews, for the Fata Morgana, or will-o'-the-wisp, liable to lead humans into the realm of the equivocal and to leave them stranded in that chimerical place. A connoisseur of this disorientating oneiric realm, like Bachelard, Welty repeatedly mentioned dream time and dream states in her fiction and associated her art quite closely with reverie. Such a state dissolved the floor of memory, admitting human beings to the mysterious underworld of time which is paradoxically our real abode. Daydreams seemed to her naturally attuned to that understanding of our temporal existence that she identified in *One Writer's Beginnings*, an understanding born of the distinctively Southern sense of time she shared with her great contemporary and friend William Faulkner:

> [Living] is our inward journey that leads us through time – forward or back, seldom in a straight line, most often spiralling. Each of us is moving; remembering, we discover; and most intensely do we experience this when our separate journeys converge. Our living experience at those meeting points is one of the charged dramatic fields of fiction. (*OWB*, 102)

It is this dimension of time that is explored in 'June Recital'.
    This substantial story interweaves the experiences and recollections of two youngsters, the boy Loch and his gawky adolescent sister, Cassie, via those dreams of yesterday that are triggered involuntarily

in them by hearing the opening bars of Beethoven's 'Für Elise' being played in the apparently empty house next door, a place unnervingly haunted for them both by the ghosts of their past. The difference between their recollections is due to a number of different factors, including their different gender, their contrasting ages and their respective temperaments. In addition, Loch's mental state is heightened by the malarial fever from which he is suffering while Cassie's disturbed equilibrium reflects in part the liminal state between adolescence and adulthood when personal identity, agitated not least by sexual awakenings, remains relatively fluid and undecided.

Riveting his attention on the house he can see from his sickbed, Loch responds to it as 'something very well known indeed. Its left-alone contour, its careless stretching away into that deep backyard he knew by heart. The house's side was like a person's, if a person or giant would lie sleeping there, always sleeping' (*GA*, 21). Like Cassie he is readily inclined to see the house as a site of fantasy, akin to the magical places of fairy tale and animated by a similarly exotic life. While Cassie aspires to a more dispassionate, 'grown-up' assessment of the property, she nevertheless finds her imagination becoming inexorably entrapped in its labyrinthine, infinitely recessive interiors and feels herself succumbing to its bewitchment, just like Hansel and Gretel in the witch's house. Drawn to the window, she stands there, her pale hair infested with paper curlers, her small head vulnerably balanced on her nakedly exposed frail neck, her feet bare, and looks 'pathetic – homeless-looking – horrible. Like a wave, the gathering past came right up to her. Next time it would be too high' (*GA*, 37). As her gaze becomes ever more fixated on the supposedly vacant building next door, she senses what she suspects to be 'agitation. Some life stirred through. It may have been *old* life . . . a life quicker' than the life of her own family, 'more driven probably, thought Cassie uneasily' (*GA*, 35). And for both Loch and his sister, the house (like the house in 'The Old Woman and the Wind') seems to mark a distinctive zone of consciousness where human life appears to be unified with, and thus inseparable from, the natural world. Indeed, in its decay, the house is in some respects 'maintained' by the natural cycle: 'Leaves and their shadows pressed up to it, arc-light sharp and still as noon all day' (*GA*, 35). As Loch's eyes scan a mattress in the old, semi-derelict property, 'A shadow from a tree, a branch and its leaves, slowly travelled over the hills and hollows of the mattress' (*GA*, 21). It is an example of what Bachelard had in mind when he spoke of '[the] coexistence of things in a space to which we add consciousness of our own existence . . . a very concrete thing' (*PS*, 203).

Gradually, both Loch and Cassie become aware of temporary inhabitants in the house – the old watchman who spends his days sleeping in one room; Virginia Rainey and her sailor boyfriend who use another room as their sexual trysting-place; and an eccentric old woman whose antics in the downstairs room which still houses the piano seem increasingly puzzling and bizarre. One-time tomboy Virginia, it turns out, looms large in the charged narrative of Cassie's memories of her childhood. Ever socially untameable, a free spirit scornful of the ways and opinions of others, the liberated Virginia was, and is, the pet hate and secret love of the inhibited Cassie. An inveterate worrier and social conformist, she yearns to emulate Virginia in her blithe insouciance and disregard for social mores. But at the centre of the story stands the nervous, awkward, unconventional figure of Miss Eckhart, an everlasting social outsider, indeed a virtual outcast, of German descent whose spinsterish occupation it was to teach Virginia and Cassie and other little girls how to play the piano that now stands abandoned and is the centre of the onlooking Loch's increasingly fascinated attention. It gradually becomes apparent that it is the eccentric Miss Eckhart's intention, in the derangement of her dotage, to set the piano alight and to burn the entire house down. However, while it is this act of arson that leads to the climactic action in the story, the real subject of the leisurely expansive and endlessly sinuous narrative is the whorl of the past and its infinite encroachments on the present. 'The space we love', said Bachelard, 'is unwilling to remain permanently enclosed. It deploys and appears to move else-where, without difficulty; into other times, and on different planes of dream and memory' (*PS*, 53).

According to Bachelard, 'The oneirically definitive house . . . must retain its shadows' (*PS*, 13), and in 'June Recital' the old house preserves its mystery to the end, the mystery of man's temporal existence. Welty allows us to experience 'the house in its reality and in its virtuality, by means of thought and dreams' (*PS*, 5), and Margiad Evans performs a similar miracle in stories like 'Into Kings'. This wondrously intense and exquisitely wrought tale is self-confessedly one that entices us, like 'June Recital', to step out of the world of ordinary place and time. Little five-year-old Harry, we're told at the outset, 'neither lived nor remembered in sequence, and life and his dreams appeared without reason. He was a busy visionary' (*OY*, 44).

It is courtesy of his consciousness that we are able to enter the twilit world of enchantment that is the living-room of 'Pewit [sic] Castle', a little cottage – whose strange misfit of a name mystifies him – occupied by elderly Mr and Mrs Lackit and their disabled daughter. And Harry's adventuring secretly over their threshold is also an enactment of the little boy's discovery of his own mysterious interiority: 'he began to be aware he was a being – a *private* being, and that he need not tell' (*OY*, 46).

The living room's dim interior is a magical zone of restlessly meta-morphosing forms, like the face of the invalid asleep in the chair, whose eyes and mouth seem to be twitching monstrously as the firelight plays over her features. The most dominant feature in this fairy-tale realm is the tall gilded mirror, in the 'poetry' of whose glass all the objects in the surrounding space seem to be strangely stilled, 'com-pacted . . . into a tilted but solid peace' (*OY*, 49). Indeed, in this living room the whole domestic world seems set permanently slightly askew. For the little boy Harry, epiphany comes in the form of a 'cheap round shaving glass' (*OY*, 49). Caught in its reflection, a vulgar golden wreath from the cheap, tired, old pier glass is transformed before his enraptured gaze into the golden crown he would have expected to find in a cottage otherwise so puzzlingly called a Castle. And once he discovers the crown, Harry instinctively garbs the old Lackits in the gorgeous glamour of regal regalia:

> Hadn't he always wanted to know why they lived in a castle? It was the greatest of marvels, the most delicious answer . . . The most real of stories seemed about to begin. He saw Mrs Lackit as queen with a great yellow ring around her brows. And driving her, in the little black tub, Mr Lackit, the king. Poor drab old Nellie the donkey disappeared, and in her place in the shafts trotted a circus pony with red harness . . .
>
> He didn't believe in the crown, any more than he believed that the excited heart he could feel was alive in the mirror. Yet, like the heart, it existed *outside*. Perhaps, yes, somewhere? (*OY*, 49)

Little Harry has, then, stumbled wonderingly on what is for Margiad Evans, like Eudora Welty, the real source of story: his entry into that shabby little living room crammed full of tasteless bric-a-brac is actually his entry into the very womb of narrative, as Evans and Welty understood it. What makes it so, is that it is the realm of what E. M. Forster, in a famous phrase, termed 'the twilit vision'. It is a region where things and people alike both are and are not as they seem. As critics regularly point out, at the very heart of Welty's fiction lies her consciousness of this doubleness, and the same could be claimed for Evans's stories. She points to this in the concluding line of 'Into Kings'. After the wonders of mirror and 'crown', the little boy next literally awakens in the invalid a wholly unexpected, clumsy and inarticulate tenderness, and is caught by old Mr and Mrs Lackit at the very moment this melting happens. Gruff Mrs Lackit is moved to quiet tears, leaving her husband as the only one who has not been turned by the affecting scene into something rich and strange. 'He', writes Margiad Evans, 'was the only person of the four to whom nothing could possibly have been otherwise than as it was' (*OY*, 50). Literalist to their 'visionary', he stands there, searching for his pipe, to remind us that the world is, indeed, mundane as well as magical. The true artist's genius lies, of course, in granting equal 'reality' to the scene in both its transfigured and its untransfigured states, and Evans was faithful to this 'double vision' in every detail of her writing. 'It was November', we learn at the beginning of 'Into Kings', 'the brown winds were visible with leaves. Yellow and tortoiseshell, grey and lacquer red, mahogany and gingerbread colour, they span and skimmed' (*OY*, 44). The first sentence, that remarkably views the leaves as a visible incarnation of the wind, is counterbalanced by the second, where the simple reality of the leaves in all the variegated colours of their ordinary, rich leafiness is reasserted.

* * *

For both Evans and Welty, it was art that frequently brought out the 'inscrutable' mystery, the unsuspected 'otherness', of people, The word 'inscrutable' comes from the concluding sentence of 'Miss Potts and Music'. Rather like 'June Recital', it is a story that pivots on the astonishing transformation that happens when an otherwise non-descript young girl sits at a piano and begins to play. And similarly in 'A Modest Adornment', who could possibly have dreamt that Miss Allensmore, ostensibly a 'fat black cauldron' (*OY*, 117) of an old 'hag', finds secret ecstatic – and indeed erotic – fulfilment by playing the oboe with breathy, sensuous lyricism. Similarly, at the climax of the collection's title story, 'The Old and the Young', the young girl Arabella stumbles on a scene where the old woman, Tilly, dances to the vigorous popular tunes being played by robust Josephine, in her gardening breeches. The scene is an idyllically communal one, embracing both the old and the young, but earlier in the same story, as little Arabella thinks wistfully of Josephine's magical playing, she suddenly recalls how her violin could suddenly change its tune. First, to Arabella's distress, would come the breakdown of melody into seeming cacophony – 'her legs would straddle and stiffen and out of the violin came the screams of a parrot in the rage. To the child it was terrible – as if the deck of the lawn tilted over a big wave and the leaves reeled' (*OY*, 157) – and then the instrument would settle to an entirely different key: 'the tune would fall, would drop half a tone as if the horizon had darkened, as if the sun had been lowered like a lamp – and Arabella knew it was Beethoven' (*OY*, 157). The change of key signifies, of course, the music's explorations of complex, subtle moods and experiences unknown to childhood and thus foreshadows the conclusion of the story, when little Esther – younger even than Arabella – breaks the charm of the innocent moment by enquiring, with semi-conscious pertness, where babies come from.

As for the otherness, the secret selves and 'virtualities' of localities, what better language could there be for exploring such uncanny dimensions of familiar 'reality' than that afforded by fairy tale, legend and myth, a narrative vocabulary in which both Evans and Welty were fluent. Such tales 'reflect upon forces and signs', as Bachelard put it (*PS*, 41). The interconnected stories in Welty's *The Golden Apples* make particularly powerful use of such rich psychic materials. The hints are already there in the very title of the opening story, 'The Shower of Gold', where the part of Zeus is taken by the elusive King MacLain, who, floating free of his family and from all the moral constraints of provincial Morgana, roams the countryside at will, mysteriously materialising on fleeting occasion like the incarnation of some amoral, sexually potent and predatory force of forest life. The very stuff of legend, MacLain is a figure ancient and distant as classical mythology yet familiar and local to Mississippi folk culture, the stories about him naturally resembling the tall tales of the south-west frontier on which Welty modelled her notable early novel *The Robber Bridegroom*. King MacLain is flesh and blood yet also exists as a figment of the feverish imaginations of the locals in whose circulating tales he looms so menacingly yet enticingly large. In this latter respect he is the means whereby Welty implicitly reflects on the origins and functions of tale-telling (and its close relative gossiping) in the 'economy' of communal existence.

His unpredictable appearances in the wood are mirrored by his unexpected appearances in the tales themselves. He returns, for example, in 'Sir Rabbit', as a kind of king of the woods entitled to exercise his seigneurial rights over all those who venture into his kingdom. When Mattie Will goes hunting with her frightened husband, aptly named Junior, and his young black helper, the party is from the outset much more apprehensive about running into MacLain than it is intent on shooting a rabbit. And when MacLain does lazily appear, drifting between and behind the trees like a stalking ghost, he has only to fire a load of buckshot vaguely in Junior's direction to scare him into a dead faint, leaving Mattie entirely at MacLain's disposal. Zeus to her Leda, he complacently has his will, and as he saunters off, so 'a dove feather came turning down through the light that was like golden smoke' (*GA*, 108). No swan he, nor shower of gold, but nevertheless he has all the attributes of a Zeus, divinely careless of human ties and obligations.

Welty's interest in communal tales is paralleled by Margiad Evans's fascination with the stories she heard on the lips of local villagers. In the footnotes to her edition of *The Old and the Young*, Ceridwen Lloyd-Morgan consistently demonstrates what an appetite Evans had for recording such materials, out of which she regularly compiled her own fictions. And, again like Welty, she was concerned to capture the actual words used by her unconscious 'informants', sensitive as both were to the fact that there could be no successful separation of oral story from the exact manner, as well as occasion, of its utterance. Evans and Welty were both connoisseurs of dialect, of inflection, of the very pace and rhythm, sound and texture, of narrative that actually constituted the very marrow of story; its core substance and meaning. And both writers placed storytelling at the very epicentre of their art. Welty, for example, stated that 'Family stories are where you get your first notions of profound feelings, mysterious feelings that you might not understand till you grow into them. But you know they exist and that they have power.'[9] While, reviewing a book on the Welsh border country, Evans could admire the photographs but very much regretted 'that there is not just an inch for the scraps of story belonging to the places they illustrate'.[10]

* * *

The interest of Evans and Welty in such matters seems to have been intensified by a melancholy intuition that such tales, in their experience, were the exhalations of a dying world. In 'The Boy Who Called for a Light', a story that is, to some extent, like some of Welty's, so constructed as to reflect on its own character as a tale, the adult narrator finds his narrative spontaneously invoking for him the vanished circumstances of its own origins:

> I'd no idea of remembering that much. It all fits in so that it is difficult to take out the pieces I need. I seem to be back there in the moon-blanched lane, standing under the tree, hearing the sounds drop out of the sky, falling clearly, with a starry stillness and shapeliness on the fields of hills. (*OY*, 63)

As is clear from a number of stories in *The Old and the Young*, the recurrent elegiac note is due, in part, to their being the anxious product of a time of war and therefore of a period of profound, and potentially cataclysmic, change. Measured in terms of its damage to the intimate relationship between young woman and fiancé in 'The Ruin', this wartime world of change leaves its physical mark, in 'The Old and the Young', on the pre-war layout that so suited slow and leisurely village life. 'The village has changed', notes Arabella, 'The bridge has been widened for traffic, and ruined, the eighteenth-century sundial has been carted away and left in a corner, a tomb without a grave' (*OY*, 150).

Arabella's worried, bewildered, question – 'Where's everybody? And what has happened to us?' – is one with which Welty may very well have sympathised. She was, after all, one of the nostalgic Southern generation of writers and intellectuals whose unease about the new, post-bellum South was so arrestingly voiced in the classic 'Agrarian' manifesto *I Take My Stand* (1930).[11] Although never committed, like her distinguished contemporaries John Crowe Ransom, Allen Tate and Donald Davidson, to its socially conservative agenda, Welty certainly sympathised with its concern to defend traditional, rural, communal values from the destructive encroachments of the aggressively individualist and functional ideology of the victorious, heavily industrialised Northern states of the Union. Along with her other contemporaries in what was a brilliant constellation of talents from across the diverse regions of the South – writers like William Faulkner, John Crowe Ransom, Allen Tate, Robert Penn Warren, Flannery O'Connor, Tennessee Williams, Cleanth Brooks, Katherine

Anne Porter and Erskine Caldwell – Welty developed her own rhetorical strategies (instanced, for example, by her preoccupation with time, memory and the past, and by the value she placed on collective imaginative enterprises such as the tale) for addressing the crisis of her South. Indeed, the very ambivalences of her 'double vision' were very much in keeping with the famous and influential concern with paradox of other Southern writers and critics of her time – a concern that spawned what became known as the 'New Criticism'.

Underlying this conspicuous privileging of creative equivocation – and the related appreciation of the pregnant indeterminacies of image and symbol (what Bachelard called 'the coalescence of images that refuse an absolute anatomy' [PS, 29]) – lay Southerners' conviction that Northern culture was so single-minded and monomaniac in its pursuit of 'progress' that it had completely lost the capacity to appreciate the rich complexities and insoluble enigmas of human existence. Believers in the straightforwardly open road to ever-increasing prosperity, the materialistic Yankees were deemed indifferent to Welty's dominant sense of 'spiralling time' and the brooding omnipresence of the past. In this context, 'the double vision' was very much understood by the Agrarians and others to be, in the US context, the unique gift of traditional Southern culture; a legacy of inestimable value to the arts. In Welty's work (as, most famously, in Faulkner's) this cultural climate is powerfully inscribed in an original style that often seems also to be evocative of the torrid body heat of the south and the miasmic quality of vision it so readily generates:

> [Like the physical climate, the style creates] an evanescent medium in which things are constantly melting into one another or dividing their identity between different levels of experience. The mind absorbs the landscape and then the landscape absorbs the mind . . . Everything . . . is animate and apparently capable of numerous metamorphoses: so much so that the metaphors lacing the description hardly seem like metaphors at all, but literal accounts of a magical environment. All is shifting, all is clear and yet somehow fluid, intangible.[12]

And while Margiad Evans's style is, of course, as markedly different from that of Welty as the climate of the Welsh border country is different from that of the Mississippi delta, it nevertheless – or so this essay has been suggesting – possesses in its own answering way

many of the salient characteristics of the style of Welty so accurately
characterised in this passage by Richard Gray.

Also like Welty, Evans is resistant to the ironing out of life to a
bland 'Yankee' flatness. Again like Welty, she is temperamentally
inclined to think of life instead as an elusive, ephemeral function
of the space–time complex. The defining characteristic of 'the space
we love', according to Bachelard, is that it 'is unwilling to remain
permanently enclosed. It deploys and appears to move elsewhere
without difficulty; into other times, and on different planes of dream
and memory' (*PS*, 53). In 'Solomon', Evans uses the fantastical
consciousness of a little boy, Albert (known in the family as Barrabas
[*sic*]), to illustrate how a cavernous house, 'filled with the green air of
the trees' but with 'too few people in it' (*OY*, 97), proves to be exactly
such a space as Bachelard specifies. So large and time-scarred is the
house that 'nobody can number what's in it or guess who dropped
and hid the things they find' (*OY*, 100). And just as its endless multiplicity of rooms is for Albert suggestive of its labyrinthine history,
so, when he joins his sisters for an imaginary tea-party in the grounds,
he informs them – 'in a voice that seems to come through the back of
his head' – that '"I'm listening to where all the little paths go to"'
before selecting from the 'skein' 'one he thinks wants to go home' (*OY*,
102). Living as he does in a world in which everything has a will and
secret purpose of its own, he laughs and then 'turns to see which way
the laugh went' (*OY*, 102). And when he looks up, he 'gazes amazed
at some sky which is coming round the corner of a steamy cloud' (*OY*,
102). There is, therefore, no fixed centre, no commanding 'point of
view' in his universe, which resembles a post-Einsteinian universe of
relativity complete with time-warped space through which it is impossible to travel in any straight line of understanding. As an electric
storm gathers overhead, little Albert makes his way out of doors to
join the old gardener, Meffy, and notices that from the back the great
house 'is ponderous age. Compared with the facade it is earthenware
compared with porcelain' (*OY*, 104). The story he demands from
Meffy is 'part of the house', and the old man's 'memory is inseparable
from the place' (*OY*, 104).

The violent storm proves to be the destabilising force that radically
unsettles the 'normality' in which Albert's parents habitually dwell,
so that they, too, are not so much drawn as harassed into sharing his
vision. His father panics at the thought that one of the children may
have got hold of his gun, with fateful consequences. His mother,

returning at a wild gallop from her visit elsewhere, roams the rooms of the house closing windows against the tempest, becoming ever more uneasy. Even the candle she holds in her hand turns sinister, and seems to release unquiet presences wherever it goes:

> And then she sees it is not light she is bringing with the candle, but only a yellow smirk like fog.
> She hears the voices in the kitchen, she hears a moan of thunder and her own shadow twirls about her as she returns. It's as though some loosened entity of the house were revolving wherever she moves, now dancing as in a cage, now fitfully concealed within her own body. (*OY*, 105–6)

Hastening to a window, and throwing up the sash, she is transfixed by the sight of little Albert sitting in the yard exposed to the lightning and stirring the embers of a fire. Suddenly he seems to her a sinister, foreign creature: 'For a moment she hardly recognizes him. That's what frightens her' (*OY*, 106). On the verge of hysteria she screams at him to come in and as he lifts his face in acknowledgement it is unnervingly caught in the 'white flash of light to earth', while thunder breaks overhead like an avalanche (*OY*, 106).

It is an eerie story steeped in a sense of the uncanny. By increasingly infectious degrees that reach their zenith when the house becomes complicit with the storm, home is inverted into a hostile, unsettling place, and intimate family ties become a source of terror rather than of consolation. Knowing that the story was written in October 1945, immediately after the conclusion of the war in Europe, I find it difficult not to associate it with the atmosphere of a period of profound dislocation, when it was clear that old ways, old values, old relationships could not simply be resumed because everything had irrevocably changed. The deep resultant sense of unease was the shadow side of the enthusiasm for change that found historic expression in the unexpected election of a Labour government at that precise juncture. In that sense, 'Solomon' may be read as capturing the last phase of an extended period of disorientation beginning with the nightmarish anxieties of the pre-war years, and continuing through wartime experiences such as those of the Blitz, when many observers were shocked and bewildered by eviscerated houses whose most intimate interiors were suddenly exposed to casual public view. A classic text of the first, pre-war, phase would be Vernon Watkins's 'Ballad of the Mari Lwyd', with its invocation of the ghosts that come ominously knocking at doors and windows on New Year's Eve and press most peremptorily for admission to the domestic hearth:

> Out in the night the nightmares ride;
> And the nightmares' hooves draw near.
> Dead men pummel the panes outside,
> And the living quake with fear.
> Quietness stretches the pendulum's chain
> To the limits where terrors start,
> Where the dead and the living find again
> They beat with the selfsame heart.[13]

As for the second phase, what text is there that more powerfully evokes the stunned air of the London streets at dawn following an air-raid than 'Little Gidding', when T. S. Eliot encounters ghosts of the distant past released by the chaos on to the streets of the present? And it is in the company of texts such as these that I feel 'Solomon' naturally belongs, as it uses a rural setting to suggest the way in which the heart of war-shocked, post-war England broods on its new strangeness to its old, familiar self.

* * *

One possible reason, therefore, for the 'confluence' of the imaginations of Margiad Evans and Eudora Welty may be their common source in an experience of radical social and cultural change. But, as this essay has already intimated, there are many more reasons than the one for the uncanny mutuality of their minds, and the enigma of their creative correspondence must ultimately be allowed to remain insoluble. What is clear, however, is that, although Welty's talent had considerably more reach and range than that of Evans – allowance having first been made, of course, for the fact that the American outlived the Welsh border writer by more than half a century – the creative imaginations of the two writers were, nevertheless, joined at the hip, unique though their respective achievements indisputably were. 'Art, then', wrote Bachelard, in another of his resonant apothegms, 'is an increase of life, a sort of competition of surprises that stimulates our consciousness and keeps it from becoming somnolent' (PS, xxxiii). And it is precisely for the remarkable power they held in common to 'increase life' in this irreplaceable way that we should value the haunting fictions of both Margiad Evans and Eudora Welty.

(First published in Kirsti Bohata and Katie Gramich [eds], *Rediscovering Margiad Evans: Marginality, Gender and Illness* [Cardiff: University of Wales Press, 2013].)

Notes

1   *Wales*, 5 (Summer 1935), 182.
2   Ceridwen Lloyd-Morgan (ed.), Margiad Evans, *The Old and the Young* (Bridgend: Seren, 1998), p. 15. Hereafter *OY*.
3   Eudora Welty, *One Writer's Beginnings* (Cambridge, MA: Harvard University Press, 1983), p. 102. Hereafter *OWB*.
4   *The Welsh Review*, 10 (1939), 285.
5   Eudora Welty, *A Writer's Eye* (Jackson, MS: University of Mississippi, 1994), p. 26.
6   Gaston Bachelard, *The Poetics of Space*, trans. Maria Jolas (Boston: Beacon Press, 1994), p. 201. Hereafter *PS*.
7   Dr Kirsti Bohata has drawn to my attention the following intriguing entry from Margiad Evans's journal for 22 August 1943: 'One of my strange house dreams, about mother. Big rooms, big beds & black staircases. the moonlight like curtain's [?] rods. All these things I must remember.'
8   Eudora Welty, *The Golden Apples* (New York: Harcourt, Brace & World, Inc., 1949). Hereafter *GA*.
9   Quoted in Jan Nordby Goetland, *Eudora Welty's Aesthetics of Place* (London and Toronto: Associated University Presses, 1994), p. 364.
10   *Wales*, 10 (October 1939), 285.
11   The most comprehensive and authoritative introductions to Southern culture during the period in question are Richard Gray, *The Literature of Memory: Modern Writers of the American South* (London: Edward Arnold, 1977) and Richard Gray, *Writing the South* (Cambridge: Cambridge University Press, 1986).
12   Gray, *Literature of Memory*, p. 178.
13   Vernon Watkins, *Collected Poems* (Ipswich: Golgonooza Press, 1986), p. 47.

3

'A GRAND HARLEQUINADE': THE BORDER WRITING OF NIGEL HESELTINE

Somewhere in Montgomeryshire, a young man named Thwaite stands meditatively by the side of a grave, staring down at his father's coffin. Then he turns around, only to see that very same father 'limping through the crowd'. And on one of the wreaths he discovers a label with the message 'An empty box' in his father's handwriting. As Thwaite gazes, his father's figure wends its way up the hill and disappears 'as the dead should'.[1] It is difficult to read this passage from Nigel Heseltine's 1946 collection of stories, *Tales of the Squirearchy*, without remembering how haunted he was throughout his life by the death (whether murder, suicide or – very probably – accident) of his own father Peter Heseltine Warlock, the talented English songwriter and notorious dabbler in the black arts, in 1931. In the writer son's experience, some dead disquietingly refused to 'disappear as [they] should'.

And now Nigel Heseltine himself is a writer who has very largely disappeared from view in Wales. He is remembered, if at all, only as the author of the occasional odd (sometimes very odd) story and a few critical pieces. But he deserves to be better served, if only for his brief but valuable contribution to his country's emergent English-language literature, and in that connection he may perhaps best be appreciated as a border-country writer, one of a large and eclectic group that includes (at random) Newtown's Geraint Goodwin, Herefordshire's Margiad Evans, Abergavenny's Raymond Williams (a great pioneer of border fiction as of border studies), Flintshire's Emyr Humphreys, and, of course, Manafon's very own R. S. Thomas. Border regions are fascinating. They are zones of conflict, regions of cultural exchange, limbo-lands, areas of negotiation, no man's land, their own place. They generate distinctive forms of consciousness. The Wales–England border is an area rich in cultural history that tends to be marginalised by 'mainstream' Welsh and English culture, and it remains for scholars to map out not only the actual geography but the symbolic geography of this region. Border studies are also currently very fashionable. In the light of contemporary postmodern and post-colonial thinking, the relationship between margins and centres has, in effect, been reversed. The former – the erstwhile peripheral and somewhat suspect border regions – now occupy pride of intellectual place as providing the most potent examples of that meeting, mingling and cross-fertilisation that is regarded as the creative essence of contemporary social and cultural life.

Moreover, from the postmodern point of view, they have the advantage of calling the very concept of fixed categories of identity into radical question, as border regions defy categorisation in 'received' terms. The cult of rootedness, that flourished half a century ago, has been replaced by a cult of fluid personal, social and cultural being. And the most subtle, sophisticated and influential cultural models of this ubiquitous 'border' identity have been produced by Homi Bhabha.[2] The key term and value in his thinking is what he styles 'hybridity'. By it he means to draw attention to the fact that, as the summary in the front matter of *The Location of Culture* succinctly puts it, 'the most creative forms of cultural identity are produced on the boundaries *in-between* forms of difference, in the intersections and overlaps across the spheres of class, gender, race, nation, generation, location'. In the body of the work this concept is more fully developed along the following lines:

> The borderline work of culture demands an encounter with 'newness' that is not part of the continuum of past and present. It creates a sense of the new as an insurgent act of cultural translation . . . The margin of hybridity where cultural differences 'contingently' and conflictually touch, becomes the moment of panic which reveals the borderline experience. It resists the binary opposition of racial and cultural groups . . . as homogeneous polarized political consciousnesses. (*Location of Culture*, 7, 207)

If Bhabha's theory is helpful in enabling us to characterise Heseltine's cultural and social positioning as a writer, so too Gilles Deleuze and Félix Guattari's concept of 'schizo' man may throw light on the creative energies of a life like Heseltine's, seemingly devoted to a bewildering multiplication of personae.

> [T]hey created the term 'schizoanalysis' to describe their own approach and goal: not the primacy of the psyche but the primacy of parts, 'schizzes' or impersonal and mobile fragments. Instead of beginning from the assumption that there are fixed structures such as language or logic that order life – this would be the 'paranoid' fixation on some external order – they argued that life was an open and creative whole of proliferating connections . . . Their 'schizo' is not a psychological type (not a schizophrenic), but a way of thinking a life not governed by any fixed norm or image of self – a self in flux and becoming, rather than a self submitted to law.[3]

Heseltine's capacity for ceaseless, lawless self-(re)invention can seem fertile, and while this 'schizo' tendency may have originated as a defensive adaptive mechanism for coping with the radically destabilising features of his early family circumstances (never knowing who was his mother; effectively abandoned early by his mysterious and mercurial father; raised by his caring grandparents in a colourful family environment that, however unconventionally stable, was vulnerable to his father's unpredictable visitations; traumatised young by his father's mysterious death) it became a powerful enabler first of his (sometimes wildly pantomimic) work as a writer and subsequently of his restless worldwide career as a government administrator. In Celia Buckmaster's 1939 review for *Wales* of *Scarred Background*, the youthful Heseltine's account of his pre-war travels in Albania, she perceptively wrote: '[this book] would seem to be in the circumstances not so much a scarred background for Albania, but a scarred background in front of which Mr Heseltine walks and suffers.'[4] That scarred background was his own childhood upbringing, an upbringing which was, indeed, to be not so much described as invisibly inscribed in much of his adult writing. Consequently, he could be seen as having lived his whole life in masquerade, providing a classic example of what Judith Butler influentially termed the 'performative' aspects of personal and cultural identity.[5]

The young Nigel Heseltine may therefore be seen as attempting to 'place' his own psychically 'scarred background' in his native border country of rural Montgomeryshire – a Wales just 'round the corner from England', as one of his characters befuddled by drink suggestively puts it. In his Welsh works he constructs it as a wild zone; a 'lawless' territory in Deleuze and Guattari's terms; a stage for zany performances of identity. Indeed, a version of what Bhabha was half a century later to valorise as 'hybridity' was celebrated by Heseltine early in his writing career. In March 1939, he published a revealing review of David Jones's *In Parenthesis*, hailing it as the founding text of Anglo-Welsh literature and comparing it with *Ulysses* as involving 'the fusion . . . between Celt and Saxon'. Jones's prose poem appeared to him to be 'the first of a new race' that was 'more likely to make our national peculiarities international than the mouthings of Dylan Thomas'.[6]

Appropriately enough, the review appeared in that explosively influential magazine *Wales*, the natural site for such a claim, since, under the crazy maverick editorship of that charlatan of genius Keidrych Rhys, it set out to provide an aggressively combative and provocatively controversial platform for the first, often flamboyantly experimental, generation of Welsh writers in English. Having first published a poem in *Wales* when he was twenty-one, and having succeeded Rhys as editor in 1939 at the age of twenty-six, Heseltine at this time clearly subscribed to the journal's main ideological aim of creating a new Wales by inciting a cultural revolution. And it is easy to see how he might have been attracted to Keidrych Rhys. That Falstaffian lord of misrule was an ideal surrogate father for a child whose own similarly renegade and raffish father had virtually abandoned him at birth, and whose beloved step-grandfather, Walter Buckley Jones, who helped raise him, was at once a conventional establishment figure and a great teller of local, and family, tales – Ian Parrott describes him as being both a JP and a magistrate to the local 'lunatic asylum'.[7] As for the rumbunctious Rhys, in signing off his first stint as editor of *Wales* with 'Notes for a New Editor' (i.e. his successor elect, Nigel Heseltine), he began with the typically baiting observation that 'The Squirearchy in most villages are of the decayed English militarist class, who settle down in Wales on account of the salmon-fishing or because they are fussed over'.[8]

It was, then, to the remarkable, self-liberating, culturally hybrid and lawless first generation of 'Anglo-Welsh' writers that the young Heseltine consciously belonged. Dylan Thomas, Glyn Jones, Rhys Davies, Idris Davies, Vernon Watkins – simply to name them is to be struck not only by the constellation of talents but by the significant fact that they were all products of the south Wales coalfield. That, too, was a border region of a kind, of course. What had the townships of the industrial valleys been but wild frontier towns? And as they gradually established a social equilibrium, it was evident that they represented a wholly new phenomenon in Wales, a rich mix of peoples ready for explosive cultural ignition. It is not for nothing, therefore, that Tony Conran entitled his recent study of the literature that was thus ignited *Frontiers in Anglo-Welsh Poetry*.[9] But while Heseltine was naturally attracted to this new, border-country 'Anglo-Welsh literature' and its liberatingly hybrid work, he was also aware that, from a Montgomeryshire perspective, these writers came from foreign parts. 'Takes longer than to go to London', remarks one of his characters who has ventured to travel from south to mid Wales.[10] One of Heseltine's aims was surely to extend the map of 'Anglo-Welsh Wales' to include his own Montgomeryshire border country.

The above comment appears in 'The Lay Reader', a story he published in *Wales* in August 1939. It concerns a chapel lay reader who arrives in deepest Montgomeryshire and is quizzed by his host: "'So you're from South Wales," I said, "it's a long way."' That immediately starts the newcomer off about pits closing and lay-offs, dole queues and unemployment, the struggle between labour and capital, until the locals grow thoroughly alarmed at a militant socialism that seems to them positively bolshie. In the end Old Davies the Lane speaks up:

> 'D'you know what they sold sheep for last year in Newton Smithfield?' he asked. 'D'you know what they were giving for fat lambs?' The lay reader didn't know of course. And most of us remembered when you could get a man to work without any of this minimum wage nonsense and insurance on top. (228)

And when the lay reader starts off again about 'the unequal bargain between employers and workers that only a strong Union could settle', Evans Cwm-llan breaks in: 'We've had to buy our farms now the landlords have sold out. Pay rates, and do our own repairs too. I tell you, young man, it's not so comfortable here either.'

There is the nub of it for Heseltine: the hidden, historically momentous revolution that has befallen the Welsh countryside but that (as R. S. Thomas also insisted) has been wholly overshadowed by the colourfully epic sociopolitical drama of south Wales industrial history. That quiet, forgotten, but momentous, rural revolution was central to Heseltine's understanding of his paternal family, of himself, of his border region and of his Wales, and it was the compulsive subject of his Welsh fiction. Using comedy as his medium, he explored this disappearing world of the border gentry directly, in a splendid collection of stories that sadly remain unpublished, thus perpetuating the marginalisation, the effective silencing, by contemporary Welsh social, political and literary history of the important story of Heseltine's Welsh place.

Tales of the Landless Gentry – the title of Heseltine's unpublished collection in a way says it all.[11] From the middle of the nineteenth century, Wales's great Tory landlords who had (mostly affably) kept the peasantry in obsequious thrall for centuries were forced by the irresistible new power of Liberal politics literally to give ground to new, proto-democratic political realities. Compelled, by a series of great people's elections, to relinquish political control, they were also gradually obliged to sell off their vast acres to the tenant farmers who had been the main sources of their wealth. The extent of the revolution may be gauged by the fact that in the 1873 census over 60 per cent of Wales 'consisted of estates of over 1,000 acres':

> these estates were in the hands of only 571 landowners, a mere 1 per cent of the total of those owning lands in some form. Beneath these great families lay a whole nexus of smaller land-owners and squireens, bound together by marriage and by commercial and social intercourse. Over most of Wales, these landowners still exercised a massive, almost unchallenged authority.[12]

The dismantling of this powerful hegemony was a process begun with the great campaigns of radical and nationalist protest of the last decades of the nineteenth century. As a result, these ascendancy landmarks 'now became beleaguered outposts of a new form of English and Anglican dominance over the countryside' (*Rebirth of a Nation*, 11). The process was subsequently accelerated, and completed, by the economic crisis during and following the Great War. At the same time a new upstart class of industrial magnates, ennobled en masse by the unscrupulous political maestro Lloyd George, turned squire, acquired land, built grand houses, and generally usurped the (much diminished) place of the great landed families some of whom had arrogantly traced their pedigrees back to Tudor times.

This was the world Nigel Heseltine entered, when he was in effect adopted by his paternal grandparents and brought up in the rambling would-be *plas* of Cefn-Bryntalch, with its thirty rooms, situated 'near the village of Llandyssil, about half way between Montgomery and Abermule in Powys (then known as Montgomeryshire)' (*Crying Curlew*, 9). Not that his paternal step-grandfather could claim ancient pedigree. Walter Buckley Jones was one of the grandsons of a Welsh hill farmer from Mochdre who had made enough of a fortune by selling flannel to Newtown to become gentrified. The old man married into the genuinely ancient but impoverished Buckley-Williams family, thus allowing his offspring to conceal the vulgar Welsh appellation of 'Jones' within a new, decently hyphenated surname.[13] Consequently, by the 1920s and 1930s, such an upstart Welsh family had acquired at least a sheen, a patina of dignified age, and an impeccable, imperially English, establishment character. Two of Walter's brothers became distinguished military figures – Colonel Whitmore and Brigadier-General Lumley Williams Jones served in India, Burma and South Africa, and Lumley was awarded the DSO. Given Heseltine's upbringing in this definitively Anglo-Welsh setting, it is no wonder that as a writer he became interested in 'hybridity'.

In the unpublished *Tales of the Landless Gentry*, a collection seemingly assembled over a period of decades, Heseltine draws heavily on the yarns of his genially eccentric step-grandfather Walter along with other family experiences. Many of the stories are for instance fictive retellings of tales about Heseltine's father, the composer known as Peter Warlock, and others that Heseltine had heard from his step-grandfather and was eventually to include in his late 1992 memoir *Capriol for Mother*, while characters such as Colonel Whitmore carry the names of actual family members.[14] Almost all the stories either directly concern, or at least mention, the typically eccentric Vaughan-Thomas family of border squires who claim direct Tudor ancestry. The family's zany modern history is traced by means of the only son, Rhys, who in some respects seems to be an amalgam of Heseltine and of his father. The dominant, and socially representative, theme of the collection is a once-great family's decline and eventual social disappearance. Indeed, the stories are a powerful comic elegy for the passing of a peculiar Welsh class and with it a way of life. Comedy prevails for most of the time, and it ranges from the subtle comedy of social manners to the robustly anarchic, even faintly nihilistic humour of outright farce. But the tone changes, and darkens, towards the end of the collection, when Heseltine sensitively identifies with the plight of a young woman who has effectively been sentenced to a life blighted by hard labour following her colonel father's squandering of what was left of the once-prominent family's dwindling fortunes.[15]

The tragicomedy of money as fecklessly handled by a squirearchy terminally bewildered by its own decline is one theme treated at times acidly and at times sympathetically by Heseltine. Rhys's incorrigibly vague mother pins her hopes on her ultimately ruinous speculations in the Wahi gold mines of South Africa, while his amiable uncle Devereux has – but whisper it not, since the family never does – fled to Madagascar to escape his creditors, having failed for years even to glance at his business ledger. Money is to them a mysterious foreign body. It is status and land alone that really matter – the land they have lost, such as the farm sold off to old Hamer, a speaker of Welsh, regarded by Rhys's family as a mere barbaric patois. But if Hamer can scarcely speak a word of civilised English, he can certainly accumulate cash, and when he sets about felling the may trees on the land he has bought from the Vaughan-Thomases, these outraged grandees treat it as if it were still theft of their own property. Mrs Vaughan-Thomas regularly bemoans her straitened circumstances, but, as Rhys notes, 'having been ruined every morning for months, his parents would set off in good spirits for Vichy and Baden Baden to recover from their worries by drinking beneficial foreign waters'.[16]

And the nouveau riche gentry lack the bearing, the manners, the grooming, the style of the Old Quality. Whereas Lord Herbert unmistakeably looks like a lord, fat Mrs Buckley with her withered eyes 'wore what looked like a sponge-bag on her head', and as for the awful, aitches-dropping Mrs McCraw, in her best get-up she resembles a bloated purple fuchsia.[17] But as they are forced to abandon their great sprawling Jacobean houses for smaller, and increasingly shabby accommodation, the old gentry, raised to fecklessness and mad eccentricity, can demonstrate a talent bordering on genius for the unkempt and the squalid. When Rhys crosses south to the wrong side of the Black Mountains to stay with the Pryses he finds himself visiting a family with bats in their bedrooms and grain in their bath; he has to fend off the cats in order to help himself to some of the rancid butter among the ruins of the breakfast table. And it isn't just the squirearchy that is bizarre, so is its supporting class, like the vicar of Llanmerewig, 'his moustache fluttering like a wounded bird'.[18]

Farce is the natural mode of this mad world, and a number of the stories are hilarious exercises in this genre, ingeniously extended so as to suggest, as does Pope's *Dunciad*, that Folly possesses its own insane energy, its own crazily creative inventiveness. There is, for instance, the story of the Mochyn Hunt, a ramshackle outfit bringing together the remnants of the Old Quality, mounted on shaggy ageing nags, and the 'arrivistes', ridiculously spruce in their new pink coats and riding fine horses with gleaming coats.

> Divided among themselves the Quality cast envious glances at certain near-squires with their polished horses and willing grooms neatly dressed, reflecting that these happy new-comers of thirty years back, now staring haughtily through the calm morning air, were financed by cotton-booms and profitable trade in fat and oils, while the remote descendants of Welsh chieftains sold off their land to them.[19]

The Master of the Hunt is Major Borrowdale, whose grandfather, the family's founding squire, came from Bradford and was known as 'Old Stink o' Brass' (a name Heseltine took from one of his step-grandfather's tales). The Hunt's Hon. Secretary is Mr Chappell, 'five days a week at his desk in Liverpool, but a jolly squire on the sixth, and tootling a horn, too' (2). And one of its most prominent members is Mrs de Morgan, a tough old biddy of 'indisputable Quality' (2). The hunt is meeting on the lawns of a new villa that aspires to be a *plas*, but lacks not only the acreage of lawns but even the imposing sweep of derelict drive that every true *plas* can boast. To cap it all, the villa's tiny lawn is dominated by the most vulgar of arboreal species, a monkey-puzzle tree. This is the abode of Mr McCraw, 'a recent immigrant from Manchester' who is so vaguely known to the assembled gentry that he is mistaken for a groom and beats a hurried retreat.

Into this scene intrudes Rhys Vaughan-Thomas, celebrating his recent return from exotic Ethiopia by being mounted not on a horse but on a camel from Duffy's Travelling Menagerie, and sporting a djellaba (5). It is a wild parody of the Empire striking back, because chaos predictably ensues as the horses take fright and in the resulting melée the camel backs into one of Mr McCraw's prize greenhouses. That is just the beginning of a whole series of mishaps, including a failed attempt to ensure that the Mochyn Hunt manages to raise a fox (a previously unthinkable triumph) by releasing the animal into a covert under the very noses of the hounds. At the end of the story the fox is indeed killed – not, though, by the hunt but by a local farmer vengefully trespassing on his neighbour's land. Major Borrowdale, now bent on retirement, is left wistfully reflecting that 'with what he

could save with no flea-bitten hounds he could go to the South of
France every year and relax at Monte Carlo' (8).

Of all Heseltine's many portraits of the parvenus, or what we might
term the new half-baked Upper Crust, the most unforgivingly biting
is that of Evans-Hughes (Lord Hughes of Llandewi). He is what
Americans colourfully call a blowhard, a Welsh *gwerinwr* made good,
and vulgar to the core. His father, the great founder of the family's
fortune, had, or so local gossip has it, started out as a mere bottom
sawyer before moving on to move a mountain in order to build first
the Cambrian railways and then Cardiff docks. There are therefore
no prizes for spotting a resemblance to the renowned Davies family
of Gregynog, that pseudo-Tudor pile in the near vicinity of Cefn-
Bryntalch, built of concrete but on Welsh coal by 'Davies [top-sawyer]
Llandinam', one of the lords of the industrial Rhondda. As for Evans-
Hughes, the bottom sawyer's son and one of the Liberal MPs elevated
to the peerage as a job lot by the cunning Lloyd George, he is renowned
primarily for being renowned. His reputation for philanthropy is
literally legendary, since it has no basis whatsoever in fact. He wraps
his avarice up in fantasies of grandiose community projects, the
latest of which is to construct a House of Re-Coordination on top of
a mountain and to make it accessible only by a funicular railway.
Don't ask what Re-Coordination means: neither Lord Hughes nor
anyone else has a clue, but they are too much in awe of him ever to
ask. A comically disastrous theatrical performance is arranged at
the local Abermule hall to raise money for this project, at which Lord
Hughes himself unexpectedly materialises to dispense not largesse
but patronising bonhomie to all and sundry. When a local orchestra
is commandeered to play at a fund-raising concert, Lord Hughes
insists on attending the rehearsals, booming advice in his megaphone
voice, bullying the distinguished London conductor hired for the
occasion, and mistaking a Mozart symphony for that non-existent
oratorio, Mendelssohn's *Elisha*. At the end of the story, Lord Hughes
disappears to Washington on urgently important government business,
leaving the locals to pick up the disastrous bills for the fiascos he
has perpetrated. But through it all the local *Montgomeryshire and
Radnor* newspaper remains cravenly, obsequiously loyal. 'None will
be found to dispute, at least among our readers,' it sententiously
pronounces, 'that in our Generous Patron we are the fortunate pos-
sessor of the summit of forward-looking progress which is the acme
of our Era.'[20]

In its humour, the unpublished *Tales of the Landless Gentry* may be considered an interesting border hybrid. It is reminiscent of an English comic genre that ranges from *Jorrocks' Jaunts and Jollities* by Robert Surtees to P. G. Wodehouse and Evelyn Waugh. But it also has some affinities with the young Heseltine's prose paraphrases of Dafydd ap Gwilym's great medieval poetry.[21] Heseltine turns many of the poems into little comic sketches of a sort, and he responds best to the extravagant, burlesque elements in the writing, as in the well-known poem about the drunk lover who stands pleadingly under his mistress's window on a freezing night, with the frost biting him like a rake. The window is opened by her 'withered oaf' of a husband who sets the whole town after him. In other poems, a pining lover emaciated by passion complains 'You could make a razor from my nose' (54), and another is so bewildered by his infatuation that he falls into a bog. It is noticeable that Heseltine's poem 'To a Girl Marrying a Man with a Wooden Leg', published in *Wales* in 1939, could easily be a crude paraphrase of Dafydd ap Gwilym. But another parallel for Heseltine's *Tales* may be found in Irish fiction, not only the Anglo-Irish great house novel, from Maria Edgeworth to Somerville and Ross, but also the contemporary work of that comic genius Flann O'Brien. In reviewing O'Brien's quirky, zany, absurdist masterpiece *At Swim-Two-Birds* in 1939, Heseltine praises the way in which 'the funniest book yet out of Ireland' 'scoffs at the sacred foundations of Celtic culture'. Heseltine exults in the maverick quality of this 'grand Harlequinade', and in celebrating the achievements of what a contemporary English reviewer had uneasily styled 'an uncomfortable book', Heseltine may well have been paving the way for the book he himself was to publish in 1946, *Tales of the Squirearchy*.[22]

As already noted, it was published by Keidrych Rhys's Druid Press, which also almost simultaneously published *The Stones of the Field*, the groundbreaking volume by R. S. Thomas, then at Manafon, himself very much a border writer. And in a way, both these books address, in their indirect and wholly singular and arrestingly grotesque fashion, the radical changes that had happened in the Welsh countryside. A weird, bizarre, work, *Tales of the Squirearchy* includes some stories that make one feel as if one has stepped into a Dalí painting.[23] It is difficult not to believe that Heseltine had been influenced by the surrealism of the previous decades, and his work has certain affinities with the strange stories in Dylan Thomas's *Map of Love*, a book Davies Aberpennar (later Pennar Davies) had reviewed for

Heseltine in *Wales*.[24] And just as Thomas invented his own imaginary
Jarvis Hill country as a setting for stories that were clearly concerned
with west Wales, so Heseltine set his stories in the county of Cariad
which is obviously a most peculiar version of Montgomeryshire. The
absurdist tales are full of an ebullient black humour, frequently
expressed through the controlled hysteria of crazy farce. Theorists
of the grotesque and of the absurd have made much of the way such
disquieting modes seem to derive from psycho-cultural factors that
destabilise normality, defamiliarising it startlingly by twisting it out
of comfortingly familiar shape. Such modes are frequently expressive
of psychic and/or cultural alienation. And such insights into the
genre seem relevant to Heseltine's case. One might phrase the same
understanding rather differently, and suggest that the grotesque
can be expressive of borderline states, of border experiences where
different cultures not only confront each other but sometimes violently
collide. That may give us a clue as to the deeper logic of stories that
might otherwise be rather difficult to comprehend. It may also aid
the placement of Heseltine in the context of his Anglo-Welsh contemporaries. In reviewing *The Map of Love* in the winter (1939–40)
issue of *Wales*, Davies Aberpennar (later Pennar Davies) proposed
that there was

> an interesting family resemblance between, say, Caradoc Evans, Arthur
> Machen, the Powys brothers, Dylan Thomas and even Richard Hughes
> – a delight in the eccentric, the luscious, the strange, sometimes the
> macabre. Reading them you find yourself in a world which has a life of
> its own but which remains unnatural according to the life of *this* world.
> There is no escapism, for their creations are rather grimmer, if anything,
> than the world you know. (307)

The Heseltine of *Tales of the Squirearchy* would seem recognisably
of that company.

It is therefore worth considering some of the points of tension out
of which these stories proceed. A character common to many of them
is a young gentleman called Thwaite, mentioned at the beginning of
this essay, whose father limps and has a hole in his head left by the
Great War. Thwaite lives in a great house.

> Raskolnikov Jones is his neighbour and is still rich and wicked, yet
> Thwaite's father has now thirty acres out of the four thousand. So

> [Thwaite's] estate is a large house, a large yard, large stables, a large
> garden; two small fields, a small wood, some scrub. (45)

And through that he walks 'with his second unnecessary servant to
the broken fence'. We enter, then, the superannuated and therefore
unnecessary world of the Welsh border squirearchy, a moribund world
which is inherently absurd because there is this gross and grotesque
mismatch between its self-image and the social reality. Add to that
another consideration. This squirearchy, whatever its cultural ante-
cedents, has become in many respects an interloping English class, a
colonial relic, not only surviving but still enjoying social privileges
and exercising social authority, although it has been shorn by an
erstwhile Welsh peasantry of the political and economic power on
which it had depended for so many centuries. One could therefore
read Nigel Heseltine's collection as a species of post-colonial literature.
In his early collection of poems, *The Four-Walled Dream*, he has a
slogan-ridden English journalist say of the people who have been
killed in a bomb blast:

They died for England
(Say no more)
died with 'God save the King' on their lips and a smile on their faces . . .
As you'll find out if you dive to the bottom of that crater . . .
and they died as well, for Scotland and Wales, and the subject races.[25]

The implication is that Scotland and Wales are also viewed by the
English as subject races – the races to the service and welfare of which
Nigel Heseltine was, in a sense, to dedicate his later life. His later work
in Africa, Madagascar and a myriad other places could be seen as the
continuation, in mature and frequently sceptical form, of his early
sympathies with his fellow-Welsh. He turned to other culturally
oppressed or colonially subjugated peoples worldwide, and showed a
practical, unillusioned interest in their transition to self-rule, while
deploring the ruinous waste of resources by self-serving native power
élites in establishing the ostentatious trappings of statehood.

It is therefore not inappropriate that *Tales of the Squirearchy* should
begin with a story about a shoot that unexpectedly ends in a bloody
massacre. Among those assembled at the country house of Cam-
Vaughan, distantly descended from Welsh princes, is an embittered
overbearing General from darkest America who exclaims at the 'ugly

face' of Owen the head keeper, grinning obliquely at him 'like a dark
and evil man (he's Welsh)' (7). The gentlemen in the shooting party
'lower their moustaches' on their guns, and start downing the pheasants.
But suddenly balloons, not birds, begin to rise out of the woods where
the beaters are at work, and then the loaders run to join the beaters
as the latter reach for guns stuffed down their trousers. It is no contest.
The Quality are quickly out-gunned, and Thwaite, who has escaped
the carnage by shinning up a tree, sees Owen below him slitting Cam-
Vaughan's throat. As Owen and his cohorts sweep up the drive to the
great house, whose door is obligingly opened for them by the butler,
Thwaite nonchalantly comes down from the tree, picks up his gun
and starts shooting rabbits. As a Welshman, he remains unperturbed
by the massacre of these foreigners.

   Heseltine's own socially and culturally ambivalent position seems
to be expressed through Thwaite. Heseltine was a rogue product, so
to speak, of the border squirearchy, a part of him rebelling socially,
politically and culturally against the background from which he
came and keen to release himself from it by exposing its grotesqueries.
So when Thwaite attends an Upper Crust party in the company of
a Miss Menzies, he views her as if anatomising a peculiar exotic
specimen:

> Thwaite slipped the skin from her and looked at her organs while they
> swelled and groaned with the burden of living; and he looked from her
> heart to her lungs to her viscera, and her pear-shaped womb. And he
> thought, shall I plant there a seed and run off with this bone-faced
> woman, and away from her when she holds me? (13)

In another story, Thwaite is excoriated because

> he has not behaved according to the traditions of his class, he has not
> acted with *esprit de corps*; he has behaved contrary to other people,
> he has behaved contrary to the principles on which good breeding,
> on which kindness or the dealing in a magnanimous way with inferiors
> is based. Thwaite does not acknowledge his inferiors, and he has no
> reverence! He has none of the milk of human kindness possessed by
> the inhabitants of the county of Cariad, who conform. (28)

In the same story, Reverend Codger, a Calvinistic Methodist minister,
is caught shooting pheasants in a squire's wood and hauled before

Sir Gam Vychan: "'In India!'", he cried, "You would be shot. In the Malay you would be flogged! In Africa you would be chained up!'" (31). Here again the Welsh are seen as a subject race, a colonised people. But the Revd Codger's friend, Mr Cambyses, objects to such treatment of the Welsh and in revenge refuses to send his ram, Owen's pride, to service Sir Gam's flock. And the local people are stirred to protest, the town band leading them through the town with banners that read: 'Defend our Antient Rights, Down with Feudal Tyranny'. When the band plays 'Land of my Fathers' there's not a dry eye in the crowd, but their conception of mass popular uprising is just a little skewed, since they proudly march in the name of Arglwydd Jones, another local grandee.

Wildly anarchic in spirit, the stories revel in the crazy energies at work in this world. Naturally, therefore, sex is treated as the most potent spirit of black mischief that sets people running amok. Pamela Blinding, in the ironically entitled 'Boring Story', is twenty-four and a proud virgin:

> Ignorance and up-bringing in ignorance managed in a mysterious way to keep down her natural passions amongst the savage surging reproductions of the herbs and the beasts of the land. She never wondered what her father did so late in London, nor what he did with the large body of Mrs Blinding in their brass marriage bed. (61–2)

Needless to say, Pam's virginity is not long for this world: she succumbs to a local pub landlord. But more surprising is the way her mother, who has been 'running the house until the floors and the walls vibrated with her energy', is seized with an importunate lust for Albert the footman. Left to his own devices and to the nagging of his tyrannically interfering crone of a mother, Colonel Blinding strikes her on the head with a hatchet. 'And with many expressions of horror on both sides, Colonel Blinding was tried for the murder of his poor old mother and sent to a Criminal Lunatic Asylum where he founded Colonel Blinding's Band of Hope' (68).

Such an episode exposes the impacted anger and violence that lie at the root of the anarchic black comedy of *Tales of the Squirearchy*. A similar anger explodes bitterly in Heseltine's wartime collection of poetry, *The Four-Walled Dream*, which for all its Modernist affectations is at bottom a young man's rant against the profiteering and the ruthlessly self-serving power-politics of the English Establishment:

the unholy alliance between the upper, ruling and military classes. There is, for instance, his acid sketch of a 'Recruiting Office':

> bodies in queue for heroes
> . . .
> From the sharks of the works, and the bumping land
> shooting its sons in a gun. (32)

Even love is seen not so much as a refuge as infected and inflected by the surrounding violence. So in a kind of allusive rewriting of Yeats's famous 'Leda and the Swan', he dramatises Leda's experience of the 'rasp of live feathers, beak dug in my neck/ tearing my breasts with his own, jabbing with bird member' (12). Alternatively, he resorts to Audenesque parody of ballad style to prophesy social revolution:

> hang up your boater till that summer comes
> when people run and rulers suck their thumbs:
> when arms are melted down for coin,
> and clubs are there for all who care to join. (47)

As for *Tales of the Squirearchy*, itself after all essentially a wartime production, a like bitterness stands revealed in the final story when the grinning, grimacing mask of comedy is allowed to slip. As already suggested, however, the tensions that find expression through this work are much older than wartime. And if they have their roots in the peculiar sociocultural study of the Welsh borders, they are also partly psychological in origin. Included in the collection is a story about a spinster who, while carrying on a lustful affair with her somewhat reluctant footman, writes steamy, bodice-ripping fiction. One day, one of her characters comes to life off the page and threatens to ravish her. The story seems to be a coded expression of Heseltine's own fears – that through the would-be exorcism of his writings he might raise up ghosts that would refuse to be laid to rest. In writing his fictions, he was risking what Freud would have termed the return of the repressed. In this connection, it is worth noting the brief portrait of his young self Heseltine included in *Scarred Background*:

> The subject of this notice, myself, represents an obscure connection
> between a suppressed desire for violence and travel, and the instinct
> that makes us kick the table when we are angry and stamp around the

room. I wander because I cannot usefully canalize my animal lust for disturbance. I am not aware of it, but it gives me itchy feet.[26]

And, one might add, an itchy pen. And when he goes on to admit that he 'has also felt an admiration for primitive lives and cultures, and the desire to seek them out and live with them' (15), it is now surely possible for us to see that he was, unaware, already intuiting at this early stage his long later career of service in Madagascar and several other countries of Africa.[27]

As already noted, the psycho-social origins of this violent restlessness, this pent-up anger, this appetite for risky adventure may well be found in his own childhood. The family circumstances were in some ways lurid. In his memoir, *Capriol for Mother*, he recalls an extraordinary turning point in his life. On a hot Italian day in the early 1950s, he visits a fortune-telling old lady who lives, almost crowded out by her extensive family, in a dilapidated concrete block, a relic of Mussolini's Rome. She leads him into a dining-room, with its damp concrete walls and cheerless centre light and cuts the cards. There stand revealed 'pictures I had never seen, and now she showed me two with faces contorted in agony. "They are in Hell," she said, "They are in agony in Hell. It is they who watch and call to you"' (23). The faces are those of Heseltine's parents and it is they, she adds, '"who are blocking you when you want to accomplish what you are capable of doing"'. This brings back to Heseltine the memory of the many pitiful dreams he had had of reconciliation with his dead father; and of the way that unease about his mother and father would rise 'like bile' any time he had a drink. He was already older than his father had been when he died. And he realised that ever since he had heard of the circumstances of that death in his adolescence, he had 'changed my pattern of life, [thrown] away many advantages, and followed a pattern that seemed to be imposed from without, rather than arising from my own character and upbringing' (24). Moreover, 'my work in distant places was banishing the dream-world of Philip' (24). But when young,

> the repetition-compulsion of Freud fought inside me against the desire to escape. To escape, however, not from reality, but into the reality of my own life . . . While the dream world had control, I lived according to [my father's] pattern, but when its control faltered and I saw reality for a while with my own eyes, I escaped. (35)

What can be sensed in *Tales of the Landless Gentry* and *Tales of the Squirearchy* is precisely the conflict between repetition compulsion and escape – a conflict felt as one between indulgent affection and bitter condemnation for this border place and its people. This is the complex psycho-social conflict that is mediated in and through comedy. And folded into that comedy is a sense of pain and of aching loneliness. It comes out briefly and shyly in his portrait of Thwaite when a boy. He is happiest when able to slink out and cuddle up to the dogs in their kennels; or when he sneaks away to a secret corner of the river.[28] The deep pathos of this desperately needful attachment to place is indirectly echoed in *Capriol for Mother*. There he recounts how he heard of his father's death. He was a public schoolboy at Shrewsbury, and was coldly informed by his unsympathetic housemaster. Heseltine duly squeezed out the dutiful tear that was expected of him, but in reality his feelings were not of loss but rather of relief and even of exultation. After all, his father had many times threatened that when he inherited Cefn-Bryntalch he would immediately sell the estate – would sell the beloved woodlands, streams and fields that in many respects had provided the boy Heseltine, as the mountains and lakes of the Lake District had the boy Wordsworth, with a kind of deep emotional consolation, a parent substitute. But mingled with this exultation at his father's death was no doubt guilt at such feelings, to be compounded by jealousy as he realised that the dead Peter Warlock had now effectively usurped his own place in his grandmother's affections. Not long afterwards, when the now-adolescent Heseltine was on leave from preliminary officer training at Sandhurst, he was initiated into sex by a slightly older woman, Katherine, who was rumoured to have been his father's mistress. The psychological charge of such a relationship is surely unmistakeable – it provided Heseltine symbolically with a form of intimacy with both his father and (given Katherine's age) his anonymous mother; it also allowed him symbolically to usurp his father's place at a time when, to his grandmother, he seemed to be hell-bent on repeating Peter Warlock's disastrous life by determining to become a writer, rather than the military man or senior civil servant she thought appropriate. This, then, is the nexus of intensely conflicted feelings that find indirect expression in his *Tales*.

It seems a wonder that, given his early background, his baleful relationship with his father and the terrible blankness where his mother's nurturing, directing and sustaining love should have been, that Heseltine ever succeeded in living a fulfilling life. That he did was, as he candidly and clearly admits in his Memoir, thanks to Cefn-Bryntalch, to his formidable grandmother, and above all, perhaps, to his step-grandfather, Walter Buckley Jones, to whom in *Capriol* Heseltine pays the warmest and most moving of tributes: 'I tell of the family of Walter, Philip's stepfather, who was like a father to me . . . thanks to Walter and Covie [Nigel Heseltine's grandmother Edith Covernton] I survived and prospered' (5–6). However, the greatest compliment of all that he paid to this stabilising background was the two collection of *Tales* he completed. Walter was himself a spellbinding teller of tales, and therefore in reproducing these, as Heseltine did in his own fashion, he was acknowledging the 'parenthood', so to speak, of Walter, and the centrality of Cefn-Bryntalch. As noted earlier in this essay, *Tales of the Squirearchy* was published in the very year (1946) in which Heseltine sold off the family estate and departed for foreign parts. And in the very last story in *Tales of the Landless Gentry*, the now-ageing Heseltine returns in imagination to Cefn-Bryntalch, and produces a powerful, haunting elegy for everything that was lost with its passing out of the family:

There are two ways of visiting my old home, Rhys pondered. One is to push my way through the rain-forest that grows where my mother's garden was, see what the concrete-mixer was doing, greet whoever is sitting in our drawing-room, watching TV where the Reynolds prints of laughing girls used to hang.

The other way is not visit it . . .

His eyes travelled over the little rounded hills of Montgomery, and the small sunny valley where the river Severn flashed sudden silver patches.

But his thoughts were on the evenings of childhood, leaning out of a friendly window of the Plas where the sky was an aquarium green, the rooks flew home against the green sky, and the blackbirds chaffered in the laurels. Then the sky mellowed into the hills, and into the night . . .

I left, and what little I left behind vanished like grass. You carry rich memories with you, and the smiling faces of people. With my eyes shut, I see it all. When I open them, there is only the beautiful empty valley . . .

The engine purred. 'What is my future?' he asked himself, thinking how the future rushes on you like a river, leaves you suddenly old and lonely, like an old stone standing unwanted in the land of your fathers.[29]

Notes

This is a revised and extended version of a lecture delivered in Montgomery at the Peter Warlock Festival, 17 December 2005. Published in *Welsh Writing in English: A Yearbook of Critical Essays* 11 (2006–7). I am very grateful to Dr Rhian Davies for the kind loan of several texts of critical importance to this discussion and for providing a wealth of biographical information about Nigel Heseltine.

[1]   'The Life and the Burial', in Nigel Heseltine, *Tales of the Squirearchy* (Carmarthen: Druid Press, 1946), p. 19.

[2]   Homi K. Bhabha, *The Location of Culture* (London and New York: Routledge, 1994).

[3]   Claire Colebrook, *Gilles Deleuze* (Routledge Critical Thinkers, London: Routledge, 2002), p. 5.

[4]   *Wales*, 6/7 (March 1939), 208.

[5]   See, for instance, Judith Butler, *Excitable Speech: A Politics of the Perfomative* (New York/ London: Routledge, 1997).

[6]   *Wales*, 4 (March 1938), 157. At this point in the text, the editor, Keidrych Rhys, inserts the tart exclamation 'Oh dear me!' in parenthesis.

[7]   Ian Parrott, *The Crying Curlew: Peter Warlock, Family and Influences: Centenary 1994* (Llandysul: Gomer Press, 1994), p. 18.

[8]   *Wales*, 8/9 (August 1939), 246.

[9]   Tony Conran, *Frontiers in Anglo-Welsh Poetry* (Cardiff: University of Wales Press, 1997). See also 'Writing Glamorgan', in M. Wynn Thomas, *Internal Difference: Twentieth-Century Writing in Wales* (Cardiff: University of Wales Press, 1992), pp. 25–48.

[10] 'The Lay Reader', in *Wales*, 8/9 (August 1939), 227. Later included (Story X) in *Tales of the Landless Gentry*, an unpublished collection of short stories (see below).

[11] I am very grateful to Dr Rhian Davies for so kindly loaning me a typescript copy of this collection. The pages are not consecutively numbered, instead each story is paginated separately. Consequently reference to the text in this essay will take the form of story title and number followed (where relevant) by page reference within that particular story.

[12] Kenneth O. Morgan, *Rebirth of a Nation: Wales, 1880–1980* (Oxford: Oxford University Press, 1981), p. 9.

[13] According to Ian Parrott, it was Nigel Heseltine's formidable grandmother, Edith (née Covernton), who, upon marrying his step-grandmother Walter, converted the plain surname 'Jones' into 'Buckley Jones' (Parrott, *Crying Curlew*, p. 20).

[14] Nigel Heseltine, *Capriol for Mother: A Memoir of Peter Warlock and his Family by his Son Nigel Heseltine* (London: Thames Publishing, 1992). In his

Introduction Heseltine states 'I began this book in Rome around 1958; I have finished it in Ziguincho, Sénégal, in 1991' (p. 5).

[15] 'Break away if you can', Story IX.

[16] 'Generous Patrons', Story V, p. 1.

[17] 'A Young Night of Love', Story III, p. 1.

[18] 'Generous Patrons', Story V, Part II, p. 3.

[19] 'Flaming Tortoises', Story VII, p. 4.

[20] 'Generous Patrons', Story V, Part IV, p. 1.

[21] Nigel Heseltine, *Twenty-Five Poems by Dafydd ap Gwilym* (Banbury: The Piers Press, 1968; first published 1944).

[22] 'To a Girl Marrying a Man with a Wooden Leg', *Wales*, 11 (Winter 1939–40), 303, later collected in *The Four-Walled Dream*, p. 37; review of Flann O'Brien, *At Swim-Two-Birds*, *Wales*, 11 (Winter 1939–40), 308–9. Heseltine refers to the (anonymous) English reviewer during the course of his own review.

[23] Nigel Heseltine, *Tales of the Squirearchy* (Carmarthen: Druid Press, 1946).

[24] *Wales*, 11 (Winter 1939–40), 306–8; the review immediately preceded Heseltine's review of *At Swim-Two-Birds*. Heseltine had earlier reviewed Thomas's *25 Poems*, *Wales*, 2 (August 1937), 74–5.

[25] 'The People of England', Nigel Heseltine, *The Four-Walled Dream* (London: Fortune Press, no date), p. 52.

[26] Nigel Heseltine, *Scarred Background: A Journey through Albania* (London: Lovat Dickson Publishers, 1938), pp. 14–15.

[27] For full information about Heseltine's extraordinary, and hitherto largely uncharted, later career, see the essay by Dr Rhian Davies in *Welsh Writing in English*, 11 (2006–7), 69–101.

[28] 'Data on the Squirearchy', *Tales of the Squirearchy*, pp. 45–53.

[29] 'Homecoming', Story XI, no pagination.

4

'THERE'S WORDS': DYLAN THOMAS, SWANSEA AND LANGUAGE[1]

'Dylan loved people and loved Swansea. Even the eccentrics and odd characters were his kinsfolk be they Swansea people.'[2] The words are those of one of Thomas's closest friends, Bert Trick, and they seem to me to be a fair summary of the positive aspects of the relationship between the poet and his home town. The negative aspects, mostly limited to that period in late adolescence when he morosely viewed Swansea as the provincial graveyard of his burgeoning talent, are lividly recorded in the self-dramatising letters he sent to his young London girlfriend, Pamela Hansford Johnson. It is still possible, in one sense, to tour Thomas's Swansea. Yet in another, more important, sense it is not. That is not only because such a substantial part of what he loved about the place was obliterated during three dreadful nights of air-raid in February, 1941. It is more importantly because a writer's town can be accessed by only one route – through that author's writings. We might even say that, as an inveterate writer, Thomas turned his town *into* words. But then, it was Swansea that had first set him on the way to becoming himself a figure fashioned out of language; a linguistic sign. Instead of word being made flesh, in his case flesh eventually ended up being made word.

This sobering realisation occurs to Thomas at one arresting point in his moving and grossly underestimated radio play *Return Journey*. Broadcast first in 1947, it is a haunting account of his post-war return to his home town in a wry, comic, poignant attempt to reconnect with his youthful self. He comes 'home' in search of what (or rather who) he had once been – a search that is also a search for the Swansea that no longer is. And his first port of call, once he's left the town's High

Street Station, is naturally one of the many pubs he had frequented
when he'd been a young cub reporter, apprenticed to language on the
local paper that became the *South Wales Evening Post*. In an attempt
to describe his one-time youthful self to the barmaid, he launches
into a virtuosic performance of linguistic self-portraiture:

> He'd be about seventeen or eighteen . . . and above medium height.
> Above medium height for Wales, I mean, he's five foot six and a half.
> Thick blubber lips; snub nose; curly mouse-brown hair; one front tooth
> broken after playing a game called Cats and Dogs, in the Mermaid,
> Mumbles; speaks rather fancy; truculent; plausible; a bit of a shower-
> off; . . . lived up the Uplands; a bombastic adolescent provincial Bo-
> hemian with a thick-knotted artist's tie made out of his sister's scarf,
> she never knew where it had gone . . . a gabbing, ambitious, mock tough,
> pretentious young man; and mole-y, too.[3]

And what is the barmaid's response? It is devastatingly uncomprehending. 'There's words: what d'you want to find *him* for, I wouldn't touch
him with a barge-pole.'

'There's words': the phrase haunts me, because in its ambivalence
it encapsulates the creative heart of Thomas's life and writing. 'There's
words' is, obviously enough, Dylan's self-knowing and self-mocking
advertisement of his irresistible way with language, voiced here in a
naive barmaid's unconsciously wondering tribute to a poet's seductive
potency of expression. And I'll be returning to this celebratory aspect
of the phrase later. But the exclamation also carries dark, disturbing
overtones. His wistful question to the girl behind the bar has in effect
been 'do you remember a young Mr Thomas?' To prompt her memory
he's launched into a bravura performance. And what is her response?
'There's words'. It is as if, horrifyingly, Thomas, the would-be home-
comer, discovers he now has existence only in language, not only as
a clever arranger of words but as a clever arrangement of them.

This is a realisation already anticipated in an earlier failure of his
in *Return Journey* to conjure up memories of his younger self in
Swansea people, this time by mentioning him by name. The blank
reply he this time gets from the barmaid, as she turns to another
customer at the bar for confirmation, is 'this is a regular home from
home for Thomases, isn't it, Mr Griffiths?' (*RJ*, 75). Even the surname
'Thomas', it turns out, is not a reliable personal signifier, an identifier
of self: 'Thomas' is after all the most common of surnames in Swansea,

a byword for all and sundry. It is much more common even than the familiarly Welsh 'Mr Griffiths' – a surname the barmaid can here confidently (even pointedly) deploy to denote a real, living, single person. It is as if Dylan the returnee finds himself lost in language. No wonder, therefore, that, as he walks the streets of his old town, he seems to have become a merely ghostly presence wandering among the 'blitzed flat graves' of shops, 'marbled with snow and headstoned with fences' (*RJ*, 73). Words, it is implied, have usurped and thus obliterated his living, individual human identity. This is a point underlined, as the radio play subtly emphasises, by the way the barmaid's phrase 'There's words' precisely echoes her earlier phrase 'There's snow'. As *Return Journey* makes graphically clear, the exceptionally heavy snowfall under which Swansea disappeared in the notoriously hard winter of Thomas's return to the town in 1947 is symbolic of the obliteration, during the terrible three-night Blitz in 1941, of the centre of the old town which had been the heartland not just of the town but of the young Dylan too.

The war in Europe had ended only some two and half years before Thomas's return to Swansea in 1947, and so much of the town still lay in ruins. Devastated by bombing, large areas from the docks to the shopping centre remained in a derelict, devastated state. 'What's the *Three Lamps* like now', asks the returning Thomas of the barmaid. And the reply comes from a customer leaning on the counter: 'It isn't like anything. It isn't there. It's nothing mun. You remember Ben Evans's stores? It's right next door to that. Ben Evans isn't there either' (*RJ*, 77). Buildings, places, these are now just names, just words. Whereas Thomas had once been able to take his substantial, material bearings from these buildings, and thus been able to orientate himself, now, disorientatingly, where there were solid shops there are nothing but 'hole[s] in space'. Those 'displaced' shops now have an existence – a 'place' – only in language. 'Eddershaw Furnishers, Curry's Bicycles, . . . Hodges and Clothiers . . . Crouch the Jeweller, Lennard's Boots, Kardomah . . . David Evans, . . . Burton's, Lloyd's Bank' (*RJ*, 78): 'there's words', just as the barmaid said. This vivid elegy for a Swansea town that is no more may remind us how aware, and how appalled, the post-war Thomas was that the age had turned nuclear since last he'd visited his home town. Bombed Swansea was, so to speak, his personal Hiroshima. It's as if the hopeless sense of nihilism by which he had been afflicted following the first nuclear explosions had fatefully heightened his sense that his beloved, Swansea-generated world of words and memories was itself likewise nothing but an endless chain reaction of signifiers.

After all, Swansea and language had always been so intimately interconnected in Dylan Thomas's experience as to be virtually interchangeable. It's therefore not surprising that *Return Journey* should from the very outset show us a Dylan who, in returning to Swansea, is brought face to face not with his younger self but with language itself. It was there that he had first been brought alive to words. I'd therefore like briefly to consider just a very few of the many important locations and occasions of his original awakening not just to the world but to the word in his home town.

* * *

Let's start with one of his best-known poems: 'Do not go gentle into that good night,/ Old age should rage against the close of day;/ Rage, rage against the dying of the light.'[4] This famous villanelle bespeaks Thomas's awareness that his father hadn't only begotten him; it was his father, too, who had made him a poet. Because what is rarely, if ever, noticed by commentators is that 'Do not go gentle' is Dylan's despairing, taunting challenge to his rapidly ageing father to assume the role of a King Lear. Behind the poem lies the aged Yeats's recently published poem 'Lapis Lazuli', a poem Thomas would certainly have known, not least because his great Swansea friend Vernon Watkins was a Yeats fanatic.[5] In that poem Yeats famously celebrates the defiant 'gaiety' with which the great Shakespearean heroes meet their end, 'gaiety transfiguring all that dread', a phrase echoed in Thomas's 'Blind eyes could blaze like meteors and be gay'. Thomas is also picking up on Yeats's use of the verb 'blaze': 'Black out: Heaven blazing into the head'.

'Tragedy wrought to its uttermost . . . Hamlet rambles and Lear rages', Yeats had written. And Thomas next proceeds to borrow yet another Yeatsian word: 'rage'. 'Rage, rage against the dying of the light.' Thus in urging his father to turn 'age' into 'rage' just like Lear, Dylan Thomas is trying to provoke the sick atheist into once more roaring the disgusted cry that had characterised him in his prime: 'it's raining again, damn Him.'[6] Via Yeats, then, Thomas is implicitly alluding to the figure of King Lear throughout 'Do not go gentle'. And why is he doing so? Well, it is in part his way of confessing himself to be, as poet, the offspring of a passionate Shakespearean – his father had actually read the Bard's poetry to him in his very cradle. 'Do not go gentle' implicitly bears witness to the vivifying effect of poetic language on little Dylan at the very beginning of his life, and so the villanelle is able convincingly to claim a like power to *re*-vivify D. J. Thomas at the very end of his life. Therefore, in being a poem about Dylan's father, 'Do not go gentle' is also inescapably a poem about origins, about Swansea as a cradle of language, and about the power of words to shape personal identity.

D. J. Thomas was, by some reports, not an easy man to live with. Aloof, frustrated and irascible, he seems to have been periodically irritated by the class difference between his sophisticated educated self and his comfortably homely chatterbox of a wife from working-class Swansea East. Young Dylan was thus encouraged early to escape and make an alternative home for himself in language, which is what he memorably did in magical Cwmdonkin Park, whose true 'keeper' was not the park keeper but, of course, the hunchback. Bent out of true, 'The hunchback in the park' is the physical image of the enticingly deviant, the alluringly monstrous, the rivetingly grotesque (*CP*, 93–4). Like the poet, he is the eternal outsider. To enter his territory is to cross over to the wild side, to join the company of 'the truant boys from the town'. Truancy must have held an irresistible appeal for a schoolmaster's son who went on to revel in the truancy of words.

Tributary influences on 'The Hunchback in the Park' are many, and obviously include the film of *The Hunchback of Notre Dame* and the William books by Richmal Crompton that Thomas devoured as a boy.[7] But all influences tend towards the same conclusion; that as a poet he feels most at home with the errant life and the wild energy of words. Those are the words that, like the truant boys, once they're clearly heard can then seem to 'run on out of sound'. This truant phrase, like so many of Thomas's, is itself a hunchback, because it wilfully distorts a well-known idiom – 'run on out of sight'. In the process it reveals all poetry to be language misshapen, like the hunchback himself. It also reminds us that, for a poet like Thomas, a poem is a device for allowing words to 'run on out of [the] sound' of their usual, ordinary usage and meaning. A poem is a magical 'park' where words are let out to play, given their head, and allowed to go wherever their exuberant energy of life may take them. 'Run on out of sound' can mean either 'run on out of the reach of sound', or it can mean 'run on propelled only by sound' (compare with 'I did that out of spite'), just like one of Thomas's poems.

'The Hunchback in the Park' is often sentimentally read as enchanting idyll and indulgently supposed to be a poem as innocent as strawberries. But stalking the text is an incipient, because pre-pubescent, sexuality, hinted at in the description of the hunchback himself as 'the old dog sleeper' – the phrase 'old dog' (with its echo of the Welsh *hen gi*) implies a dirty old womaniser, the roguish aged twin of the 'young dog' Thomas himself boasted of being in his *Portrait of the Artist as a Young Dog*. Of course the poor old hunchback can be such only in his sleep, and even then he is capable only of a eunuch dream of 'a woman figure without fault', the old man's pathetic twist on the Pygmalion story. The sublimated sexuality of his frustrated making is paralleled and contrasted with the activity of the incipiently sexual boys who 'made the tigers jump out of their eyes/ to roar on the rockery stones,/ and the groves were blue with sailors'. The word 'blue' there refers not only to the colour of the sea and the uniform of sailors, but also to their blue language and thus by connection to the docks from which the Cape Horners sailed in the heyday of Swansea as Copperopolis. This dockland area, with its adjacent red-light district of the Strand, was distantly visible from Dylan Thomas's window away at the far end of town from his home in the affluent genteel suburban Uplands. Indeed, wickedly hidden in that phrase 'the groves were blue with sailors' is a subversive allusion to the bourgeois neighbourhood in which young Dylan lived, because the name of the triangle of streets directly adjacent to Cwmdonkin Park is 'the Grove'. In exultantly making the groves 'blue with sailors' Thomas is therefore slyly using his power as poet to turn the respectable Grove into a district of low repute.

For Thomas, Cwmdonkin Park was both nursery of the imagination and an adventure playground for language. That it was so may have been in part due to its proximity to what in those days was referred to as a School for the Deaf and Dumb, the significance of which for Thomas was pointed out in an important but neglected essay by my late friend Vic Golightly.[8] It was awareness of signing that lay behind such phrases as 'the rows/ Of the star-gestured children in the park'. Hence, from earliest days, Thomas was aware of language not as voiced, fixed and given, but as a system of flexible signs, a nimble means of signifying. That words could be produced in all forms, shapes and sizes would have been self-evident to one who grew up in a bilingual environment. Welsh was the first language of both his parents, and his country relatives were virtually monoglot Welsh-speakers. There were Welsh-language dictionaries, grammars and poetry anthologies on his father's shelves. And the English spoken all around him as a boy would have been colourfully influenced by the Welsh language. Indeed, the very phrase 'there's words' is a good example of this. A familiar form of Welsh English, it derives from the use in Welsh of *dyna* ('there') where in English an exclamatory 'What' or 'How' would be used. Hence 'There's posh', 'There's lovely' and so on. The young Dylan would also have been very familiar with code-switching – a primitive example of it in the text of *Return Journey* being the use of 'Tawe water' to denote a pint of beer – 'Tawe' being the Welsh name of the river at whose mouth – Aber-tawe – Swansea stands.

To mention code-switching is to be reminded of an intriguing fact. Thomas's two closest friends at Swansea, the poet Vernon Watkins and the musician Daniel Jones, went on to work during the war at the government's secret code-breaking centre of Bletchley Park. They seemed to share with Dylan an exceptional sensitivity to the complex patterned character of closed signifying systems such as language. Thomas's was an interestingly hybrid model of poetry. He repeatedly spoke of it in organicist and biological terms suggestive of natural processes. But he also described his poems as laboured assemblages, which is why of late they've caught the attention of the L=A=N=G=U=A=G=E school of poets. Thomas could represent poems as word machines for multiplying meaning. In the interests of the latter he did not respect the individual integrity of a single word but was happy to reduce it to its constituent parts if this served his purposes. This is most evident in the case of his only known Joycean, multi-lingual pun. His notebooks record his discovery that the Welsh word *amser* (meaning 'time') could be split into the two syllables *am* (which normally means 'around') and *sêr*, which means 'stars'. The outcome of this bizarre nuclear splitting of a word to release its arbitrary additional signifying possibilities was the line he included in 'The force that through the green fuse', about 'how time has ticked a heaven around [*am*] the stars [*sêr*].' He has treated *amser* as if it were a code word, a miniature cipher that needed to be cracked to reveal its secret meaning.

Had I time I'd like to explore the broad analogies between both the making and the reading of Thomas's poetry and those of cipher-construction and cipher-breaking. Central to all these processes is the construction and deconstruction of patterns of equivalence. But if Thomas can be read as a maker of codes, he can also be read as a maker of anti-codes, since while his poems operate, like codes or ciphers, on the principle of equivalence, they knowingly resist the reduceability to singleness of meaning that any code or cipher pre-supposes.

* * *

After the 'Cwmdonkin' period in Thomas's development came the period of Warmley, the substantial middle-class Sketty home of Dylan Thomas's great friend and fellow artist Daniel Jones. It was there that two lads crossing the threshold into their teens conspired to create their own theatre of the absurd out of the incorrigible zaniness of language. If Cwmdonkin Park was the nursery of Thomas the poet, then Warmley was the nursery of Thomas the comic writer – and I'd even venture to suggest that he may have had a greater natural genius for comedy than he had for poetry, because comedy allowed (and indeed positively encouraged) him to gleefully exploit the sheer glorious silliness of words. He revelled in the anarchic accidents of meaning and loved the adventitious character of words. In later years he was, after all, shrewdly and glumly to surmise that he might be more 'a freak user of words than a poet'.[9] In Warmley Dan and Dylan (even their names conveniently rhyme) mirrored the Marx Brothers' films and anticipated the Goon Show, that madcap classic of post-war British radio, by inventing characters outrageously named Miguel Y. Bradshaw, Waldo Carpet, Xmas Pulpit, Paul America, Winter Vaux, Tonenbach and Bram (CL, 196). Across the sky of their Warmley world there flew 'panama-shaped birds from the Suez Canal', and the 'Radio Warmley' they invented broadcast rhymes of which Lewis Carroll or Edward Lear might not have been entirely ashamed: 'a drummer is a man we know who has to do with drums,/ But I've never met a plumber yet who had to do with plums,/ A cheerful man who sells you hats would be a cheerful hatter,/ But is a serious man who sells you mats a serious matter?' (CL, 5). The adult Thomas was to view Warmley nostalgically as the epitome of 'the queer, Swansea world, a world that was, thank god, self-sufficient'. And of his Warmley alter ego Percy he was to write 'Percy's world in Warmley was, and still is, the only one that has any claims of permanence . . . his was a world of our own, from which we can interpret nearly everything that's worth anything' (CL, 197). To which I'd add the question, What is Llareggub, after all, but a Warmley for grown-ups?

Cwmdonkin Park, Warmley; these were then two Swansea locales important for Thomas's evolution in language. To these can be added an unexpected third: the Paraclete Congregational Chapel, just around the bay from Swansea in Newton, a corner of the sometime fishing village of Mumbles. It was there that the boy Dylan was regularly subjected of a Sunday to a strong dose of chapel religion administered by his mother's brother-in-law, who was a local minister. And that made him aware that for more than a century in Wales, the word had been the preserve of the great preachers of the Welsh pulpit, the lords and masters of language who had been allowed the last word on every aspect of life.[10]

Realising that if he wanted to become a writer, he'd have to wrestle language out of the iron control of the pulpit, he began early to wage his own war for the word. One of the most celebrated of his attempts to displace what remained of the erstwhile regnant discourse of Nonconformist, chapel-mad Wales is 'After the Funeral: in memory of Ann Jones' (*CP*, 73–4). The poem openly presents itself to us as the very site of a linguistic struggle between Dylan, 'Ann's [Dionysiac] bard on a raised hearth', who commands the power to 'call all/ the seas to service', and the ministers and deacons of a repressed and repressive patriarchal culture, with their 'mule praises, brays' and 'hymning heads' as they soberly preside over Ann's chapel funeral service. In this inverted version of the Old Testament story about the contest between Elijah and the pagan priests of Baal, it is the pagan champion of nature, the anti-chapel Thomas, who emerges triumphant. That triumph is variously expressed in the poem as a power to raise an 'alternative', verbal tombstone in Ann's memory, and as a power to resurrect the dead fox, so that its 'stuffed lung . . . twitch and cry Love/ And the strutting fern lay seeds on the black sill'. The outrageous phallic thrust of that final image is, of course, utterly unmistakeable.

It is already evident in 'After the Funeral' that, to coin an image from *Under Milk Wood*, Dylan Thomas is a Polly Garter of a poet. He defies the respectable chapel-cowed community not only by flaunting the fecund sexuality of his poetry but by delightedly indulging in promiscuous verbal liaisons, encouraging words to copulate and thrive so as to breed unpredictable and uncontainable meaning: 'I like contradicting my images, saying two things in one word, four in two words and one in six. . . Poetry . . . should be as orgiastic and organic as copulation, dividing and unifying . . . Man should be two tooled, and a poet's middle leg is his pencil' (*CL*,182). Implicitly imaging Nonconformist discourse as authoritarian, univocal to the point of being totalitarian, this poetic Polly Garter rebels by becoming a connoisseur of polysemy, a subversive proliferator of meanings.

From the beginning Dylan Thomas consciously uses puns, double entendres and a whole wild menagerie of suspect forms and socially proscribed kinds of 'language' to reflect on the profligate, uninhibited nature of 'language' itself. 'Llarregub/Llarregyb' – a word he had already coined and patented as his own in the stories of the early 1930s – was always Thomas's true native place, a place made exclusively out of the potentialities of language to turn itself back to front, inside out, upside down. In his poetry topsy-turvy language proves itself to be an incorrigible contortionist and shameless shape-changer. 'Every device there is in language is there to be used if you will', he told a Texan postgraduate in 1951: 'old tricks, new tricks, . . . paragram, catachresis, slang, assonantal rhymes, vowel rhymes, sprung rhythm'.[11] 'Poets have got to enjoy themselves sometimes', he added disingenuously. But there was always much more to it than that. To the Calvinistic minister's implicit model of human words as solidly and respectably underpinned by the Divine Word, Thomas, from his teens onwards, opposed an alternative, radically different model – of the ungovernable liquefactions of language, 'the sea-slides of saying', as he suggestively phrased it. His lifelong infatuation as poet, as short-story writer, and even as letter-writer, was with 'the procreant urge of the word', to misquote Walt Whitman, one of his poetic heroes.[12] In a poem like 'After the Funeral', Thomas adopts an openly confrontational stance towards the dominant discourse of Nonconformity and constructs what sociolinguists term an 'anti-language'; an alternative discourse of his own.

And if 'After the Funeral' is the key text in Thomas the poet's struggle for mastery of the word, then its equivalent for Thomas the comic writer is 'The Peaches', the first story in *Portrait of the Artist as a Young Dog*.[13] Based on Thomas's boyhood recollections of visiting his relatives' farm in the rural west, it features a wonderfully comical sermon, solemnly delivered by the would-be preacher Gwilym, a twenty-year-old 'with a thin stick of a body and spade-shaped face'. He has a captive audience of one – his cousin Marlais, Dylan's alter ego, a little Swansea townie. Obediently seated on hay-bales in the barn that passes for Gwilym's chapel, little Marlais listens to his country cousin's 'voice rise and crack and sink to a whisper, and break

into singing and Welsh and ring triumphantly and be wild and meek',
until the sermon reaches its grand solemn climax:

> 'Thou canst see and spy and watch us all the time, in the little black
> corners, in the big cowboys' prairies, under the blankets when we're
> snoring fast, in the terrible shadows, pitch black, pitch black; Thou
> canst see everything we do, in the night and day, in the day and the
> night, everything, everything; Thou canst see all the time. O God, mun,
> you're like a bloody cat.'

In the silence that follows 'the one duck quacked outside'. 'Now I
take a collection,' Gwilym said' (*CS*, 128). Then, as the story proceeds,
Gwilym's Calvinistic sermon (the emphasis is on a humanly distant,
prying, preying God) is implicitly trumped by the alternative, secular,
story-weaving power of little Marlais from Swansea town, as he plays
with his Swansea friend Jack Williams in the secret dingle on the farm:
'There, playing Indians in the evening, I was aware of me myself in
the exact middle of a living story, and my body was my adventure
and my name.'

* * *

By the end of his teens, Thomas was understandably beginning to
feel distinctly isolated in Swansea. In 1933, when he was nineteen, he
could write like this, in one of his outrageously pretentious letters to
Pamela Hansford Johnson. 'In my untidy bedroom, surrounded with
books and papers, full of the unhealthy smell of very bad tobacco, I
sit and write' (*CL*, 47). In one way, his Swansea had shrunk to a single
cramped room 'by the boiler', to which he regularly retreated between
1930 and 1934 to fill notebook after notebook with remarkable drafts
of poems, steeped in adolescent eroticism, many of which, duly
reworked, would find their way into his first two published collections.
By now, he could superciliously describe his Swansea as a 'dingy hell'
from which he longed to escape, 'and my mother is a vulgar humbug,
but I'm not so bad, and Gower is beautiful as anywhere' (*CL*, 63). In
a letter to the *West Wales Guardian* he expressed disgust at 'this over-
peopled breeding box of ours, this ugly contradiction of a town for
ever compromised between the stacks and the littered bays' (*CL*, 142).
   By this time, the Thomas who yearned to escape the confines of his
home town and who had ostensibly retreated from its philistinism

into the safety of his own bedroom, was also the Thomas who had for a couple of years been a 'young dog', cutting a figure in the local pubs, on the stage of the Swansea Little Theatre, and in the mildly bohemian company of his acquaintances at the Kardomah Café. As a cub reporter on what became the *Evening Post*, Thomas was wholly unreliable and frankly irresponsible. But, as James A. Davies has emphasised, it

> increased his knowledge of Swansea and particularly of its crisis areas and low life: the hospital, the police station, the mortuary and its sad cargo, and the docks area with its sleazy pubs and loose women. He cultivated a 'reporter's image' influenced by American films; a pulled-down porkpie hat, dangling cigarette, and check overcoat. (*RG*, 21)

And it was during this period that the habit of trawling the pubs began. He captured the atmosphere of his life at this time in the last two stories of *Portrait of the Artist as a Young Dog*.

The old Kardomah Café was conveniently situated directly opposite the *Evening Post* buildings (diagonally opposite the Castle), and so at lunch times Thomas and his fellow trainee journalists like Charles Fisher could always slip across the road. Once again, he therefore occupied a frontier zone, a sociolinguistic positioning that contributed significantly, time after time, to the development of his distinctively hybrid imagination. This cultural situation is again conveniently represented for us by the Kardomah's physical location and accordingly mixed clientele at that time. It was located in Castle Street, at the bottom of High Street, adjacent to the red-light district of the Strand and the racy docks area of Swansea. But it was also in the heart of the old Swansea's downtown shopping area, next to prestigious stores like Ben Evans, and so patronised by middle-class and working-class shoppers alike.

The strong development of the Swansea Art School under Grant Murray after the First World War meant that the town was home to a young artistic set, and from the late 1920s onwards one of the favourite haunts of young artists was the Kardomah. It was to this set that Thomas the cub reporter attached himself. Those gathering periodically at the café included the two young artists Fred Janes and Mervyn Levy, a young man who spoke Yiddish at home (that frontier zone again) because he was the grandson of the refugee Russian Jew who had opened the first cinema in Swansea. Other regulars were aspiring writers Tom Warner and Charles Fisher, who was to enjoy a very colourful career as a globe-trotting journalist and died in Canada at the beginning of the twenty-first century. Daniel Jones, Thomas's boyhood friend who would go on to fame as a symphonic composer, would also sometimes join the company. The model for them all were the Viennese and South Bank Parisian cafés frequented by intellectuals and artists who had contributed so notably to the development of the modernist arts.

The Kardomah was, for Thomas, the successor to Cwmdonkin Park and Warmley – a congenial space within a comfortingly protective, intimately knowable, but ultimately philistine town where his imagination could be allowed full play, and find stimulation in the company of others. The informal café setting also promoted cross-fertilisation between different art forms. This fluid, highly informal group consisted of painters and musicians as well as poets, many of them fascinated by the modernist experimentations that had foregrounded the formal, compositional properties of art at the expense of the old, traditional, representational paradigms. And these interests, too, chimed with those of the young Thomas, reinforcing his instinct to treat words rather as, say, the Cubist painters treated objects. He captured the flavour of their meetings in the story 'Old Garbo', from *Portrait of the Artist as a Young Dog*:

> Most of the boys were there already. Some wore the outlines of moustaches, others had sideboards and crimped hair, some smoked curved pipes and talked with them gripped between their teeth, there were pin-striped trousers and hard collars, one daring bowler . . . 'Sit by here,' said Leslie Bird. He was in the boots at Dan Lewis's.[14]

'Sit by here' is an example of the young men's self-mocking affectation of the Welsh English that was the vernacular idiom of this cultural frontier town, situated on the very edge of the thoroughly Welsh-speaking industrial Tawe (Swansea) valley. And it is obvious that the language spoken by the youths in the café was a mix of the standard 'educated' English of their grammar-school backgrounds, the Welsh English of the streets, the high 'literary' language of the modernist writers with whom they were obsessed, and the flavoursome slang of the American gangster movies they so loved. Whereas the language used by the leading English poets of the day, such as W. H. Auden, tended to be very much the limited product of an English public school, middle-class milieu, a Swansea Welshman like Dylan Thomas was early exposed to a variety of linguistic registers, class sociolects and cultural discourses that helped make him the distinctively 'hybrid' poet he became.[15] And conversations around the tables in the Kardomah obviously featured a constant switching between these many different examples of language usage. No wonder therefore that one of the places Thomas revisited so movingly in imagination, and indeed in implicit homage, in *Return Journey* was the site of the Kardomah, reduced to rubble in the Blitz:

> I haven't seen him since the old Kardomah days . . . Him and Charlie Fisher – Charlie's got whiskers now – and Tom Warner and Fred Janes, drinking coffee-dashes and arguing the toss [. . . about] Music and poetry and painting and politics, Einstein and Epstein, Stravinsky and Greta Garbo, death and religion, Picasso and girls[.] (*RJ*, 81)

* * *

These were also years during which Thomas was active with the Swansea Little Theatre, 'based in Mumbles . . . close to congenial pubs', as Jim Davies has astutely noted. This was a breakaway group from the Swansea Amateur Dramatic Society, interested in staging more sophisticated plays, such as classics by Shakespeare, Chekhov and Ibsen.[16] During his time with the group, Thomas had roles in William Congreve's *The Way of the World*, Noel Coward's *Hay Fever* and a couple of other contemporary plays. He attracted good notices for his performances, but was also criticised for his inability to adapt his accent and mode of delivery to suit the different parts he was required to play. But the experiences that he gained through his acting obviously contributed very substantially to his subsequent career of public performance, both as a brilliant radio broadcaster (who first took the microphone at the Swansea studios of the BBC) and as an incomparable reader of his own poetry.

His theatrical experience enabled him to perfect his public persona – or rather, his public personae, as he actually proved far more adept in life than he did on stage at changing his personality to suit his various audiences. One of the leading figures in the Little Theatre was Thomas Taig, at that time lecturer in the English department at the fledgling University College of Swansea, and after Thomas's death, Taig was to stress how consummate an actor he had become in the street theatre of life itself. 'I think of him as infinitely vulnerable,' Taig wrote, 'living from moment to moment a heightened awareness of sense-impressions and emotional tensions, the victim rather than the master of his environment.' It was his acting skills, Taig added, that eventually enabled Thomas to overcome these handicaps and eventually to achieve a mastery, of sorts, of his environment – but at considerable, and eventually tragic, cost to his inner self (*DR*, 100–4).

Eerily enough, Daniel Jones was to paint a very similar picture of Thomas in one of the last interviews he gave before his death. He spoke of the Dylan he knew so well as a lost soul, one who could never reconcile public performer and inner being. Jones's Dylan is one who never really knew who he was – he's the lost soul we've already met, who in that opening passage from *Return Journey* returned to Swansea in a vain attempt to reintegrate his present with his past. Never lost *for* words, Daniel Jones's Dylan was consequently condemned to be forever lost *in* words, doomed to be a garrulous performer for all and sundry to the very last. So maybe the barmaid had indeed innocently seen him for what he was, when she'd exclaimed 'There's words'.

After his first departure for London in 1933, Thomas was never again really a native of Swansea. And then, over those three terrible nights in 1941, the centre of Swansea was razed to the ground. It's scarcely an exaggeration to claim that the erasure of his home town's heartland was a traumatic event in Thomas's life. After it, he felt imaginatively orphaned. The umbilical cord connecting him to the richest and most dependable source of his creativity had been cut for ever. He'd always been restless, but after the war he became a displaced person.

There's even a sense in which both of his most popular works – *Under Milk Wood* and 'Fern Hill' – are elegies for the lost Swansea of his boyhood. In *Under Milk Wood* he recreated, after an adult fashion, the zany world he invented with Daniel Jones during those years of high-spirited collaboration in Warmley. And 'Fern Hill', although of course a poem nostalgically recalling boyhood holidays on his aunt's west Wales farm near Llansteffan, is also a poem directly responding to the two events that changed Thomas's world for ever. The first was the bombing of Swansea; the second was the bombing of Hiroshima and Nagasaki. In Thomas's mind they tended to merge into a single nightmare – the irreversible loss of what had remained to him of human hope and innocence. 'Fern Hill' is an elegy for such a lost world. And his radio play, *Return Journey*, about his imaginary journey back to Swansea in the terribly cold winter of 1947 in search of an irretrievably lost town and an irretrievably lost self, is a memorable elegy for both self and Swansea that also darkly foreshadows his own imminent death.

Rooted in his Swansea experiences, then, are Thomas's great affirmations of language, such as the great magnificat to words he sent to an enquiring obscure Texan postgraduate in 1951. Recalling his early discovery, once more in his Swansea childhood, of 'such goings-on in the world between the covers of books' (the sly insinuation of verbal sexual shenanigans is interesting), he wrote of:

> such sand-storms and ice-blasts of words, such slashing of humbug, and humbug too, such staggering peace, such enormous laughter, such and so many blinding bright lights breaking across the just-awaking wits and splashing all over the pages in a million bits and pieces all of which were words, words, words, and each of which was alive forever in its own delight and glory and oddity and light. (*EPW*, 156)

But Thomas was also ever aware of being 'Shut, too, in a tower of words' – a tower that could be phallically creative but could also be humanly imprisoning. It is telling, I think, that at the time of his death, one of the projects Thomas was contemplating undertaking was entitled 'Where Have the Old Words Got Me?'.[17]

* * *

As I started this discussion with *Return Journey*, let me also finish with it, ending with its immensely moving conclusion. It features Thomas, the returnee, wandering Cwmdonkin Park as twilight falls and the park prepares for closure. In one, final attempt at coming face to face with his young self, he asks the lugubrious park keeper, now turned gatekeeper of tenebrous regions, the same plaintively insistent question he'd asked the barmaid earlier: does he remember a curly-haired youngster? 'Oh yes, yes I knew him well', comes the reply: 'He used to climb the reservoir railings and pelt the old swans. Run like a billygoat over the grass you should keep off of. Cut branches off the trees. Carve words on the benches.' This seems promising, at last, not least that memory of a boy whose very identity yearned to take the form of words. But even as the park keeper goes on to fill in the rest of the picture – of a boy who used to 'Climb the elms and moon up the top like a owl. Light fires in the bushes' – he is, we discover, preparing the way not for a revelatory disclosure but rather for an anticlimax. 'Oh yes, I knew him well. I think he was happy all the time', the park keeper poignantly repeats, before fatally adding: 'I've known him by the thousands.'

> [Dylan Thomas]: We had reached the last gate. Dusk grew around us
> and the town. I said: What has become of him now?
> Park Keeper: Dead.
> [Dylan Thomas]: The Park keeper said: (*The park bell rings*)
> Park Keeper: Dead ... Dead ... Dead ... Dead ... Dead ...
> Dead. (*RJ*, 90)

That is indeed the play's very last word; the last word on the play; the last word on Thomas's search; the word that marks the end of language itself; the dead end. And behind this concluding passage we are surely meant to hear the ironic echo of yet more words, as memorable as they are ultimately futile; the words of John Donne in the great, famous, prophetic utterance that had ignited the young Swansea Thomas's imagination and helped turn his entire life into a fateful adventure in language: 'Ask not for whom the bell tolls: it tolls for thee.'[18]

Notes

1 This is the text of a keynote lecture delivered at an International Dylan Thomas
   Conference held in the University of Bordeaux (Autumn 2014). Published as
   '"There's Words": Dylan Thomas, Swansea et la langue' in *Lire et Relire Dylan
   Thomas, Cycnos* 31:2 (2015).
2 Quoted in James A. Davies, *A Reference Guide to Dylan Thomas* (Westport,
   CT and London: Greenwood Press, 1998), p. 24. Hereafter *RG*.
3 'Return Journey', in Dylan Thomas, *Quite Early One Morning: Poems, Stories,
   Essays* (London: Dent, 1974), p. 76. Hereafter *RJ*.
4 Walford Davies and Ralph Maud (eds), *Dylan Thomas: Collected Poems
   1934–1953* (London: Dent, 1988), p. 148. Hereafter *CP*.
5 'Lapis Lazuli', *The Collected Poems of W. B. Yeats* (London: Macmillan, 1963),
   pp. 338–9.
6 Constantine Fitzgibbon, *A Life of Dylan Thomas* (London: Dent, 1965),
   p. 13.
7 For the influence of Crompton, see Betty and William Greenway, 'Just Dylan:
   Dylan Thomas as Subversive Children's Writer', in *Welsh Writing in English:
   A Yearbook of Critical Essays*, 5 (1999), 42–50.

[8]   Vic Golightly, '"Speak on a Finger and Thumb": Dylan Thomas, Language and the Deaf', in *Welsh Writing in English: A Yearbook of Critical Essays*, 10 (2005), 73–97.

[9]   Paul Ferris (ed.), *Dylan Thomas: The Collected Letters* (London: Dent, 1985), p. 130. Hereafter *CL*.

[10] In the discussion that follows, I draw upon two earlier publications of mine: the chapter entitled 'Marlais: Dylan Thomas and the "Tin Bethels"', in M. Wynn Thomas, *In the Shadow of the Pulpit: Literature and Nonconformist Wales* (Cardiff: University of Wales Press, 2010), pp. 226–55; and 'Marlais', in Hannah Ellis (ed.), *Dylan Thomas: A Centenary Celebration* (London: Bloomsbury, 2014), pp. 30–41.

[11] Walford Davies (ed.), *Dylan Thomas: Early Prose Writings* (London: Dent, 1971), p. 156.

[12] 'The procreant urge of the world', Francis Murphy (ed.), *Walt Whitman: The Complete Poems* (London: Penguin, 1977), p. 65.

[13] Leslie Norris (ed.), *Dylan Thomas: The Collected Stories* (London: Dent, 1983). Hereafter *CS*.

[14] *The Dylan Thomas Omnibus, Under Milk Wood, Poems, Stories and Broadcasts* (London: Phoenix, 2000), p. 242.

[15] This aspect of his poetry has been highlighted most recently in John Goodby, *Dylan Thomas: Under the Spelling Wall* (Liverpool: Liverpool University Press, 2013).

[16] There's useful information about this period in Colin Edwards and David N. Thomas (eds), *Dylan Remembered, Volume One, 1914–1934* (Bridgend: Seren, 2003), pp. 260ff. Hereafter *DR*.

[17] Ralph Maud (ed.), *Where Have the Old Words Got Me?* (Cardiff: University of Wales Press, 2003).

[18] John Hayward (ed.), *John Donne: Complete Poetry and Selected Prose* (London: The Nonesuch Press, 1972), p. 538.

5

'A HUGE ASSEMBLING OF UNEASE':
READINGS IN *A MAN'S ESTATE*

A vengeful wife (Mary Elis) murders her unfaithful husband (Felix Elis) with the tacit complicity of her secret admirer (Vavasor Elis). That gaunt suitor, a cousin of the deceased, subsequently marries her. Their sin is visited upon the children of both her marriages. The son (Dick) born to the grim pair, indulged by his mother, proves wilful and dies in war; his life is a 'judgement' on his parents, his story makes for 'a puny provincial tragedy'.[1] Philip, the son of the original union, is separated from his sister Hannah at birth. Growing up scarcely aware of each other's existence the siblings are nevertheless eventually united. This marks the fateful culmination of the sister's long-cherished dream of the arrival of a saviour who will release her from the house ('Y Glyn') and family that have long held her spirit captive. Reluctantly returning to claim his 'estate', her impecunious brother finds himself nightmarishly entangled in a past about which he knows nothing. And when the gruesome truth about the family history finally surfaces, their ageing mother escapes incontinently into madness, while their stepfather commits suicide. The atmosphere throughout is doom-laden; a judgemental God hovers ominously over the scene; gloom seems to pervade every corner of the action.

Reduced to the bare essentials of its plot, *A Man's Estate* (1955) proves to be massively built on an ancient substratum of legend – the primal stuff of which Greek tragedy was made, and Shakespearean and Jacobean drama likewise. The dominant stories of the Old Testament – so relevant to this novel about a 'biblical' society –are also of the same 'archetypal' character. During the period he was writing the novel, Emyr Humphreys was in the grip of a fascination with

myth, with classical tragedy, and with plays such as *Hamlet*.[2] 'A huge
assembling of unease' (*ME*, 84) – a phrase used by the sentimental
young minister, Idris Powell, bewildered by the dark complexities of
love – is a fair description of *A Man's Estate* as a whole, with its
labyrinthine rootedness in human passions. There is something repellent
about even the most marginal characters:

> Katie is thin and rodent: she scuttles about the house, always too fast
> to do anything properly, her small head carrying a flopping flappy
> cap, and when she speaks, her teeth seem very sharp as she makes her
> indistinct squeaks and noises (*ME*, 155).

Not only does this highlight unsavoury physical signs of Katie's
spiritual deformity, it reflects the sour, twisted soul of the neurotic
and 'barren spinster' who is here viewing the maid through jealous,
jaundiced eyes.

Much that was best in modern Welsh literature, Emyr Humphreys's
great friend and exemplar Saunders Lewis once observed, derived
from the Calvinist strain in nineteenth-century Nonconformity.
Through its insistent recognition of the evil ingrained in human
nature, Calvinism nurtured an unillusioned consciousness creatively
alive to the moral ugliness of the human condition. War experience
refocused attention on the lurking presence of evil within the human
soul – William Golding's *Lord of the Flies* (1954) was a memorable
1950s fable emphasising this. Likewise indirectly a product of Emyr
Humphreys's wartime experience, *A Man's Estate* is a classical Welsh
Calvinist tragedy (even a kind of 'revenger's tragedy') in two senses.
It deals with the morbid, decaying Calvinist culture of the chapels
midway during the first half of the twentieth century; and it views
that culture from the standpoint of an author capable of empathising
with the tough realism of Calvinist belief in original sin. As such,
the novel is the radical Welsh Nonconformist complement to the
Catholic novels of sin and guilt written by Humphreys's early friend
and mentor, Graham Greene.[3] It may also be revealingly juxtaposed
with another important 'Calvinist' novel of the 1950s, Robin Jenkins's
The Corn-Gatherers (1955), set in the Calvinistic society of Argyll-
shire.

One possible consequence of the replacement of a Calvinist vision
by a more tolerant post-Calvinist theological outlook is explored in
A Man's Estate through the character of the young idealistic minister

Idris Powell. Devotee of a facile liberal theology of universal love, he crushingly discovers that he lacks the moral, psychological and spiritual resources to deal with the harsh realities of devious human existence. Like the spiritually lightweight Merton Densher in Henry James's great novel *The Wings of the Dove*, Powell is judged in the sombre light of human tragedy and found wanting. 'Murderer' and hypocrite though the morally weathered and withered Vavasor Elis may be, in his daily implicit recognition of the severe Puritan values by which he will eventually be implacably judged he possesses a compelling moral weight; a monstrous integrity.

The very title of the novel bears the heavy burden of its central preoccupations. As the epigraph makes clear, the phrase 'A Man's Estate' alludes to the opening lines of a familiar Welsh Calvinist hymn by Dafydd Jones of Caio: 'Plant ydym eto dan ein hoed/ Yn disgwyl am ystad'. The translation provided in the novel reads: 'We are all still children/ waiting for an inheritance'. As modified in Humphreys's title, the theological meaning is double. *A Man's Estate* alludes to the state of sin that is the inheritance of all the sons and daughters of Adam. But the reference is also to that other 'state', of Divine Grace, to which spiritually infantile mankind as a whole should aspire, but which can be entered only by the elect; by the few mysteriously chosen as sole beneficiaries of Christ's self-immolation. In some important respects, the action of the novel oscillates between these two meanings. If the 'barren spinster' Hannah, daughter to Mrs Elis and her first (murdered) husband, is in one sense manifestly an innocent victim of her mother's tyrannical grip on life, she is also (as she recognises) 'bound' to her mother and stepfather 'in the blood-cement of likeness. I have their coldness, their calculation, their trained hypocrisy, their perpetual misery, their unexpiated guilt' (*ME*, 156). Recognising her own 'sinfulness', Hannah dreams euphorically of a salvatory act of secular grace in the form of the return of her long-lost brother. But in its vengeful aspects, such a messianic expectation in turn evokes uneasy memories of the strong-leader cult of the 1930s. To the domestic fascism of her everyday life on the family farm, 'Y Glyn', she secretly opposes her own fascist fantasy of supreme personal empowerment. Finally, having begun as a victim of her circumstances, Hannah ends up guilty of perpetuating the status quo; a 'feudal' biblical order grown rotten to its core.

* * *

If, then, *A Man's Estate* is modelled on classical tragedy, it is set not
in ancient Greece but in the morally decadent chapel culture of rural
Wales during the first half of the twentieth century. In this society
relationships involve the kind of ruthless power-struggles so nakedly
and memorably illustrated in some of the primal stories of the Old
Testament. And just as, for all its roots in 'universal' human legends,
Greek tragedy is actually woven out of the conflicting values of ancient
Greek society at a particular historical juncture, so Humphreys's novel
specifically addresses the tensions within the dying 'Nonconformist
nation', a century after its mid-nineteenth-century prime. In this
connection, it is useful to register the pivotal place *A Man's Estate*
occupies in the development of Emyr Humphreys as a novelist.

The novel was written some three years after Humphreys's return
from London to teach at Pwllheli, on the Llŷn peninsula. A teacher
in Wimbledon, but living in Chelsea, and a coming young writer with
three novels already to his name, he had spent four years mixing with
aspiring, talented young writers, artists and actors in a metropolitan,
cosmopolitan, atmosphere heady with the excitement of new beginnings after an exhausting war and the establishing of a welfare state.
The return of this native to Wales was prompted by a commitment
to the Welsh language and the values it had nurtured. This was the
result of the schoolboy Humphreys's 'conversion' to cultural and
political nationalism in the 1930s. But his move 'home' was at a
considerable price – Graham Greene strongly advised against it,
forecasting the miscarriage in the 'provinces' of Humphreys's talents
as a novelist. The resulting tensions within the ambitious young author
found expression in *A Man's Estate*, a novel that subjects the concept
of 'rootedness' (to which Humphreys nevertheless remained tenaciously
faithful) to sceptical scrutiny. Cross-examined about his 'pietas' by
his prospective father-in-law, the odious Master of an Oxford college,
the scientifically minded Philip dismisses all discussion of family (as
opposed to property) inheritance as nonsensical superstition, 'un-
scientific fascism' (*ME*, 19). He acknowledges blood groups but not
blood lines. The novel, however, calls Philip's supposedly objective,
'scientific', outlook into doubt, exposing it as simplistic by indicating
its compromised origins in family and society. Meanwhile his sister,
the claustrophobically cloistered Hannah, is aware of how the Elis
family farm has remained in stubborn, decaying stasis while life in
the surrounding Welsh countryside has been undergoing revolutionary
change. Although resentful of her parents' glowering dominance, she

is nevertheless willing prisoner of the 'old dispensation'. In its apparent immunity to springtime's infectious revivifications, the rural scene almost completely filling her window, and blocking her 'view', resembles a consolingly timeless frieze:

> I sit watching through my square bedroom window a man ploughing a field that slopes upwards. If I lean back this field fills all the window space except the top right which gives me a further horizon and a small view of the bay. The white gulls wheel perpetually around the tractor and the plough. (*ME*, 27)

'Rootedness' here appears in the form of the arrested development of a personality fearful of facing up to the challenges of life.

Life at 'Y Glyn' acts as a corrective to the younger Humphreys's weakness for rural idyll. In his teens, he had embraced the conservative social ideology of Plaid Cymru under Saunders Lewis's leadership, with its anti-industrial bias and alternative valorisation of rural, 'yeoman' life. While wartime work on the land, as a conscientious objector, had modified his ideal, it had been reaffirmed by the happy experience of working on the Llanfaglan estate, near Caernarfon (1941–3). Memories of that period were, no doubt, gilded by recollections of his courtship there of his wife-to-be, Elinor Jones. But the family's return from London to Pwllheli, a small seaside town on the Llŷn peninsula, prompted a more mature, and nuanced, estimate of rural, traditional Welsh society. *A Man's Estate* is therefore, for Humphreys, what *Return of the Native* was for Thomas Hardy: an ambivalent affirmation of 'roots', of 'origins', of 'belonging'. This takes the form of a fictional balance-sheet scrupulously weighing the advantages of staying against those of leaving; of social memory against forgetting.

Humphreys's ambivalent meditation on people's stubborn, complex, compromised, and often problematic allegiance to place was no doubt also informed by his experience, as charity worker, of administering a 'transit camp' for displaced peoples in Italy at the close of the war. These were vast encampments – temporary cities of transients housing not just individuals but virtual populations, some desperate to return to (frequently obliterated or forcibly appropriated) 'homes', others equally anxious to start anew by making a 'home' in any welcoming country. Humphreys's sensitivity to their refugee condition may have been all the more acute given his own angry discovery, as a sixth-former, that he had hitherto been living as a 'displaced' person in his own country. That unwitting displacement had been cultural rather than geographical in character. Humphreys's exposure to the 'colonial' reading of Wales offered by Saunders Lewis and Plaid Cymru had opened his eyes to his own 'disinherited' condition as a monoglot English 'Welshman'. He suddenly saw himself as a subaltern colonial subject, effectively prevented from 'reading' the history of his own country inscribed in its (Welsh-language) place names, instanced by its distinctive (Welsh-language) religious history, and tenaciously recorded in its (Welsh-language) literary culture. By setting to and learning Welsh, Humphreys further felt he was equipping himself to counter the enormous centrifugal forces generated by the wartime British state. Even while serving as a Save the Children Fund officer first in Egypt and then in Italy, he was able to continue reading Saunders Lewis's weekly, Welsh-orientated, commentary on political events in *Y Faner*. But if Humphreys thus became, as he has remained, a committed nationalist, *A Man's Estate* is his dark 1950s reflection on a Welsh nation whose future existence was in real jeopardy, because its only potent sustaining image of its own modern identity (the seminal nineteenth-century concept of the 'Nonconformist nation') was in monstrous terminal decline.[4] As Humphreys was to make clear in his later fictions, the image of its 'proletarian', industrial self adopted by early twentieth-century Wales in preference to its outmoded nineteenth-century religious self-image was, in his view, a destructively Anglocentric one, spuriously masquerading as 'internationalist' in character.

But nationalism is not given an easy ride in *A Man's Estate*. Mrs Elis's version of that ideology is fanatical, chauvinistic and paranoid, a grotesquely pathetic echo of the brutally swaggering 1930s nationalism of Germany, Italy and Spain. Not so that of Humphreys. As developed through his exposure to wartime European conditions, his nationalism became internationalist in its implications. The transit camps helped him realise the universality of the 'Welsh condition' – of a small national culture's struggle to retain a separate identity in the face of (linguistic, cultural, economic and political) powers 'innocently' intent on its obliteration. To members of a dominant, seemingly omnipotent, anglophone culture immeasurably reinforced, in the aftermath of victory, by the world dominance of the USA, such a struggle might seem to be the product of an outmoded and futile kind of petty, 'provincial' self-preoccupation. But the transit-camp experience had taught Humphreys that such an endangered condition was in fact the post-war European norm. And soon it would become the common fate of nations worldwide vulnerable to the culturally corrosive processes of 'globalisation' and its attendant anglicisation.

Nor is this the only 'international' dimension of the novel's concerns. In *A Man's Estate*, Humphreys fashions a Welsh 'family saga' suitable for obliquely exploring a Europe-wide post-war crisis: how to deal with a 'guilty', humanly destructive past; but also how to apportion 'guilt' in such morally opaque circumstances. There is a striking resemblance between the terms in which Humphreys recalled the experience of serving in Italy in the immediate aftermath of war and those used in his novel by a Hannah bewildered by her family situation. Her problem is that:

> I must somehow, out of myself like an industrious silk-worm produce the thread that will bind the fragments together, or lead me back through the labyrinthine wood of incidents behind whose apparently solid trunks sinister outlines seem to move in the dark. (*ME*, 48)

Speaking in interview about post-war Italy, Humphreys uses a similar image: 'in the terrible situation Europe was in at the time, we were moving around like children in the forest to a great extent.'[5]

Like the characters in some Ibsen play, the Elises are so obsessed with their terrible secrets they seem little more than pallid ghosts helplessly haunting the site of a violently vivid family crime. And in their gloomy moral paralysis, Humphreys seems to see, more locally, the state of a Welsh nation unable either to connect with its past in a way that would guarantee its future, or to break with it in ways that could offer a way forward. The other side of the coin represented by the monstrously deformed chapel 'morality' of the Elises is the vigorous self-interested resourcefulness of predatory 'survivors' like the scornfully anti-chapel Wally Francis and Winnie Cwm. Winnie's daughter, Ada, is a much more complex character –sympathetic, attractive, even heroic perhaps, but with her tragic aspects. She pays the price for being both genetically and socially a product of both the world of the chapel and the world of her mother. Thus internally torn, she is only imperfectly able to turn her moral instincts into an opportunistic amorality. Willing herself to be manipulative, she struggles to get the better of the born, and therefore instinctive, manipulators (including

Hannah's half-brother Dick) by whom she is surrounded. To her
irritation, she senses that compared with them she remains little more
than a sheep in wolf's clothing.

The novel is thus coolly open-eyed in what is its nevertheless (guarded)
advocacy of a committed concern with 'belonging' and with the
difficulty of establishing an honest, appropriate, responsible, creative
connection with the past. This becomes apparent if one considers its
treatment of the alternative – an opting for a 'rootless', culturally
amnesiac existence. Such is the life of Mrs Elis's first husband, the
ambitious young Liberal politician, Elis Felix Elis, loosely modelled on
the morally and physically footloose career of the brilliant opportunist,
Lloyd George. Greedily allured by London's promise of office and
power, Elis maintains the merest cynical token of a connection with
his Welsh home and family, just sufficient to allow him to continue
to be the darling of the chapels. Such a metropolitan path had, in
Humphreys's opinion, proved the headlong highway to national
destruction for the Welsh and their country ever since the assimilationist
Act of Union. During the first half of the twentieth century this well-
trodden route had been enthusiastically followed not only by ambitious
Liberal and Labour politicians but by the professional classes, including
generations of Welsh teachers like Gwendoline Esmor (who has
discreetly jettisoned that shameful brand of Welsh identity, the vulgar
surname 'Jones'). Miss Esmor and her secret lover Elis Felix Elis, MP
are well matched in lamenting 'the misfortune of being Welsh' (*ME*,
215), in their desperate attempt to escape 'that octopus country, that
cannibal mother country' (*ME*, 216). The MP's middle name, 'Felix',
nicely conveys his conscienceless and insouciant blitheness (*felix* being
Latin for 'happy'), while the repeating of 'Elis' perfectly captures his
ruthless narcissism. Nurtured in the outlook of this pair, Felix's son,
Philip Elis views his journey to the family 'estate' as a descent into a
pit of 'Calvinistic sadists and hypocrites' (*ME*, 231). Nor is he far
wide of the mark.

* * *

Like Philip, when Emyr Humphreys returned to Wales he was brought
into intimately close contact with Welsh Nonconformity. His wife,
Elinor, was the daughter of a highly respected minister with the
Annibynwyr (Welsh Independents), and, although Humphreys had
been raised an Anglican – he had even considered taking holy orders

as a teenager – on his marriage he was accepted into membership by his wife's denomination. As her father grew older, Elinor assumed responsibility for his care, and this culminated with the Reverend Jones spending his declining years with the Humphreys family. This afforded his son-in-law an opportunity to acquaint himself thoroughly with the richness and complexity of Welsh Nonconformist culture. As a respected liberal, the Reverend Jones provided Humphreys with an excellent example of the effort made by the chapels after the First World War to remedy the damage that had been done by the publicly vociferous, jingoistic support for wartime recruitment of some of the more prominent conservative ministers. Partly in response to this, and to the perceived indifference of the denominations to the condition of the industrial working class, disillusionment and disaffection gripped chapel members during the post-war period, and mass defections followed. A generation of young, progressive, ministers, sympathetic to liberal theology, reacted by attempting to reconnect Nonconformity to the political radicalism that had characterised it during the later nineteenth century. While Humphreys greatly respected his father-in-law as embodying the impressive qualities of this generation, in Idris Powell he examines not only the challenges faced by any young minister who commits himself totally to a humanly unexamined and untested gospel of love but also the challenge such a Christian idealist represents for the majority of us who settle for a much more pragmatic approach to life. Is Powell disastrously naive, or is he spiritually pure? Does he mistake *eros* for *caritas*? Is he a danger not only to himself but to others? What are we to make of a 'holy fool'? Urgent questions of this kind have continued to trouble Humphreys throughout his long writing career, and the enigma represented by Powell has been re-presented time after time in his fiction by similarly puzzling, morally indecipherable characters.[6]

A related issue explored through the character of Powell, and one that would again continue to haunt Humphreys for half a century thereafter, is whether a resolutely pacific approach to life is a sign of weakness, in a world so evidently governed by power and violence, or a sign of spiritual strength. This issue had presented itself in particularly anguished form in Humphreys's own life when he had to choose whether or not to stand by his pacifist beliefs during the Second World War. And having opted for pacifism, he was faced with a related dilemma as a committed Welsh nationalist. Determinedly opposed to any kind of resort to force, he nevertheless had to admit that history seemed to offer no reassuring example anywhere of national liberty won without the shedding of blood. These moral dilemmas are clearly focused in *A Man's Estate* by the placing of Idris Powell in a society entirely at the mercy of the fierce struggle for power within the Elis family and between it and the community it dominates. Puzzled, moved, attracted and irritated in equal measure by the singular, stubbornly non-violent character of the young minister of Bethania, Ada intuits that his gospel of love represents a serious threat to her. Briefly infatuated by his sweet difference, she comes to regard him impatiently as an ineffectual naïf, a dangerous incubus likely to compromise her independence and liable to leech away her precious power of survival. She particularly resents, and fears, his attempt to treat her as an adored, redemptive figure at the centre of a new religion of romantic love. Ada's reaction is, of course, significantly shaped by the feeling that she has twice previously fallen victim to her own dreamer's weakness for ideals. Viewed in this light, Idris Powell is only the latest instance of this recurrent inner temptation she has previously failed to resist.

* * *

Although the action of *A Man's Estate* covers more than thirty years, the novel was published in 1955 and can therefore usefully be viewed in the wider context of fiction's response to British society during that decade. Long regarded as a pallid period in the history of a British novel exhausted by the exhilarating modernist experimentations of earlier decades and resorting to drearily familiar and superannuated realist conventions, the 1950s has recently undergone substantial revaluation and rebranding.[7] The decade's literary culture is now styled 'late modernist', or 'intermodernist', and emphasis has shifted to an appreciation of how the post-war generation of novelists can best be understood as engaged in a range of textual conversations with their celebrated modernist predecessors. For instance, as was noted by William Cooper, one of the significant writers of the decade, some of this new fiction was concerned to recognise the claims of its society upon it. Whereas the modernist 'Experimental Novel', Cooper later observed, 'was about Man-Alone . . . we meant to write novels about Man-in-Society as well'.[8]

This was a distinction with which Emyr Humphreys strongly identified. Just two years before the publication of *A Man's Estate* he published a seminal essay in *The Listener*, one of the leading periodicals of the age. Entitled 'A Protestant View of the Modern Novel', it began by recognising that all 1950s novelists were working in 'a post-Joyce era of English fiction'.[9] Acknowledging Joyce's genius, Humphreys proceeded to criticise the Irishman as a driven aesthete, intent on maintaining an 'extraordinarily detached' attitude towards life. Such an attitude, Humphreys argued, was no longer possible after 1945, because Joyce was a man of the 'pre-atomic age' who had also ante-dated the rise to power of the working class. The latter 'have become a key factor in the technique of political power: monstrously large, frighteningly gullible, defenceless as a jelly fish – the raw material of the dictator's or the advertiser's art' (*CR*, 70). The urgent function of the contemporary novel, the essay implies, is to educate this new mass society by providing it with a moral compass. Otherwise, the impressionable population will continue, as during the 1930s, to fall victim to unscrupulous demagogues and populist manipulators of public opinion. The danger of a socially empowered but morally directionless working population is indicated in *A Man's Estate* by Humphreys's treatment of the amiably exploitative garage-owner Wally Francis and his family and cronies. Raised in the chapel, Francis has long abandoned it, recognising that its moral, as well as its social, authority, has crumbled away not least through inner corruption. His alternative gospel, like that of all those who lie within the orbit of his petty dictatorship, is one of shrewd opportunism.

In adopting his formalist attitude to human experience, Joyce was, Humphreys further argues in his essay, wholly at odds with the great tradition of the European novel as instanced by Dostoevsky, Tolstoy and others. For them, 'human life was not [as it was for Joyce] the raw material of art; it was a strange sea in which humanity thrashed about like a powerful, bewildered whale, harpooned by death, and still consumed with a desire for immortality' (*CR*, 70–1). This vision of mankind finds expression in the tragic action of *A Man's Estate*. In any tragedy, Humphreys observes in his 1953 essay, 'a lifetime leads to a meaningful crisis of disaster' (*CR*, 71) – a comment that brings the Elises immediately to mind.

Both Vavasor and Mary live out their lives to their tragic conclusion with a conscious sense of living under divine judgement. Theirs is a religious tragedy, as well as a personal and social one. And like many another writer and intellectual of the 1950s, Humphreys attributed the dangerous moral disorientation of his society to the decline of religion. Unlike his contemporaries, however, he refused to indulge in fantasies of 'restoring the myth', of defying science in order to reinstitute an 'organic society' of faith. 'Religion', he roundly insisted, 'must embrace what is true in science' (*CR*, 74).The dangers of divorcing the one from the other had been manifest in the terrible uses to which scientific knowledge had been put during the Second World War, culminating in Hiroshima and Nagasaki.

And the issue of how to handle scientific understanding –in particular of how to deal with a human mind irreversibly refashioned in the image of science – is a very live one in *A Man's Estate*. Could Vavasor have so arranged the scientifically undetectable murder of Felix Elis had he not possessed a chemist's understanding of the exact consequences of ceasing medication and withholding water? Isn't Hannah Elis's wish to become a chemist an expression of her wish to evade responsibility for confronting the complex mess of human motives and actions? Doesn't the coolly cynical Dr Pritchard afford an excellent example of a medical man's untroubled adoption of a materialist and hedonistic philosophy on the questionable assumption that science has demonstrated there is no more to life than such pleasures and satisfactions as can be wrung from one's mortal span? And isn't Philip's claiming of the scientist's prerogative of 'objectivity' and 'dispassionateness' likewise clearly revealed, by the end of the novel, to be an abrogation of moral duty, a failure of imagination, conscience and nerve, and a refusal to face up to the bewildering claims upon him of the human condition? These instances of science's failure to recognise key constitutive features of human existence are, of course, complemented in the novel by the failure of the chapel faithful to recognise science as religion's challenging partner in human-kind's endless pursuit of truth. As is noted in 'A Protestant View of the Modern Novel', 'Religion cannot ignore science on the so-called spiritual plane any more than science can ignore religion on the material' (*CR*, 74).

Central to Humphreys's important essay is his plea for the re-instatement of the 'Protestant principle of personal responsibility' (*CR*, 74). His is partly a reaction to the subordination of the individual to the mass will, evidenced so appallingly by both Fascist and Com-munist regimes. Humphreys's concern was not, however, primarily with these vestiges of past ideology; rather, he shared the worry famously articulated by George Orwell in *Animal Farm* (1945) and *Nineteen Eighty Four* (1949), that democratic states, too, were liable to turn authoritarian, even totalitarian, as they grew more dominantly systematised and centralist. Although in sympathy with that child of the 1950s, the Welfare State, Humphreys saw both in it and in the state rhetoric of a society fearful of the Communist threat, the seeds of a totalitarian democracy. It is worth bearing in mind that *A Man's Estate* is roughly contemporary with the McCarthy witch-hunt of 'Reds' in a United States hysterically convinced it was at risk from Communist fifth-columnists.

'The artist', Humphreys observed in his 1953 essay,

> has shied away from the crude strength of the Protestant conscience – that constant, hoarse, dynamic whisper. But it possesses an exciting paradoxical combination of simplicity and complexity: an awareness of the great mystery, the infinite unconditional nature of God, and the egocentric solitude and sin of man in his trap of time. (*CR*, 74)

The core subject of *A Man's Estate* is the Protestant conscience, that stern guardian of a sense of personal responsibility. Many of the main characters are urgently aware of being finally answerable for their own lives and actions. The novel is a sustained study of the history of the Protestant conscience in a period of moral confusion and uncertainty. Those consequences are various, ranging from the case of Vavasor and his wife, who finally fall tragic victim to the moral conscience that has worn their minds to tatters and their bodies to the bone, to that of Wally Francis, in whose comfortably corpulent case moral self-scrutiny has metamorphosed into wily self-interest. Ada's tragedy, of course, is that she is internally divided, trapped between the one principle and the other. As for Idris Powell, sexual passion and an attractive human compunction threaten to soften the iron backbone of his spiritually progressive principles.

* * *

Revisiting 'A Protestant View of the Novel' some fifty years after its publication, Emyr Humphreys concluded he would still stand by the insights and commitments in that text but would now prefer to substitute the term 'Dissident' for 'Protestant'. It's an interesting substitution because when writing during the 1950s about the contemporary novel Kenneth Allsop suggested that, whereas it had become common practice to speak of the fiction of 'angry young men' as a phenomenon of the period, 'a more accurate word for this new spirit that has surged in during the fifties is dissentience' (*Pelican*, 485). *Room at the Top* (1957), *Saturday Night and Sunday Morning* (1958) – and even *Lucky Jim* (1954) – all feature rebellious young male characters. These novels remain familiar landmarks of the period, and continue to be accepted as symptomatic of the social revolution afoot in Britain at the time. It was the coming of age of the social outsider. The war had effectively marked the end of Imperial Britain, and some of the scarce resources and energies of a weakened and exhausted country had to be devoted to the (frequently bloody) dismantling of Empire from India to Africa. Along with the implementing of the Welfare State and the social impact of the grammar schools, decolonisation accelerated the erosion of traditional respect for the authority of the middle class.

During the 1950s, the novels of Braine, Sillitoe and Barstow were primarily (and rightly) understood as demonstrating the right of the largely neglected English working-class to serious social and fictional attention. But in retrospect, they may also be regarded as instances of a new decentralising process at work within a post-war British state that, under the pressures of wartime, had reverted to its authoritarian centralist instincts. These northern 'working-class' novels were unmistakeably 'regional' in character, and as such they may now be usefully re-viewed in the light of other fiction of this period. The two decades immediately following the war saw the appearance of such classic texts as Chinua Achebe's *Things Fall Apart* (1958), V. S. Naipaul's *A House for Mr Biswas* (1961) and Jean Rhys's *Wide Sargasso Sea* (1968). Emanating from Africa and the Caribbean, they were the forerunners of what later, following the landmark publication of Salman Rushdie's *Midnight Children* (1981), came to be classed as post-colonial fiction. This was the exhilarating result of the appropriation of the English-language novel by natives of the erstwhile 'colonies' who thus gave expression to their own, distinctively non-English, experiences and concerns. English backlash took the form of the 'Little Englandism' exemplified in the fiction and poetry of Kingsley Amis and John Wain and in the 'Movement' poetry most powerfully instanced by Philip Larkin.

Given Emyr Humphreys's early tutelage under Saunders Lewis, and his resultant sensitivity to the colonial aspects of the Welsh condition, *A Man's Estate* may also reasonably be regarded as broadly anticipating the Welsh 'post-colonial' fiction Humphreys went on to write. It was an early product of his identification (implicit in his turning of his back on the metropolis) with a Welsh nation acquiring a consciousness in English, during a decade of rapid decolonisation, of its long cultural and political subordination by England. In looking to Philip for salvation, Hannah is also looking to England, as the servile Welsh had repeatedly done ever since the Act of Union. She busily weaves her self-protective fantasies out of materials from the Bible and from fairy tales.

> In my thirty-sixth year I wait and I am skilled in waiting. But it is danger-ous. It is easy to confuse the coming of a knight errant with the coming of the Saviour, and I sometimes see myself among the idolators throwing palms before the short nervous steps of the frightened ass. (*ME*, 54)

Needless to say, her callow dreams of rescue are rudely dashed, and at the end she is left to her own resources, however impoverished and dubious they may be. Recognising himself to be an outsider, disqualified on many different grounds from intervening, her anglicised and alienated brother returns 'Y Glyn' to Hannah's care. She is left to make what she can of her personal and cultural inheritance. The idiom of the novel likewise refuses to compromise with any respected English discourse of its day. *A Man's Estate* respects the rural religious society with which it is dealing sufficiently to judge it by its own best light and not by those of any supposedly more advanced cultural 'centre'.

* * *

One significant sign of Humphreys's mental orientation at this time was his adoption as role model not of any of the leading fiction writers of the British and Irish modernist tradition but of a confirmed American decentralist: William Faulkner was the great novelist of the defeated, subordinated culture of the southern states of the USA.[10] Cleanth Brooks opens his classic study, *William Faulkner: The Yoknatawpha Country* with the following paragraph:

> Most writers associate William Faulkner with the South quite as auto-matically as they associate Thomas Hardy with Wessex, Robert Frost with northern New England, and William Butler Yeats with Ireland, and perhaps more naturally than they associate Dylan Thomas with Wales. The regions and cultures to which these writers are linked differ in character, but they all stand in sharp contrast to the culture of the great world cities of the twentieth century. They have in common a

> basically agricultural economy, a life of farms, villages, and small towns,
> an old-fashioned set of values, and a still vital religion with its cult,
> creed, and basic norms . . . for all their differences, each provides its
> author with a vantage point from which to criticize, directly or perhaps
> merely by implication, the powerful metropolitan culture.[11]

Replace the name of Dylan Thomas with that of Emyr Humphreys
in this paragraph and one begins to understand why he was so powerfully impressed during the 1950s by the fiction of the great Southerner.

Faulkner was first fully 'discovered' in his own country with the
publication in 1949 of Malcolm Cowley's anthology *The Portable
Faulkner*, but he came to worldwide attention the following year
when he was awarded the Nobel Prize for Literature. Exactly when
Humphreys became aware of his work cannot be established, but he
has testified to an intensification of his appreciation of Faulkner's
work during the period he spent in Salzburg in 1954 in the company
of the great American critic, Edmund Wilson. A recent recipient of
the Somerset Maugham Prize, Humphreys had repaired to Austria
with his family to spend a year there working on what was to become
A Man's Estate. But a number of factors – including serious concern
about the condition of his eldest son, who developed peritonitis during
this period – meant he was unable to embark on the novel until he
had returned to Wales. Nevertheless, the work had been incubating
throughout his stay in Austria and therefore his discussions with
Wilson about Faulkner's novels must have been directly influencing
the development of his ideas.

Humphreys seems in part to have encountered in Faulkner a like-
minded writer whose singular, and signature, modernist innovations
of style and expression were driven, like Humphreys's own much more
modest experimentations in *A Man's Estate*, by a compulsion to access
the deep truths of his own culture. Robert Penn Warren, another great
critic of Southern literature, like Cleanth Brooks, feelingfully noted:

> as a technician, Faulkner, except for his peers, Melville and James, is
> the most profound experimenter in the novel that America has produced.
> But the experiments were developed out of – that is, were not merely
> applied to – an anguishing research into the Southern past and the
> continuing implications of that past.[12]

For instance, the stylised, poeticised, internal monologues that characterise such classic novels as *The Sound and the Fury* (1929) and *As*

I Lay Dying (1930) convey the weight, complexity and intensity of the characters' embeddedness in a stiflingly conservative society. In *A Man's Estate* Humphreys uses a similar device, most conspicuously when probing the state of mind of Hannah. By such means he is able to resolve one of the most pressing difficulties facing a writer seeking to fashion a modern tragedy out of lives lived in a democratic, egalitarian, levelling society – how to imbue the characters with the density, gravity and high seriousness that would effectively heighten the tone of their lives in the manner necessary for producing the rich, resonant tragic effect. Conscious of this problem, the great American dramatist Arthur Miller first attempted to solve it in *Death of a Salesman* (1949) by staying faithful to a naturalist, demotic style, but went on to draw memorably on scriptural speech when writing *The Crucible* (1953), which appeared just two years before *A Man's Estate*. Both Faulkner and Humphreys similarly drew extensively in their fiction on the cadences of the Bible – the sacred 'founding' text of their respective, originally biblical, societies. And in the cases of both writers, accessing this resource helped make possible their central achievement – what André Malraux described, with reference to Faulkner, as 'the renewal of tragedy' (*F*, 205–6).

Critics likewise spoke approvingly of the 'primal' quality of Faulkner's writing and, as has already been noted, this is a feature of *A Man's Estate*. The novel is concerned to demonstrate that human life tends to approximate to 'archetypal' patterns, a characteristic underlined by the way we make our lives intelligible both to ourselves and to others by shaping them into the form of familiar narratives. So Idris Powell images the abortive relationship between himself and Enid, his friend Lambert's wife, in terms of a medieval chivalric romance:

> Like legendary lovers, woven on the edge of a medieval wood, too poor to trouble about time or place, we walked in the garden of the hotel at night as if it were a rich man's castle that would admit only our most innocent dreams. (*ME*, 89)

And when the virtuous Powell begins to consort oddly with the far-from-virtuous Frankie (Ada's brother), village tongues begin to wag: 'Housewives wondered to see Frankie's turned out steps alongside my untidy strides, their myth-making minds having more to make of so untoward an alliance' (*ME*, 95).

Humphreys actually causes his novel to reflect on this storytelling and myth-making propensity of the human mind, and in the process causes it to reflect on its own narrative strategies, by including a story within his story. Owen Owens is a traditional Welsh *cyfarwydd*, an enthralling rural storyteller who acts as communal remembrancer. He holds his audience spellbound as he weaves his narrative, while 'the wind rushed through the cobbled yard outside the long window and the flames of the wide fire stretched into the cavernous mouth of the chimney' (*ME*, 65). Owen's story feeds the mind of his listeners as surely as the table laid for the morning's breakfast promises to satisfy their stomachs. He tells of a treacherous young farmer's wife whose unfaithfulness drives her innocent husband to suicide but who lives on to enjoy a prosperous life with her lover, a cowman. The tale has been repeated by him many times, and honed to a gratifyingly familiar shape. The episode ends with a comic reprise of Owen's story when Dick, Hannah's unruly half-brother, and his friend Willie, frighten Hannah by persuading her that, like the cowman, Dick has hanged himself from a beam in the barn. But then Owen Owens's story is later reprised in an entirely different key. His tale echoes that of Vavasor and Mary Elis, while the cowman's suicide foreshadows that of Vavasor, who poisons himself. He is discovered by Hannah collapsed over the sink he had been struggling to reach in an effort to alleviate his pain with a drink of the water he had, of course, murderously denied Elis Felix Elis. Story, like history, has an uncanny, unnerving, habit of repeating itself in human experience.

Also significant for Humphreys was Faulkner's genius for devising stylistic means of conveying the omnipresent, suffocating pressure of the past – felt too in the oppressive heat of the South – on the lives of his characters. Such a sense of the inescapable burden of cultural history corresponded to Humphreys's ambivalent sense of the significance for Wales of its inheritance: its Nonconformist 'estate'. Faulkner's achievement is of course different from that of Humphreys, and as the past of Southern history is immeasurably more terrible than that of Wales, so is its sinfulness and guilt proportionately more massive. But the felt parallels between Humphreys and his Wales and Faulkner and his South are nevertheless an important strand in the dense weave of *A Man's Estate*.

Humphreys attributed his recognition of himself in Faulkner to the fact that both the Southern states and Wales were defeated 'nations', subsequently incorporated into the victorious alien state (*DPR*, 85–6).

The values and practices of that nation-state were fundamentally different from, and inimical to, those of the cultures it had so comprehensively defeated. It was natural for the victorious to espouse a confident ideology of progress and of self-fulfilment that it was difficult for the defeated to share.

The consequences of the defeat of the Confederate cause are everywhere, and obsessively, explored by Faulkner. One recurrent structural feature of his fiction is the contrast between relics of the 'old order' – the impoverished, socially disempowered, and impressively flawed members of the cultivated classes that had traditionally sustained the ethos, the elaborate courtesies and the ethical codes of the antebellum South – and the creatures of the new order. The latter consisted not only of those carriers of Northern commercial values, the original 'carpetbaggers' who entered the former Confederacy as entrepreneurial interlopers to dismantle a semi-feudal society and to open the South up to the modern, thrusting world of capitalist competition, but also of their native allies, the lower-class Southerners who profited by allying themselves with this new 'foreign' culture of enterprise. Prominent instances of such creatures of the new post-bellum South in Faulkner's fiction are the semi-literate and nakedly opportunistic members of the large Snopes family. They roughly correspond to the members of Wally Francis's clan and their associates who occupy a not dissimilar position within the structure of *A Man's Estate*. Their relationship to those decadent representatives of the old Nonconformist 'aristocracy', the Elis family, is broadly similar to that of the grossly fecund Snopes family to the decaying leadership of the old antebellum South. Hannah Elis disdainfully dismisses Winnie Cwm, Wally Francis and their promiscuously intertwined families as 'a low family scheming to rise' (*ME*, 196). How, she asks herself, can she 'allow our family pride to be fouled by gutter people like Winnie Cwm and Frankie Cwm?' (*ME*, 197). She consequently refuses to acknowledge Ada as her half-sister, and so fails to grasp the social implications of the fact that they both actually have the same father.

* * *

These, then, are some of the matters with which Emyr Humphreys was concerned when writing *A Man's Estate*. But they can matter to us as readers, of course, only if they are fully grounded in the fiction; in other words, if they are fully inscribed in the text, are discursively

constructed, and are thus rendered convincing in fictional terms. Take
the dominant figure of Vavasor Elis, a candidate for tragic stature.
That there are repellent aspects to his character is evident enough.
Yet he remains a compelling, if forbidding, figure because virtually
alone among the main characters he is afforded the dignity of reticence.
Whereas we are made privy to the inner feelings of Hannah, Philip
and Ada, any insight into Vavasor Elis's state of mind is denied us
until the late, and therefore memorable, scene, when he voices his inner
torment through the heightened, measured, biblical rhetoric of public
confessional prayer.

> Elis' lips trembled as they always did before he began. His eyebrows
> twitched rapidly. But tonight I noticed his head moving slowly from
> side to side as if he were rocking some crying sleepless grief within
> himself.
>   'Almighty and . . . Almighty . . . O Lord in the words of Cain, my
> punishment is greater than I can bear. . . year after year . . . from the
> day my eyes grew dim to this thou hast visited me with these afflictions
> . . . Must I speak O Lord . . . Must I confess as a criminal still when I
> have accepted each affliction as a just punishment?' (*ME*, 393)

Even this climactic scene is carefully counterbalanced by an emphasis
on the bathos of Vavasor's punctilious observation of the rituals of
the prayer-meeting and on his affectingly uncoordinated, ungainly
physical presence: 'He pushed open the door and sat down on the
nearest seat exhausted, slowly removing the black hat he always wore
to come to chapel. It was too big for him and almost rested on his
large ears' (*ME*, 391). And in his electrifying confession before the
Lord, Vavasor demonstrates an impressive indifference to any effect
he may have on the solitary adult listener, Idris Powell: 'I was an aider
and abettor in his untimely death: the waters of succour trickled away
between my opening fingers as they approached his mouth' (*ME*, 393).
The weighty authority of the judgement he unsentimentally passes
on himself is palpable: he is speaking not just of 'murder' but of
mortal sin. There is a terrible fatalistic composure about him to the
end. 'He hurried off towards the door as he always did as if he had
endless business affairs waiting for his attention. "Good night now
then," he said, as he always did leaving chapel' (*ME*, 396).
    That obliviousness to the impression he is making is, in fact, one
of Vavasor's most impressive characteristics. His semi-blindness

emphasises his unconcern with social interaction, and, in its way, figures his bleak self-arraignment. There is a permanent unconscious helplessness about him, and he is unnerving because his obliviousness to anyone's gaze seems to prompt the observer (and thus vicariously the reader) to subject him to bold, guilty scrutiny. Yet for all this Vavasor baffles one's understanding. This is evident in Hannah's obsessively focused evocation of his gawky, helpless appearance:

> He is very thin, but the tweed suits he wears are so thick that you do not at first notice this, until you observe the loose skin of his neck is untouched by the stiff white wing-tipped collar that encircles it. His head is large and bald enough to appear flat along the top. The eyebrows above his deep-set staring blue eyes are thick and red, and seem to blink themselves when he exposes his old false teeth – beneath a broad moustache that my mother trims, after shaving him – in a constant nervous smile that is meant to disguise the hopeless intensity of his stare. (*ME*, 33)

Vavasor's old-fashionedness is here painfully obvious and embarrassing, yet his complete indifference to it bespeaks an implicit moral judgement on all those who follow the prevailing currents.

Vavasor remains a lonely enigma. In taking his own life he leaves no note – that would have been totally out of character. He is answerable only to God. Implicit in everything he is and does is an acceptance that he alone must take responsibility for what he has done and therefore is. His wife breaks down; he does not, not because of any psychological robustness but because of a stubborn moral strength. He is even more isolated in the terrible sanity of his unsparing self-indictment than she in her wild madness. Unlike him, she can take a kind of crazy comfort in the fantasy that hers had been an act of moral retribution, that she had sent her baby son away to protect him from knowing (what? about his father's sinful adulteries or about her own guilt?), and that she had similarly shielded her daughter by effectively imprisoning her. In killing the chickens that are her favourite 'children' she finds symbolic expression for her guilt, and so finds a kind of irrational relief. There is for her a kind of relief in the bloodiness of it – it contrasts with the bloodlessness of her silent, secret murder, just as her melodramatic voicing of the act contrasts with the muteness of that murder. And her killing of the chickens combines a re-enactment of her murder of her husband with a ritualistic punishing

of herself for that crime. It is also her symbolic admission that with
the killing of Felix she had effectively killed her capacity to love the
children born of their union. They had become the innocent scapegoats
for her husband's infidelities. In turn, of course, her frustrated need
to love had found an outlet in her doting indulgence of Dick, with
eventually disastrous effects.

Philip, a man who preens himself on his scrupulously 'scientific'
objectivity, is naively disturbed to realise how slippery a concept 'truth'
is outside the confines of the laboratory:

> I was thinking about truth. And how maddening to realise the difficulties
> when by instinct you felt that somewhere absolute truth existed, waiting
> for your arrival however long you delayed on the journey. There lie
> waiting your life's meaning and the secret of your unrest. (*ME*, 338)

If only it were as simple as that. While, in detective-story fashion, the
novel maintains suspense for much of its course by prolonging uncertainty about whether or not Felix Elis was actually murdered by
his wife and her admirer, as local rumour supposed, this 'mystery' is,
of course, solved well before the end. That is because *A Man's Estate*
is not centrally interested in soluble mysteries. It is concerned not with
the issue of (theoretically) ascertainable 'facts' but with the wholly
insoluble enigma of judgements – with the enigma, in other words,
of any life's 'meaning'. Vavasor Elis may, in his prayer and suicide,
pass 'definitive' judgement on the meaning of his own life, but the
novel refuses to pass final judgement on him: it cannot second-guess
the verdict of the God in whom Vavasor believes with such terrible,
fervent, devotion. Perhaps all tragedy is rooted in enigma; that is, it
may be a terrible manifestation of the unfathomable character of
human beings and the incalculable implications of their actions.

Compared with Vavasor and, to a lesser extent, his wife, Hannah Elis
and Idris Powell are diminished characters. Their inner tensions and
torments may generate pathos, but lack the dignity of tragedy. Ada,
however, commands much greater respect, and if the tragedy of Vavasor
and Mary Elis is an old-fashioned religious tragedy, hers may be a
secular tragedy after the modern fashion. In several important ways
she is the mirror image of that of the murderous couple. It is partly
because their language of self-understanding is religious that hers is
secular. It is in part their hypocritical ethics that fires her ambition to
be amorally selfish and opportunistic. Of their self-deception and

deceptions is born her own ruthless honesty. But beyond these super-ficial divergences between her life and theirs lie much deeper con-vergences. It is from the lives of the Elises quite as much as from the example provided by her mother, Winnie Cwm, that Ada learns the lesson that life is all about survival, and is therefore no more than one long unremitting struggle for power. No wonder that when she breaks the news to Hannah that her mother and stepfather are murderers she seems to be acting the role of one of the avenging Furies of ancient Greek tragedy. Her wailing 'coiled itself as smoothly as a trained snake into the empty spaces in my knowledge of the past', admits Hannah. 'It was very familiar as soon as I heard it in the way that only Truth can be' (*ME*, 206).

Ada enters her half-sister's world like the Reality Principle itself, exposing not only the 'Truth' about Vavasor and his wife, but also Hannah's long, wilful suppression of any sense of misgiving about her family. In a sense, Ada thus reveals Hannah's tacit complicity in the concealment of her father's murder. And if the 'barrenness' of which Hannah, the self-styled spinster, bitterly accuses herself is a metaphor for the desiccated moral and emotional state in which she has chosen to live, then Ada's 'promiscuity' is its complement, as well as its opposite, because it, also, is a defence against being trapped in any complex relationships of committed attachment. And in mourn-ing Dick, Ada is harbouring her own fantasy and lie, refusing to acknowledge his chronic selfishness and unreliability.

It is by rebelling against the patriarchal character of the Elises' religion that Ada takes on the role of the New Woman. This figure had fascinated Emyr Humphreys ever since childhood. He had grown up in the years immediately following the First World War, a period that saw a dramatic extension of the freedoms, rights and opportunities that women had been granted during wartime when they were allowed into the workforce as replacements for the men who had marched away, never to return. Although the social and political liberation of women had been a subject of fiction ever since the concluding decades of the nineteenth century, Humphreys became fascinated with the figure's increasing prominence during the period between the two world wars and beyond. A great admirer of independent women, he nevertheless struggled in his fiction to come to terms with them and to calibrate the implications of their growing social power. Time after time, a female figure of this powerful kind is uneasily twinned in his novels with that of a seemingly ineffectual, 'emasculated' man. Such, of course, is Idris Powell in part in *A Man's Estate*. It is the ambivalence of feeling manifest in such twinning that makes the portrayal of Ada so complex, and therefore so compelling.

As for Hannah, she takes refuge throughout the novel in loving her 'place'. She knows her very character has been formed in its image. Of herself and her mother she reflects that 'Out of our basic landscape our figures lost their recognisable shape and we became foreign to one another' (*ME*, 185). Others may treat 'Y Glyn' and its acres merely as property, but for her it constitutes identity. It exists sensuously – a displacement of her frustrated sexuality:

> A good year for blackberries. With the aid of a walking stick a quart gathered in a few minutes. The horses free of work galloped around the salt pools in the rough fields near the shore. Smoke from the chimney of Miss Aster's cottage blown about. Wet sheaves still out sticky to touch. A slow corn harvest. (*ME*, 197)

Hers is the kind of passionate identification with territory ('estate') that is the product of the Nonconformist emphasis on place as the sacred locale of a people, a notion based on the biblical (and particularly Old Testament) notions of land. But hers is also a decadent and perverted version of that Nonconformist 'theology' of place and nation.[13]

So what are we to make of the conclusion of the novel, when Hannah inherits 'Y Glyn' and 'A Man's Estate' thus becomes 'A Woman's Estate' instead? Does this bode well? Does it indicate that evil has been purged through the storm of tragedy? Does it signify that restoration of sound order that allowed Shakespeare to end his tragedies reassuringly with such firm, quiet conviction? That is difficult to believe. Hannah may have been released from enthralment to her parents, but she remains the prisoner of their world – the only world she has known or has ever wished to know. In the end, she can offer only a more humane continuation of the old, exhausted, 'feudal' dispensation. As the new mistress of the Glyn, she resumes the ritual of greeting the faithful retainers. 'My response echoes my uncle's. The voice is different but the formula must be the same' (*ME*, 410). Her earlier comment proves prophetic: 'Spinsters, it is their function and their fate, are custodians of family history. They knit the temporal net with ropes of their heart's blood' (*ME*, 195). And so the novel seems unable to imagine through Hannah a substantial, vibrant, living new future for the moribund, not to say morbid, Welsh Nonconformist world of which she is the belated representative. For any hint that such might be possible, one must turn instead to Idris Powell and his faithful pursuit of Ada. Such an unconventional pairing might yet augur hope for the future of the chapels. But whereas the minister very evidently needs her, it is far from clear that she needs him – nor is it clear that, even should she accept him, such a union could possibly work and endure.[14] In being entirely open-ended, or noncommittal, about the prospects of this relationship the novel also concludes without resolving the question of whether there can be a future for Nonconformity or not. And so, *A Man's Estate* offers us no confident reassurance that its Wales has come to terms with its past and is thus well 'placed' to face its future.

(Published in Katie Gramich [ed.], *Mapping the Territory: Critical Approaches to Welsh Fiction in English* [Cardigan: Parthian, 2010].)

Notes

1   Emyr Humphreys, *A Man's Estate* (London: Eyre & Spottiswoode, 1955; repr. Cardigan: Parthian, Library of Wales, 2006), p. 162. References hereafter (*ME*) to the latter edition.

2   In an interview about his fiction, Humphreys noted that during his London period he was reading Robert Graves, *The White Goddess*, and that he even took a copy of F. L. Lucas's study of *Greek Drama* as 'light reading' for his wife who was in hospital preparing for the birth of their child! He also mentions attending Shakespeare productions at the Old Vic featuring Olivier and Richardson: R. Arwel Jones (gol.), *Dal Pen Rheswm: Cyfweliadau gydag Emyr Humphreys* (Caerdydd: Prifysgol Cymru, 1999), pp. 68–71. Hereafter referred to as *DPR*.

3   See in particular *The Heart of the Matter* (1948) and *The End of the Affair* (1951).

4   For the contribution of literary texts to the construction, and eventual de-construction, of the 'Nonconformist nation' see M. Wynn Thomas, *In the Shadow of the Pulpit: Literature and the Nonconformist Nation* (Cardiff: University of Wales Press, 2009).

5   My translation of comments made in *Dal Pen Rheswm*, p. 64.

6   The great example is that of the minister J. T. Miles in *Outside the House of Baal* (London: Eyre & Spottiswoode, 1965; rev. repr. Bridgend: Seren, 1996).

7   See the following: D. J. Taylor, *After the War: The Novel and England Since 1945* (London: Flamingo, 1994); Brian W. Shaffer (ed.), *A Companion to the*

British and Irish Novel, 1945–2000 (London: Blackwell, 2005); and Marina MacKay and Lyndsey Stonebridge (eds), *British Fiction After Modernism: The Novel at Mid-Century* (London: Palgrave Macmillan, 2007). None of these makes any mention of the novel in Wales. This is, however, given cursory attention in Dominic Head, *The Cambridge Introduction to Modern British Fiction, 1950–2000* (Cambridge: Cambridge University Press, 2002) in a chapter dealing with 'National Identity'.

8   Quoted in *British Fiction After Modernism*, p. 5.
9   M. Wynn Thomas (ed.), *Emyr Humphreys: Conversations and Reflections* (Cardiff: University of Wales Press, 2002), pp. 67–76. Hereafter *CR*.
10 Humphreys acknowledges his debt to Faulkner in *Dal Pen Rheswm*, pp. 85–6.
11 Cleanth Brooks, *William Faulkner: The Yoknapatawpha Country* (New Haven: Yale University Press, 1966), p. 1.
12 'Introduction: Faulkner: Past and Present', in Robert Penn Warren (ed.), *Faulkner: A Collection of Critical Essays* (Englewood Cliffs, NJ: Prentice-Hall, 1966), p. 5. Hereafter *F*.
13 Such ideas are discussed with subtlety and penetration in Dorian Llywelyn's important study, *Sacred Place, Chosen People* (Cardiff: University of Wales Press, 1999).
14 The not-too-dissimilar union between J. T. Miles and Lydia in *Outside the House of Baal* ends in sadness.

6

OUTSIDE THE HOUSE OF BAAL: THE EVOLUTION OF A MAJOR NOVEL

One evening in the early 1960s, while driving his elderly mother back to her home after a family visit, Emyr Humphreys was greatly struck by an innocent remark she made as she gazed through the car windscreen. It was bad luck, she flatly assured her son, to look at the moon through glass. The comment made him realize she was a survivor from an earlier, 'horse and buggy' age, whose picture of life had been significantly different from his own. He suddenly saw her as the personification of historical changes and as yesterday's fragile witness. Out of his consequently urgent impulse to explore aspects of the disappearing past his mother had known, came in due course *Outside the House of Baal* (1965), Emyr Humphreys's most impressive attempt not only to describe but also to calibrate the changes that had drastically refashioned Welsh society during the first sixty or so years of the twentieth century. In the novel he skilfully interweaves two distinct timelines. The first is confined to a single day in the early 1960s and concentrates exclusively on the life of an elderly couple; J. T. Miles, a dreamy, mild-mannered, retired minister, and his crabbily practical sister-in-law, Kate. The second spans some six eventful decades, from the closing years of Victoria's reign to the early 1960s, when the novel was written, and, by tracing the extensive network of events and relationships that have constituted the life-experiences of J.T. and Kate, it succeeds in offering a compelling, ambitiously inclusive portrait of Welsh social, cultural and political history during a period of turbulent changes that included two world wars and a great economic depression.

Emyr Humphreys's experience with his mother had alerted him to the fact that important features of these momentous sociocultural transformations in the life of his nation were conveniently focused in the history of his own maternal family. His grandfather, who had been widowed relatively early, owned a prosperous hill-top farm within comfortable cycling distance of Emyr Humphreys's boyhood home in the village of Trelawnyd (then called Newmarket), a few miles inland from Rhyl.[1] Like Pa in the novel, this grandfather was an old-style, philoprogenitive patriarch, puritanically stern and somewhat of an autocrat. In their own adult lives his numerous children found various pragmatic ways of modifying the tenets and practices of his brand of high Nonconformity – which had been heroic and hypocritical by turns – to suit the spirit of a new, secular, and complaisant society. Like Lydia, Pa's headstrong younger daughter in the novel, Emyr Humphreys's mother was in her youth a free spirit, lively, strong-willed and unconventional, who eagerly embraced marriage to a schoolmaster as a convenient escape from a claustrophobic home background. The marital tension that predictably ensued may well have given rise to scenes similar to the one in the book when Ronnie, the little son of J.T. and Lydia, returning from school with a friend, is aghast to hear his parents quarrelling loudly, and tries to cover both the noise and his confusion by raising his voice and banging the gate. He ends up – as perhaps did the young Emyr Humphreys himself – wretchedly taking refuge in books.

In an earlier scene in the novel Ronnie is warned by his mother to hide his war-comic under a cushion before his father returns from chapel. Emyr Humphreys's own father bore in general very little resemblance to the minister J.T., but he had seen service at the front in the First World War, spent the rest of his life suffering the after-effects of poison-gas, and was so reluctant to recall his war experience to mind that he absolutely forbade his sons, when they were children, ever to play at being soldiers. Partly in consequence, the First World War has long exercised a powerful fascination over Emyr Humphreys's imagination. At its simplest, this can be seen in his attempts in *Outside the House of Baal* to enter this potently secret, forbidden territory of paternal experience by sending the central character, J.T., to the trenches. Then again, at its most complex, this fascination with war – and related forms of violence – is an active element in the creed of pacifism, to which both J.T. and Emyr Humphreys are lifelong adherents. After all, pacifists are, paradoxically, fixated on war because it is the principal evil in terms of which they define themselves morally and because it offers the ultimate challenge to everything in which they believe. Finally, and in a sense most importantly, the First World War marks, for Humphreys, a turning point in recent Welsh history, and it is treated as such in *Outside the House of Baal*. Born in 1919, he has repeatedly attempted to reconstruct, in his fiction, the conditions of life of his parents' pre-war generation, as if seeking an explanation, in the very strangeness of that period, for the bewildering historical changes he has himself lived through.

Outside the House of Baal, unquestionably his major novel, is perhaps most centrally about the decline of Welsh nonconformity, which can be conveniently dated from, and may partly be attributed to, the First World War.[2] Indeed, in an interview Humphreys has gone on record as describing this as an unqualified cultural catastrophe, since he believes that, in its spiritual prime, Nonconformity provided the basis in Wales for a distinctive 'civilisation', of substantial value.[3] The novel, of course, tells a somewhat different story, and is compelling precisely to the extent that it problematises the issue, locating the character of the Calvinistic Methodist minister J.T., for instance, at the exact point where different judgements come most hauntingly into conflict. And it is here, in the complexity of his treatment of one of the central components of Welsh culture, that Emyr Humphreys most significantly, and most successfully, departs from established practice. For upwards of fifty years before his novel was published, Welsh authors writing in English had by and large contented themselves with reproducing a crude identikit picture of the Nonconformist: cunning, lecherous, avaricious and of course invariably hypocritical. Caradoc Evans, a bilious genius, had first devised and patented the picture in 1915, using it to inspired effect in the propaganda war he waged in his fiction to liberate Wales from chapel 'Prussianism'.[4] Later writers, however, from Dylan Thomas to Gwyn Thomas, inherited from him a crude stereotype which made it next to impossible for them to engage meaningfully with one of the most powerful and subtle aspects of their own culture – powerful not only in terms of the institutions it controlled, but also because the moral climate it created affected every aspect of social and political life.

Emyr Humphreys's altogether more complex approach to this whole subject may be due in part to his being that rarity in twentieth-century Wales, a convert (of sorts) to Nonconformity – although in his case the 'conversion' had a cultural as well as a spiritual provenance. He was raised an Anglican, his upwardly mobile parents having moved away from a Nonconformist background they associated primarily with the social backwardness of Welsh-language culture. It was therefore perhaps inevitable that when the young Humphreys, inspired by the militant cultural and political nationalism of leading Welsh intellectuals during the 1930s, began to learn the Welsh language, he should also begin to follow in reverse the path his parents had taken. This process was no doubt accelerated when, in 1946, he married the daughter of a minister with the Annibynwyr (the Welsh Congregationalists, or Independents). It was many years, however, before he was able to translate his growing understanding of and qualified sympathy with Welsh Nonconformity into fully effective fictional terms. The eight novels he published before *Outside the House of Baal* include occasional examples of a fairly superficial treatment of the subject, and the new complexity of approach that is one of the most outstanding features of this novel may be due in no small part to the fact that for several years before it was written Humphreys's father-in-law had been living permanently with him and his family.

The period spent apprenticed to a blacksmith before entering the ministry; the eventful journeys from north Wales to preach in the strange and turbulent mining valleys of the south; these and other episodes in J.T.'s fictional life had their origin in the facts of the Revd Jones's actual career. Much more importantly, however, Emyr Humphreys encountered in his father-in-law's principled mildness of character those aspects of the Nonconformist heritage that were to him most attractive and most admirable. They were also, it should be noted, the antithesis not only of the stereotyped picture but also of what Nonconformity had largely, in actual historical fact, become by the time – around the last quarter of the nineteenth century – it had indisputably developed into the established religion of Wales. By then the chapels had become the Liberal Party at prayer, social institutions that facilitated the triumphant rise of the Welsh bourgeoisie. Pa's fear, in the novel, of the foundry workers; his elder daughter Kate's scorning of her ardent wooer, Maldwyn Birch, a mere carpenter; the irritation of Lydia and her avaricious brother Dan Llew with the striking miners; all these are signs of the difficulties many of the chapel-bred had in coming to terms with the experiences of the new working class, particularly in the industrial areas.[5] When Lloyd George, the darling of the chapels, became the great war-leader in 1914, many of the leading ministers used their awesome cultic power to mobilise their congregations, and proved to be deadly effective recruiting sergeants.[6] Both the jingoistic atmosphere of the time and the 'Christian' arguments used to justify the war are captured by the novel, in scenes that include J.T.'s argument with the principal of his theological college and his courageous (or foolhardy – one has to double one's terms, it seems, whenever one assesses his actions) protest in the eisteddfod against the pro-war rhetoric spouted by the Lloyd George-like figure on the stage.

There was, though, another strain of nonconformity that shows in J.T.'s character, as to some extent it did in the case of Emyr Humphreys's father-in-law. Broadly speaking, it can be described as Nonconformist in the root sense of that term: radically dissenting, both in spirit and in actual social practice, from the comfortably established order of things. In the case of some major nineteenth-century issues, like parliamentary reform, the land question, the anti-tithe campaign and education, this progressivist brand of Nonconformity quickly blended into mainstream political activity. But this was not so in other cases that most famously included Samuel Roberts (S.R.)'s concern with 'public witness by the individual conscience, with peace, free trade and the limitation of the state'; Michael D. Jones's attempt to set up a new Welsh homeland in Patagonia; and of course Henry Richard's tireless work to ease international tension, which earned for him the sobriquet of the 'Apostle of Peace'.[7]

After the First World War, Nonconformity, its moral authority virtually destroyed by its indirect participation in the carnage, tried to regroup spiritually on the ground of its radical first principles, and at least one of the fascinating leaders that then emerged later influenced Emyr Humphreys's portrayal, in *Outside the House of Baal*, both of the central figure J.T. and of the minor character Bayley Lewis.[8] George M. Ll. Davies was a charismatic, if controversial, personality during the inter-war period. A strikingly handsome man of impeccable integrity, he was imprisoned as a conscientious objector during the First World War, thus embarking on what he was later to call a lifetime's 'pilgrimage of peace'. His denomination, the Calvinistic Methodists, disapproved of him as much as they did of the fictional J.T., refusing to let him be ordained until his pacifism had become socially accept-able. He went on to play a leading part in the work of the Peace Pledge Union – an organisation Emyr Humphreys himself joined in the late 1930s. Davies was as opposed to class war as he was to actual war, and in 1932 he joined the settlement of Maes-yr-Haf which the Quakers opened in the Rhondda in an effort to improve the plight of the mass unemployed by other than militant political means. A gentle,

other-worldly reconciler both by instinct and by conviction, he turned
his outrage at the social dereliction in the south Wales valleys during
the 1930s into an exhausting labour of non-denominational Christian
love for the people, but in the process laid himself open to the very
charges – of naivety, presumption, self-deception and ineffectuality
– that the seasoned political agitator Bill Mabon wittily levels in the
novel against Bayley Lewis.

In the opening sentences of his autobiography, George M. Ll. Davies
quoted Emerson's remark: 'we are always hoping to get settled down.
There is only hope for us so long as we are unsettled.'[9] It is precisely
this 'selfish' and 'irresponsible' spirit of unsettledness that irritates
both his wife Lydia and his sister-in-law Kate, in their different ways,
about J.T. He, in his turn, is made restless by Davies's vision of the
way in which 'the ancient paganisms, the worship of Mammon, Mars,
Demos and Eros still survive under highly modern names, while
persons become workers, or conscripts, voters, or film addicts'
(*Pilgrimage*, 14). In short, modern society lives all too cosily, J.T.
believes, in the House of Baal. As for the novel, it refuses to take sides,
preferring to dwell in what E. M. Forster once called 'the twilight of
the double vision'. In so doing, it is true to the creative spirit of
uncertainty that informs one of the jottings in Emyr Humphreys's
working notebook: 'Geo M LL D – an idiot busy body – or a saint?'

* * *

The drafts and working notes for *Outside the House of Baal* throw
interesting light on the development of the novel from its inception
in early summer, 1963, to its completion almost exactly a year later.[10]
Most of the main characters, spanning three generations, are there
from the beginning and the network of relationships that connects
them is already fairly clearly defined. Governing the whole enterprise
from the outset is what one note calls the 'thesis' of the novel: 'view
of life of two – J.T. and Kate – in their seventies – the life of the last
70 years – the feel of human effort struggling to be trapped in that
semi-detached house'. The sympathetic, yet unsparing, depiction of
old age in all its crabbiness of spirit and its painstaking, often laboured,
physical movements, is there in the original opening, which concerns
Kate rather than J.T. Also recorded early is the intention to ensure
that the novel covers four distinct historical periods – 'before War 1;
between wars; War II; after War' – the difference between them being

summed up as follows: 'What will you die for – c.f. 1914, your country; 1930s the workers and Spain; 1941, civilisation versus Hitler; 1960, Wales.' But although the main features of many of the leading characters are established from the beginning, the exact course of several of their lives remains to be fixed. There are plans, for example, to allow Lydia to have affairs; and to let her leave J.T. and settle in London. In particular, the fates of their children Ronnie, Vernon and Thea remain undetermined – and remain in the balance, since the death of both brothers is canvassed as a serious possibility – until quite late in the process of composition, although a socially significant contrast between the characters of the two brothers is planned from very early in the writing.

Indeed, the elaboration of contrasts is consciously adopted by Emyr Humphreys as a fundamental method of construction. Sometimes he scribbles down antitheses that are, one feels, to be operative throughout the whole novel: 'It's sin that makes the world go round. It's love that makes the world go round.' 'All is meaningful: all is meaningless.' At other times, he has his central pair of opposites – Kate and J.T. – specifically in mind: 'she can't believe, he can'; 'J.T.M. – failure and fear: Kate – no faith and [is] content. Purpose – survival'; 'In action she is useful. In repose his spirit moves – he is the useful one – balance.' This last contrast is later translated from idea into motif, with J.T. associated primarily with the head (as in the opening phrase of the first paragraph in the published novel) and Kate with the hands (as in the second section). Such open identification by the author of one of the secret motifs – whether they be physical gestures, or objects such as J.T.'s collar, his Gladstone bag, or the photograph of Ma – that provide the novel with its texture as well as its infrastructure, is however a rare occurrence in the manuscripts.

'Events every time – ideas in background', says one of the memos Emyr Humphreys wrote to himself. It is partly a reminder of the importance, to him, of story, a point he underlines elsewhere in his notes: 'story animates, therefore events, it is true, must be described in detail, but the story must hook you compulsively and animate the entire functions of the . . . imagination. This is essential.' At the same time, however, he suggestively speaks of his wish 'to hold the story like a face that turns slowly to keep in the sun'. Although the metaphor mentions one face only, it actually highlights, and in a sense explains, the multifaceted structure of a novel in which attention seems to fall upon different objects, different locations, different characters, different events, almost as impartially as light (so Whitman puts it) 'falls about a helpless thing'.

The effect of serene, lucid impartiality is, the notes show, one that Emyr Humphreys consciously aimed (and strove) to produce. 'I am absent and I do not pass myself on to you', he reminds himself, addressing an imaginary reader, in one entry. Another time he admonishes himself sharply: 'don't presume to know what they [i.e. the characters] think. The intimacy of their own thoughts.' Write, he instructs himself, 'without claiming infinite knowledge', and in one striking manuscript passage he seems acutely aware of having evolved what is for him a new kind of writing, whose 'grace of accuracy' (to borrow Robert Lowell's phrase) marks it off from the style of his previous novels:

> Late in life I took upon myself the burden: to say what is true. That is wrong. I always knew that the primary element of the beauty of a saying was the 'yes indeed that is so element.' What I had not reckoned with until now was the discipline involved in sustaining 'the saying' over a book of 100,000 words. So it is that I wake up compelled by the spirit of dedication, living as this book lives, and my dreams are dominated by physical effort.

As the very earliest drafts show, however, Humphreys did at first find it difficult to resist the temptation to trespass on the consciousness of his main characters. In its original form, the opening section describing J.T.'s slow awakening to the day included passages like the following, which register his mental reactions to the sound of Kate's busyness downstairs:

> It was always necessary to keep in touch with the woman's movements ... The fall of the lavatory seat after the chain pulling. And the ultimate sweet but final warning of the tinkling of tea cups. Whether he could or he couldn't, that was the time to start moving.

The very next paragraph cuts, without warning, back to the time, half a century earlier, when J.T. was a youngster apprenticed to Isaac Dafydd the blacksmith (see chapter 4, section 3 of the published novel). It therefore seems that Emyr Humphreys did not start out with the clear intention of setting up a twin-track narrative, one devoted to the past and the other to the present, and each proceeding at a different pace.

The notes also allow us to pinpoint one of the sources of his new spare style of writing. In 1958 he had been introduced, by his friend Walter Todds, to the philosophy of Ludwig Wittgenstein, some of whose familiar gnomic utterances are recorded in the notebooks for *Outside the House of Baal*. 'What we cannot speak about we must pass over in silence' was one ascetic remark that motivated Emyr Humphreys to aim at a chaste integrity of expression.[11] At the same time he was fascinated by the wealth of meaning which Wittgenstein had stressed every word, however humble, possessed. 'To utter a word', the Austrian had written, 'is as if a note were struck on the keyboard of the imagination'; and Emyr Humphreys briefly entertained the idea of entitling his novel 'The keyboard'. In fact, the final title emerged quite late in the day. Much of the writing was done under the working title of 'Of the event', and among other ideas entertained were 'Where is now?' and 'A Welsh dream'.

Two more of Wittgenstein's aphorisms are to be found in the notebooks. 'Not how the world is, is the mystery, but that it is', he wrote in the *Tractatus* (6.44),[12] and, particularly in relation to the laboured, painfully deliberate movements of J.T. and Kate in their old age, Emyr Humphreys is able to bring out the power and the pathos of the sheer mute existence of objects – what one writer has called 'the terse epiphany of the things in themselves, which already results from the poetry of their names'.[13] Central to Wittgenstein's philosophy was the realisation that 'The limits of my language mean the limits of my world' (*Tractatus*, 115), and central in turn to the novel is the perception that profound historical changes are accompanied by fundamental shifts in the language of people's understanding. J.T.'s religious language of sin and forgiveness is virtually unintelligible, for instance, to the self-made man Dan Llew and his miserably cuckolded son Norman, as to members of the younger generation in general, whether they live in Wales or America. Even the importance to J.T. of the Welsh language itself is something which is essentially incomprehensible to someone like his son Ronnie, who is intent on social advancement. But virtually from the beginning of his ministry J.T. himself, of course, speaks a language of faith which is scandalously different from that traditionally used by his theologically conservative denomination. Hence his reluctant emergence, in the novel, as the leader of the 'new', and politically progressive, wing of Calvinistic Methodism in opposition to the reactionary views of Machno Jones and his followers. As the notes for the novel remind us, this liberal outlook continued to gain ground within Nonconformity after the Second World War, up to the very time when *Outside the House of Baal* was being written, thanks partly to the impact of the posthumously published writings of Dietrich Bonhoeffer, who advocated a 'religionless Christianity' of the kind that manifestly appeals to the ageing J.T.[14]

'Time after all is the chief character in a novel' is one of the observations Emyr Humphreys makes in the notes, and the way in which time is managed is one of the outstanding features of *Outside the House of Baal*. Of its twenty-six chapters, ten are set in the present and sixteen in the past, but the latter are given four pages, on average, to every one of the former. In the first quarter of the novel there is a regular pattern of alternation between past and present, but thereafter the arrangement is irregular, with the maximum disparity occurring after chapter 18, when there are four chapters in succession dealing with past events. Most striking of all, perhaps, is Emyr Humphreys's success in devising techniques for distinguishing between the pace of living during youth and vigorous prime, and the slowing down, not only of physical movement, but of the very metabolism (so to speak) of consciousness itself, that is part of the ageing process. Life, and all the contents of living, seem to take on a greater specific gravity in those chapters that deal with the period that Kate and J.T. spend together in their old age in 8 Gorse Avenue.

As one would have expected, the manuscripts show that some of the original sections and chapters had to be rearranged in a different order before the present convincing pattern emerged. For example chapter 1 was at first followed by a chapter (now chapter 8, section 2) describing how Kate was most embarrassingly up to her elbows in soapsuds when the young auburn-haired J.T. first called at Argoed. Dramatically effective though this juxtaposition was in one way, it had the disadvantage of forcing the author from the very beginning into a non-chronological treatment of such events, which is presumably one reason why it was abandoned. And when this episode was eventually transferred to chapter 8 it took its place alongside other sections, scattered through chapters 7 to 10, which had previously been tried in different locations and in different permutations.

There are also one or two other differences worth noting between the first version in manuscript and the text as published. As has already been explained, Emyr Humphreys originally drafted episodes hinting at Lydia's extra-marital affairs, but the subsequent omission of this material may have necessitated the addition of two scenes which underlined by other means the tensions within the marriage. The first is the opening scene of chapter 19, which concludes with Lydia begging her neighbour Jenny Leyshon not to tell J.T. about the money she has had to borrow in order to make ends meet because her (saintly?) husband has spent all the family's meagre earnings on alleviating the distress of the miners in the south Wales valleys to whom he is ministering during the Great Depression; and the second is section 2 of chapter 20, in which Lydia shocks the young doctor by tearfully announcing that she cannot stand her husband and that, had she but the money, she would leave him tomorrow. In addition, the manuscripts provide interesting examples of phrases and sentences added, particularly at the conclusion of sections, for incisive effect. So, for instance, chapter 13 originally ended with J.T., nonplussed by Kate's tart reaction to his sorrow at hearing of his old friend Ifan Cole's death, limply holding up for inspection the letters that have just been accidentally soaked in sardine oil. In the published form, however, the chapter concludes with a splendidly climactic and combative one-liner: '—What if we all just lived for ourselves, Kate said.' Such changes emphasise the distinctiveness of the 'scenes' of which the novel is composed. In their compression of meaning, and with their heightened air of significance, they resemble short stories more than they do casual vignettes.

The notebooks mention actors and actresses of the post-war period, with whom Emyr Humphreys had worked and aspects of whose personalities helped him construct the character of Thea. There is also abundant evidence of the effort Emyr Humphreys put into historical research for the novel, including references to newspaper articles, to *cofiannau* (biographies of eminent ministers and the like), and to theologians from Augustine to Bonhoeffer. But one entry puts all this material into perspective, and reminds us, as it was intended to remind the author, where the main burden of interest consistently lies. 'Y thema yw bywyd J.T. a K.[:] peidio colli golwg ohonyn nhw yn nghoedwig hanes. ['The theme is the life of J.T. and K.: not to lose sight of them in the forest of history.'] In the dark forest of history I saw two white figures stumbling through the trees.'

Several versions survive of the opening paragraph of the novel, and they show the way in which it was reworked to produce the present rich ambivalence of tone. Originally the first sentence referred not to 'venerable' hair, but to hair that was simply, neutrally, 'white'. And only in the final text does the printed second sentence appear, with its

fine patina of irony: 'The pillow-case was lightly stained by the halo
of white hair.' At the same time revision saw the removal of simpler,
cruder examples of irony, for instance the description of J.T.'s forehead
creasing 'cautiously as if into deep thought', as he strains to break
wind. Mere details though these changes may seem to be, they are in
fact examples of the even-handed care Emyr Humphreys takes, from
the outset, to present J.T. to us in a double focus that complicates
judgement. His character is suspended somehow, somewhere, between
vanity and humility, between comedy and dignity; and our judgement
of him is in turn suspended between admiration and condemnation.
To the very end of the novel his essential identity is as uncertain as,
at the beginning, are the letters needed to fill the enigmatic blanks
between his 'initials . . . stamped at a distance from each other across
the front' of his collar box.

Also omitted from the printed text was the sentence, 'If he were to
move his head sufficiently, and if he opened his eyes, he would see
what time it was.' This makes the mistake of appearing to impute to
the sleepy J.T. a lazy unwillingness to look at the clock – precisely
the convenient habit of wilfully selective vision which enables him,
according to hostile witnesses as different as Lydia, Isaac Dafydd,
and his son Vernon's wife Sandra, self-indulgently to avoid seeing
people and situations as they really are. The novel itself, however,
never fully endorses this view – hence the omission of that offending
sentence. Instead, the narrative discourse in general carefully allows
for the possibility of J.T.'s being selfless rather than selfish, and balances
unquestionable disasters like the death of his fellow stretcher-bearer
Cynwal at the Front (thanks to J.T.'s insistence on a virtually suicidal
mission to help a wounded soldier) against occasions of unalloyed
altruism, such as when he gives away his grandmother's cottage.

Something of a spiritual Quixote, he seems oblivious to the havoc
he creates around him, whether in the comical form of a shattered
butter-dish, or in the tragic shape of an embittered wife and an alienated
son. The morally equivocal nature of the world J.T. inhabits is delicately
suggested by the description of him waking: 'He saw the haze of light
that took the colour of warmth and sunshine from the worn curtains,
although it was in fact a dull day outside.' The indefatigably practical
Kate has, of course, long since been downstairs, cleaning the grate,
preparing breakfast, and philosophically taking the gloomy August
day just as it is. Is she then the very embodiment of the reality principle
– a Martha to his Mary, and a Sancho Panza to his Quixote? Dumpy

Kate, fishing her glass eye out of the prunes, would seem to be an altogether more robustly sensible character than the elderly J.T. who mouths benedictions, preens himself rather in front of the mirror and pores over his ancient sermons. Like his, her strengths, however, turn out to be inseparable from her weaknesses. Her indomitable matter-of-factness makes her refuse to see the quiet despair behind Mr Hobley's attempted suicide. And although she is admirably stoical, she has never ceased to be her tyrannical father's dutiful daughter, able to fulfil herself only through docile service, while irritably resenting the fact. The jealousy (of Lydia's success in ensnaring the handsome young J.T.) which was the suppressed aspect of her devotion to her rebellious sister is given full expression through her resentment of her niece Thea, Lydia's daughter.

In fact, the working notes suggest that *Outside the House of Baal* has been deliberately provided with a sexual subtext, the subconscious of the novel as it were, since the text rarely acknowledges its presence. 'When I write', says Emyr Humphreys in one jotting, 'I try to be aware of Joyce and Wittgenstein, of Freud and Marx, and even of Bartok and Stravinsky and Roger Hilton' (Hilton being an artist whose abstract paintings are admired by the author). The diluted influence of Freud is, I believe, particularly evident in the key scene where the love-making of Lydia and J.T. during their courtship is interrupted by the news that Kate's eye has been scratched out by a thorn. Kate it was, and not Lydia, who should have brought J.T. his food that afternoon, and throughout the novel the preparing and the eating of food is implicitly associated with strong emotions such as love and sexual passion. Indeed, the later scene when his neighbour Jenny Leyshon prepares a meal for J.T. in Lydia's absence is closely modelled on this earlier scene of sexual encounter where the youthful J.T. returns to his half-derelict cottage, tired, wet and hungry, and finds that Lydia has lit a fire and filled the house with the delightful smell of freshly baked bread. The fact that Lydia has effectively usurped her place and completed the seduction of J.T. may mean that Kate's simultaneous loss of an eye is an unconscious act of self-mutilation, a gesture both of sexual revenge and of self-punishment, of the kind she perhaps repeats when she later masochistically marries the drunken wastrel Wynne Bannister.

But Bannister first presents himself to her, of course, in the respectable guise of a father-figure, when he comes to make arrangements for Pa's funeral. The influence of Pa on Kate's emotional life, including her sexual preference, is very deep, as can be seen from the terms of her rejection of her various suitors. Appropriately enough, she is washing Pa's drawers when she first hears J.T.'s voice – he having been brought to Argoed by Griff when Pa is away from home – and the irritable affection with which she treats J.T. in old age replicates the relationship between herself and Pa when they two alone are left in the old family farm, Argoed. Lydia, on the other hand, is initially drawn to J.T. in part because Pa disapproves of his supposed levity; but her attachment to him is reinforced not only by the rivalry for his affections that develops between Kate and herself but also by the closeness between J.T. and her favourite brother and fellow rebel, Griff. In these ways, J.T. is from the beginning involved, unawares, in the relatively innocent sexual politics of the Argoed family.

The intricate system of relationships that binds the family together is brilliantly suggested in the opening section of chapter 2 where scarcely a word is spoken as Ma leaves Argoed to die. As in silent films, meaning is conveyed almost entirely through an eloquent code of movements and gestures. This is a mode of signification sensitively and suggestively used throughout the entire novel – as when Griff, having just confessed to J.T. that he is no longer a Christian believer, puts his arm on his shoulder, as J.T. clambers up the slope to join him, so that as 'J.T. came level with him . . . Griff's arm was lifted upward by the movement' – but in this particular scene it reaches a height of balletic perfection. The powerful impression given of a close-knit family functioning as an organic feudal unit serves partly to offset the subsequent impression formed of exploitation and dissension, and so lends some colour of credence, at least, to the later nostalgic yearnings of Lydia and Kate for the good times at Argoed. Equally important is the way Emyr Humphreys follows this scene with a picture of young Joe disconsolately sitting alone on the window-sill of the classroom, keeping watch while his father is secretly refilling his whisky flask. The contrast between the two scenes is further pointed up by the way they are made to interlock. At the end of the Argoed scene Ned looks down at his trouser-leg because 'Ma had reached out to tug his trousers'. At the beginning of the schoolmaster scene, Joe rubs 'his chin against the darnings on the knees of his stockings' – in a self-comforting gesture that is thus made poignantly expressive of his motherless state. Later, it is precisely this unselfconscious air of helplessness that makes the adult J.T. so attractive to certain types of women. At the same time, the habit of self-sufficiency, which he has had to learn early, helps him develop into a spiritual loner, an inner-directed character.

This arrangement of short scenes to chime, contrast, cross-refer and interact is, of course, the primary means by which Emyr Humphreys 'makes meaning by moulding form' in *Outside the House of Baal*. He himself felt the technique was similar in some ways to the exploration of consonances and dissonances in modernist music (hence the references to Stravinsky and Bartok) and in particular to the language of form and colour in abstract art – a feature he specifically discussed, when working on the novel, with his friend the eminent painter Patrick Heron. Undoubtedly, however, the extensive experience he had gained during the 1950s from working in radio and television drama greatly influenced his method of working. Most strikingly, it caused him to revise his opinion of the way in which novels were now being read – and to deduce from this a theory of how they should be composed. He formed the view that the new media were sensitising audiences to certain signs, or signifiers – close-ups, cuts from shot to shot, attitudes, gestures, undertones – and felt a novelist should be taking advantage of the current economy of meaning made available through a sophisticated general awareness of these conventions. At the same time there were older novelistic conventions – of authorial omniscience, dense dialogue, psychological analysis, etc. – which, he believed, were now superannuated.

Whatever the validity of these theories when regarded as a general principle, they undoubtedly served Emyr Humphreys well as working hypotheses. His scenic structure proved flexible enough to produce a brilliant variety of interpretative effects, as well, of course, as making it easy for him to range over extensive time and space. Note, for instance, the way in which Pa is caught, in an early scene, as his tears are dropping into the clock he is mending. This endears him to us in a way that is never completely cancelled out by all the succeeding episodes in which he almost invariably appears overbearing and mawkishly self-pitying. One of the latter is the scene where Kate mollycoddles him with hot milk and whisky – an incident resonantly juxtaposed to the one in which J.T.'s father is found dead on the mountain, an empty Lysol bottle by his side. A poignant impression of mutability is created by the way Aunt Addy makes her one and only appearance in the novel, in the scene describing Ma's departure from Argoed, which follows on from the moment when the elderly Kate, startled by the sounds of J.T. flushing the toilet upstairs, clumsily

lets slip and breaks the butter-dish that 'was a present from Aunt
Addy of Denbigh, given to her thirty-four years ago'. Water connects
the end of one scene in which Ifan Cole, suffering from a hangover,
vomits over the small anvil, with the beginning of another in which
the romantic adolescent Lydia takes Ma's picture apart, in her frantic
search for Pa's supposed secret lover. And once this connection is
perceived, the reader can reflect that, in their different ways, both Ifan
and Lydia are natural rebels. Little Thea, playing on her uncle Ned's
northern farm, where her mother has taken refuge from the south
Wales valleys, exclaims that 'everything is hungry'. She is referring to
the pigs and the hens and the cattle, but in context her childish cry
serves to underline the difference between this rural region of plenty
and the social deprivation in the depressed industrial areas she has
just left. Examples could be multiplied endlessly of the ways in which
some of the subtlest effects in the novel are the product of the fluid
interrelationship of scenes.

It is, however, equally instructive to notice the gaps in the narrative
structure, and precisely where they occur. What is remarkable is that
silence falls at several of the most crucial points. Ma's death, Kate's
reaction to losing her eye, the marriage of Lydia and J.T., the death
of Pa, J.T.'s reaction to the death of Lydia – these and other seminal
events are bypassed. Considered in conjunction with the scenic structure mentioned above, this practice reminds us that *Outside the House
of Baal* is, in Roland Barthes's now familiar terms, a 'writerly' rather
than a 'readerly' text. In other words, the reader is called upon to
participate very actively in the process of producing meaning – and
thus in effect 'writes' the interpretative script for himself or herself.

Barthes was led to this distinction partly through the study of the
theory and practice of Bertolt Brecht, and it is worth noting that
during the period leading up to the composition of *Outside the House
of Baal*, Emyr Humphreys had himself become very interested in
Brecht's work. The aspects of the plays that most fascinated him were
those well described by Catherine Belsey:

> Brecht's solution [to the reader's passive, uncritical acceptance of the
> world as pictured in a text] was to write a new kind of text, foregrounding
> contradiction rather than effacing it, and distancing the audience from
> both text and ideology. In . . . the interrogative text there is no simple
> hierarchy of discourses such that the reader is offered privileged access
> to the work's 'truth'. Instead the reader constructs meaning out of the

contradictory discourses which the text provides. Barthes speaks of the multiplicity of voices of indeterminate origin in the writable text, the polyphony which deprives the implied author of authority so that the truth of any one of the discourses is not guaranteed by a knowledge of its origin or source.[15]

Compare this with the full text of a notebook entry by Emyr Humphreys, part of which has already been quoted: 'The voice that tells the tale colours everything and invalidates each event. Therefore I am absent & I do not press myself on you.'

It is only by ignoring the polyphony of the text that, it seems to me, readers can, without hesitation or qualification, reach conclusions like the following about *Outside the House of Baal*:

> The book is a full-length portrait of J. T. Miles – a Calvinistic Method-ist minister who is the very type of 'the good man' . . . The unfolded narrative shows him 'betraying' Argoed – here the symbol for the older Calvinistic Wales – by marrying the light-minded Lydia rather than her elder sister, Kate.[16]

There is, surely, at the very least, much more to be said for Lydia than this, and moreover the novel, in one of its voices, says it. And if one is interested not in the least that can be said for her but in the most, then a powerful case could be made for regarding Lydia (along with other women from Kate, through Mrs Bayliss and Jenny Leyshon, to Norman's neglected Marjorie) as the tragic victim of a complacently masculine world. She escapes from servitude with Pa only to become the 'slave', as she angrily puts it, of the ineffable J.T. Already a rebel, a generation ahead of her 'liberated' daughter Thea, she is allowed no scope for the exercise of her considerable energy; a feminine version of her independently minded brother Griff, she is denied the opportun-ities he is given to develop in her own way.

Of course, this is a novel in which every thesis is accompanied by its antithesis, and so a persuasive case counter to the above could be made on behalf, let us say, of J.T. But what is important to realise is that readers are not only openly encouraged (by the way the novel is structured) to enter into the 'debate', they are also made to reflect on the terms of their own preference. This, again, is a Brechtian feature of *Outside the House of Baal*: the novel is designed to bring readers face to face with their own presuppositions and hidden value systems.

Moreover, it contextualises these, showing them to be not uniquely personal to its readers, but rather embedded in a specific period and social background. In other words, like Brecht's plays, the novel not only shows us 'history', it leads us to experience ourselves as historical beings. So, for instance, our sneaking preference for J.T. (or, alternately, for Lydia) is represented to us by the noncommittal text in a manner which makes clear the social origins and ramifications of our judgement. The novel deals as equivocally with time as it does with the main characters, refusing to let the past entirely get the better of the present, or the present of the past. The title would seem to endorse J.T.'s view of contemporary Wales as pub-and-club land, but even in the matter of drink the inhabitants of the past seem scarcely more abstemious than those of the present, and J.T.'s fierce hostility to the 'House of Baal' is understandable in view of his alcoholic father. When an aged Pa querulously complains about the new maid, Kate reminds him of the sharp practices of Mary Parry Rice in the old days. The advances made in medicine are emphasised, and J.T. himself is impatient with the nostalgic maunderings of Henry Bowen, with his lament for the loss of law and order and his complaint about the disrespect of the young. But at the same time, J.T. cannot suppress a pang when he realises the young photographer with the pigeon on his shoulder has no idea that the dove is the symbol of the Holy Spirit.

The younger generation in the novel is in most other respects more knowing, and also sometimes more honest, than its elders. Thea openly flirts with her father, teasingly treating him as her beau. His nephew Norman is more honest about his contribution to the breakdown of his marriage than J.T. ever managed to be. Such frankness, particularly in sexual matters, is graphically suggested by the wartime scene in which J.T., crossing a field on his way to visit Vernon, finds his attention unwillingly riveted to a woman's half-naked body: 'Her white belly and her black pubic hair that were meant to be hidden, had become the centre of the whole landscape.' But his subsequent (and consequent) argument with his errant son Ronnie (the woman's lover) in that same scene brings out the glibness, flip reductiveness and selfishness of his son's outlook on life.

Change itself is shown by the novel to involve unexpected continuities as well as differences. Vernon is very much his father's son, idealistic to a fault. Even Dan Llew's 'modern' mercenariness has its antecedent in his Pa's lifelong habit of lifting the stair-carpet, and the old tyrant of Argoed is indeed proud of a son who has prospered because he followed the biblical injunction not to 'bury his talent'. The sad Christian farce performed at Oberammergau is paralleled by what has long been going on in Nonconformist Wales. Yet when all is said and done, some of the most powerful scenes in *Outside the House of Baal* are those which plangently convey a scene of the passing of a world, memorably instanced by J.T.'s heart-breaking attempt to speak, on tape, to Lydia's relatives in America. Emyr Humphreys sketched in his notebooks the kind of change he there had in mind: 'Man lives longer – no other physical change but the world frame of his imagination shattered [. . . J.T.'s] children lose faith; his country decays; his family becomes estranged – like Job long ago.' Nevertheless the relationship between past and present in the novel as a whole is more complex and subtle than this. In the last scene but one in which J.T. is featured, we see him poignantly at a loss to prevent the mistakes of the past from being repeated, but this time in a harsher key.

That scene revolves around the incident in which a forlornly lost little boy dirties his pants, and so after a fashion there is a reference right back to the opening paragraph, in which J.T. breaks wind. It is, in fact, noticeable how often 'gross' bodily functions are mentioned in *Outside the House of Baal* – farting, defecating, urinating, vomiting and so on. These are strong reminders that human life, however spiritualised a view of it one takes, inescapably involves an existence in and of the body, an existence which thereby has its comic, distasteful and grotesque aspects with which any serious spiritual philosophy has got to come to terms. The novel shows traditionally puritanical Nonconformity, in the shape of the main characters, endeavouring to recognise that, as one of the notes has it, 'the body [is] not an evil thing'. When, therefore, J.T. comes face to face with these physical facts of life, or is simply juxtaposed with them, the maturity of his spiritual vision is implicitly put to the test, as it is when he is seen to struggle, along with Kate, to cope with the potentially humiliating physical disabilities and general bodily decrepitude that accompany old age.

If *Outside the House of Baal* is, as I believe it to be, the best novel that has yet been written in English about Wales, then that is due in no small measure to the central division of mind and of feeling out of which it came, and which it clearly reflects. This division has already been explored, in several of its different manifestations, in the main body of this essay, but in conclusion it may be approached once more via the comments Emyr Humphreys made about the novel *Traed*

Mewn Cyffion by his late friend, the great Welsh short-story writer Kate Roberts. His remarks about her talent, and her achievement, apply almost equally to himself as author of *Outside the House of Baal*:

> Kate Roberts belongs to that select category of artist whose work emerges from a given landscape and society with the numinous power of a megalith or a stone circle. This is a status not easily achieved. It requires a combination of servitude and revolt which reflects the relationship between the artist and her society. In retrospect, it is the product of a life-long struggle and a life-long commitment: the unceasing urge to be both a free artist and a responsible member of a society under siege from hostile historical forces . . . On the surface the novel would appear to be in the mould of the 'three generations sagas' of popular fiction. But because of the special nature of Kate Roberts's gift and her response to the crisis in the life of her community and the wider upheavals of her time, the novel takes on several of the features of an epic in the classical sense. For example, although her style is bare and her prose is deliberately unadorned, there is throughout the work a note of intensity, a quality of song, that echoes the timeless celebration of tribal and social qualities characteristic of epic poets from Homer to the Hengerdd. Almost in spite of the modern critical mode there is an underlying current of praise-poetry. With all their faults and shortcomings, these are her people to whom she is tied by indissoluble bonds of attachment.[17]

When the publishers first received the typescript of *Outside the House of Baal* they announced their enthusiasm for it in the form of a telegram to the author which read: 'VERY PLEASED STOP WRITING'. Since Emyr Humphreys happened to be away at work when the telegram arrived, it was opened and read by his young daughter, who then excitedly reported to her baffled father over the phone that his publishers had told him to stop writing immediately. Fortunately, Emyr Humphreys did not take that advice – indeed during the half century since the novel appeared in 1965 he has published more than a dozen more novels, including the impressive Amy Parry sequence. But *Outside the House of Baal* remains the single best work he has ever produced; a masterpiece among Welsh novels, and a marvellous combination of 'servitude and revolt'.

(First published in Sam Adams [ed.], *Seeing Wales Whole: Essays on the Literature of Wales* [Cardiff: University of Wales Press, 1998].)

Notes

1 The novel places the decay and eventual sale of a corresponding farm at the very centre of its concerns, treating it implicitly as an allegory of the decline of the family values promoted, for better and for worse, by Welsh Nonconformity, with a resultant erosion of social conscience and cultural commitments. For the name of his fictional farm, Humphreys turned to 'Argoed', a great poem by the renowned strict-metre poet T. Gwynn Jones, recording the story of the casual erasure of a Gallic tribe's language and way of life by the implacable legions of imperial Rome.

2 This aspect of Emyr Humphreys's fictional output is considered at length in '"Solid in Goodly Counsel": The Chapels Write Back', in M. Wynn Thomas, *In the Shadow of the Pulpit: Literature and Nonconformist Wales* (Cardiff: University of Wales Press, 2010), pp. 294–330.

3 The remark was made during a discussion with R. S. Thomas in the programme *Mother's Tongue, not Mother Tongue*, presented by M. Wynn Thomas (BBC Radio 4, August 1986).

4 See John Harris (ed.), Caradoc Evans, *My People* (Bridgend: Seren Books, 1987).

5 For the general background, see Kenneth O. Morgan, *Rebirth of a Nation* (Oxford: Oxford University Press, 1980).

6 Emyr Humphreys's own view of this period is to be found in *The Taliesin Tradition* (Bridgend: Seren Books, 1989).

7 For further information about these figures see Meic Stephens (ed.), *The Oxford Companion to the Literature of Wales* (Oxford: Oxford University Press, 1986).

8 Another notable 'rebel' Nonconformist minister of the inter-war years mentioned by Emyr Humphreys in his notes for *Outside the House of Baal* was Tom Nefyn (Williams) (1895–1958), whose controversial life furnished models for certain events and characters in the novel. Tom Nefyn saw action both in the Dardanelles and in the Middle East during the First World War, and in the process underwent a religious conversion which influenced the remainder of his life. On his return he entered the Calvinistic Methodist ministry where his unorthodox theology, allied with his evangelical readiness to preach a radical social gospel, made him a figure revered by some but disapproved by others.

9 George M. Ll. Davies, *Pilgrimage of Peace* (London: Fellowship of Reconciliation, 1950), p. 13. Hereafter *Pilgrimage*.

10 In this section I draw heavily on the working notebooks which Emyr and Elinor Humphreys kindly allowed me to consult and that are now in the National Library of Wales. References to *Outside the House of Baal* are to the revised and expanded text published by Seren (1996) for which I furnished extensive notes.

11 Ludwig Wittgenstein, *Tractatus Logico-Philosophicus*, trans. D. F. Pears and B. F. McGuinness (London: Routledge & Kegan Paul, 1966), p. 151.

[12] This quotation is taken from Emyr Humphreys's notebook. In the translation by Pears and McGuinness the sentence reads: 'It is not *how* things are in the world that is mystical, but *that* it exists' (p. 149).

[13] Claudio Magris, *Times Literary Supplement* (7–13 December 1990), 1332.

[14] Dietrich Bonhoeffer (1906–45) was arrested by the Nazis in April 1943, imprisoned in Buchenwald and hanged two years later at Flossenburg.

[15] Catherine Belsey, *Critical Practice* (London: Methuen, 1980), p. 129.

[16] Entry on *Outside the House of Baal* in Meic Stephens (ed.), *The New Companion to the Literatures of Wales* (Cardiff: University of Wales Press, 1998), p. 546.

[17] Emyr Humphreys, 'Under the Yoke', *New Welsh Review*, 3 (Winter 1988), 9–10; collected in M. Wynn Thomas (ed.), *Emyr Humphreys, Conversations and Reflections* (Cardiff: University of Wales Press, 2002), pp. 77–83.

7

'Yr Hen Fam': R. S. Thomas and the Church in Wales

'Poet and priest': when John Ormond was making his celebrated film profile of R. S. Thomas for television in 1971 that was the title he gave it.[1] And it was while being interviewed for that film that R.S. made those celebrated, not to say notorious, remarks to the effect that, for him, poetry and religion were much the same thing. Insofar as sustained attention has been paid to Thomas as poet and priest it's tended to consist either of an exploration of the implications of this controversial statement, or an attempt to uncover the roots of his notoriously casual decision to enter the priesthood, usually in his relations with his mother and her own clerical background and leanings.[2] But I've come to feel that that doesn't do justice to his complex dual identity. And I've also come to suspect that critical discussion of the matter has been seriously hampered by an ignorance of its subject. Has anyone noticed, for instance, that R. S. Thomas was actually eight years older than the Church he served as priest for some forty years?[3]

We need, it seems to me, to get back to basics, which means beginning at the beginning – the beginning not so much of the Church of England as of R. S. Thomas's Church: the Church in Wales. We need to start by fully registering the fact that he belonged to virtually the first generation of priests in Wales to serve a newly *disestablished* Church. Throughout not only his period of training but also his early years as a priest, his new Church was in process of radical restructuring. But – and much more importantly for the young curate and vicar – it was also in the throes of the effort to come to terms with its problematical new status and role. R.S., I believe, came gradually to feel an immense personal investment in this latter dilemma. And, indeed, an interesting, if in the end only doubtfully persuasive, case could be made for reading those numerous early poems of his, many of them figuring Iago Prytherch, that agonise over the relationship of a priest to his people, primarily in the light of the much larger cognate crisis of his Church. What was the new Church in Wales to make of *its* relationship to the nation?

But, resisting temptation to at least toy with that passingly seductive but reductive reading, I'd like to highlight instead two long-lasting concerns of what might be styled R.S.'s disestablished mentality and then show how they seem to me to have left their mark on some of his poetry. The first might be succinctly designated 'the issue of independence'; the second 'the case of Yr Hen Fam/the Old Mother'. Disestablishment became fact in 1920 when the Church lost its long, and frequently bitter, rearguard action against the socially and politic-ally powerful onslaught of nineteenth-century Welsh Nonconformity on its privileged and supposedly predatory status. It now had to recognise the legally accomplished fact of its disestablishment and disendowment. Viewed by leading Anglican clergy and the faithful alike at the time simply as an accursed example of the trumping of spiritual authority by crude political power, this profound change in the Church's status came, in the fullness of time, to be viewed by some as an unlooked-for blessing. R. S. Thomas, in particular, came to regard this change not as a historical catastrophe but rather as a historical turning point – no less than a de facto assertion of Welsh independence. In 1970, for instance, he published a letter in the Church's Welsh-language weekly, *Y Llan.* It objected to a clause in the Church's constitution that specifically denied a priest the right to a clerical pension were he to be imprisoned for any offence against the law. With his own case very obviously in mind, R.S. points out that this harsh penalty clause would inescapably apply to any priest currently engaging in law-breaking activities in active support of the morally admirable campaign of Cymdeithas yr Iaith Gymraeg for full legal recognition of the Welsh language. And he concludes by arguing that such a clause should no longer be acceptable to a Church that had, after all, declared its separation from England and was no longer a dutiful handmaiden of the state.[4]

In other words, R.S. had come to view the Church in Wales as, at least potentially, a wholly separate, and therefore truly national, Welsh Church. But implicit in his very letter, of course, was evidence to the contrary – evidence that is of the Church's continuing reluctance to face the implications of its new status. Indeed, as R.S. very well knew, a substantial majority within the Church was stubbornly devoted to the continuation of what he regarded as unreconstructed 'English', statist, norms. It was an attitude that had been not only passively condoned but effectively 'sponsored' from the very beginning by the inaugural Archbishop of the new Welsh Church, Archbishop Alfred George Edwards (erstwhile Bishop of St Asaph), memorably characterised by the unfailingly waspish W. J. Gruffydd, a leading Welsh-language intellectual of the day, as 'the most disastrous man that Wales has ever seen'.[5] And priests and people alike of this dominant opinion were prone to manifest in practice, if not in cautious word, a hostility to the Welsh language of which R. S. Thomas was such a prominent champion. The resultant 'civil war' within the Church in Wales is fascinatingly chronicled in the columns of *Y Llan* throughout the 1960s and early 1970s. During the later part of that decade the tension between the two factions was greatly heightened, at least until the enthronement of Glyn Simon[6] in 1968 as Archbishop and his game-changing inaugural address, by the controversial activities of Cymdeithas yr Iaith Gymraeg.[7] And I'd like to draw attention to the implications of this for R.S.'s poetry by first homing in on one prominent clash between Welsh-speakers and the Church establishment, and then using it to read one of his well-known poems in a rather different light.

An editorial in *Y Llan* on 14 June 1974 launches a stinging attack on St David's Cathedral, which is accused of treating the Welsh language with contempt. Nothing, it states, at St David's is calculated to disturb the peace of the visiting English, save for an occasional Welsh phrase on the ancient tombs. The situation is, it vehemently declares, little short of a disgrace in a diocese where Welsh is still a living and lively language. 'Gall ymweld â Thyddewi', it movingly concludes, 'fod yn fendith i'r Cristion; ond mae'n wayw i'r Cymro' ('Visiting St David's may be a blessing to a Christian, but it is agony for a Welsh-speaker').[8]

The sheer exasperation so powerfully voiced in this editorial is the product of years of ever-growing discontent amongst Welsh-speakers, also liberally chronicled in *Y Llan*, of this *soi-disant* 'national' cathedral's treatment of the national language. The most prominent example arose in 1967. That year the Church was celebrating a momentous event: the 400th anniversary of the translation both of the New Testament and Book of Common Prayer into Welsh. And in

May, the *Llan* carried an angry letter from the Revd Terry Thomas
of St David's College Lampeter, protesting at the fact that the official
service to mark the event at St David's Cathedral had been conducted
almost entirely in English.[9] This sparked off a variety of responses,
defenders of the service arguing that it was only one commemorative
event out of many, that it was intended to draw the attention of non-
Welsh-speakers to an important national occasion, and so on.[10] But
many correspondents remained unconvinced, among them two heavy-
weight Anglican laymen of the day, T. I. Ellis, son of the late, iconic
Cymru Fydd MP and Chief Liberal Whip, and Aneirin Talfan Davies,
by then Head of BBC Wales.[11] The latter was insistent that the St
David's event was symptomatic of a serious malaise in the Church as
a whole, its dereliction of its duty to serve its nation.[12] And another
correspondent, Revd Tom Bowen, vicar of Llanegwad, called for the
creation of 'Cymdeithas Gymraeg yr Eglwys yng Nghymru', a Welsh-
language society of the Church in Wales. He was to prove as good as
his word as, over the next few years, he worked successfully and
tirelessly to establish and to develop exactly such a ginger group.[13]

So what, one might wonder, has all this controversy of the passing,
and now long-past, day to do with Thomas as a poet? Well, by way
of focused illustration, I suggest we revisit one of his poems, 'A Line
from St David's', in the light of these intense debates, and set the text
alongside a hitherto unrecorded St David's Day radio talk by R. S.
Thomas networked by the BBC in 1969 and printed in *Y Llan*.[14] It
recalls his pilgrimage to St David's, a spot once centrally situated, he
points out, on the pilgrim route from Ireland and Scotland to Jerusalem
but now, although by no means inaccessible, relegated to the margins
of the busy world. He emphasises the dedicated, austere life of the
Celtic saint and his brethren but then moves on, after meditating
appreciatively on the sacred stillness and quietness even of the present-
day St David's, to recall Gerald the Welshman's period of association
with the church. Why single out Giraldus Cambrensis? Because he
was for R.S. a culture hero, almost one might say an alter ego. How
so? Because the Cambro-Norman Gerald, grandson of the legendary
Welsh aristocratic beauty Nest and the local Norman warlord, had
fought tenaciously, if unsuccessfully, for that very independence of the
Welsh Church from the suzerainty of Canterbury that the Church in
Wales had at long last achieved in the twentieth century. 'In Wales, the
church is now independent', R. S. baldly emphasises, and for him that
legitimises his church's claim to be heir to an ancient national tradition.

More of that later, but for now, let's note that such an awareness of an inheritance of ancient beliefs, practices and customs is implicit in the poem R.S. had written several years earlier:

> the old currents are in the grass,
> Though rust has becalmed the plough.
> Somewhere a man sharpens a scythe;
> A child watches him from the brink
> Of his own speech[15]

Concerned as it is to register brinkmanship, that last line is, of course, ambivalent in meaning. It could be referring to a small child's imminent acquisition, as it crosses over into speech, of the ancient, invaluable, Welsh idiolect of north Pembrokeshire or of neighbouring Ceredigion, thus safeguarding its continuation. But also, and to the contrary, it could also be referring to an older child, already a monoglot English-speaker, who is thus excluded from the workman's local Welsh-speaking world and doomed to the experience of personal loss and cultural rupture.

R.S. ends his radio talk by suggesting that David is the perfect patron saint for Wales, because he represents the importance of little unregarded things and of little powerless people. I find it difficult to believe that at this point his text isn't silently haunted by two of the most famous lines written by the legendary, saintly Waldo Williams, the great Welsh-language poet of St David's and its Pembrokeshire whom R.S. knew personally and revered: 'Daw dydd y bydd mawr y rhai bychain./ Daw dydd y bydd bach y rhai mawr' ('Come the day when the small will be great./ Come the day when the great will be small'). The lines occur in 'Plentyn y Ddaear' ('The Child of the Earth'), a visionary poem about peaceful human fellowship eventually prevailing over the whole war-ravaged globe.[16] As R. S. Thomas well knew, his own St David's Day talk was to be broadcast in parallel, so to speak, with Neges Ewyllys Da – the annual St David's Day message of Good Will broadcast by Welsh schoolchildren to the whole world. Indeed, there seems to be oblique mention of this in his radio talk, when he notes that 'neges Cymru i'r byd' ('Wales's message to the world') is peace, in the spirit of its patron saint.

Indeed, for Thomas, Dewi's gospel, not least as mediated by Waldo and echoed in the St David's Day message, vindicates and hallows his own vision of a Wales dedicated not only to peace but to pacifism.

Like Waldo's poem, both R.S.'s poem 'A Line from St David's' and
his radio talk seem to me to be composed in full awareness of the
aggressive post-war 'occupation' of the cathedral's surrounding area
by the UK, US and European military, through the establishment of
large bases crucial for the Cold War at Castle Martin and Tre-cwn.
And so R.S., again closely paralleling Waldo's poem, pointedly turns
his back in his radio talk on the military banners displayed in so many
Anglican cathedrals, including even the 'disestablished' St David's. As
he puts it in his radio address,

> Nid oes gennym ymerodraeth i'w amddiffyn, ac mor ychydig yw ein
> hanghenion. Felly, tangnefedd yw ein cri . . . Nid y baneri a'r catrawdau
> yn crogi mewn ysblander llipa, na'r to gemog a ddaeth â'r meddyliau
> hyn i mi, ond y rhedyn bach a dyfai o'r garreg.

> (We have no empire to defend, so little are our needs. So, peace is our
> cry . . . It was not the banners and the battalions [*sic*] hanging in limp
> magnificence, nor the bejewelled roof, that brought these thoughts to
> me, but the little fern that grew from the stones.)

That last reference directly echoes the lines in his poem about 'the
wall lettuce in the crevices', while the banners and roof both, of course,
relate to the interior of the cathedral.

There was, at the time, considerable feeling among the champions
of Welsh and of Welshness within the Church, on this subject of its
continuing alliance with what was perceived as the militaristic tradition
of England and its state Church. For example, an eloquent letter
appeared in *Y Llan* in 1968 from a group of young ordinands at the
church hostel in Bangor. It protested against their Church's treatment
of Welsh, and particularly objected to the continuation in Wales of
the English state Church's practice of prominently parading a bellicose
panoply of military banners – the Church militant in all too literal a
sense.[17] For these young priests, those banners are the unmistakeable
signs of the survival of an English statist mentality amongst the
hierarchy of the Church in Wales.

Now, we know that R.S. was extremely touchy on this subject, not
least because it re-activated his guilt, clearly recorded in *Neb* and *The
Echoes Return Slow*, at his own perceived failure, as a young pacifist,
to speak out against the Church's support for the military during the
Second World War.[18] And this guilt erupted again during his time as

vicar of Eglwys-Fach, where he found himself parish priest to an impressive squad of ex-military big-wigs. It's therefore particularly relevant to note that both his radio talk and his poem were produced during his period at Eglwys-Fach (which he left in 1972).

It's not surprising, then, that in his talk R.S. specifically turns his back on conspicuous ecclesiastical displays of support for the military. Nor is it surprising, given such feelings as these about the Church establishment, that in his poem he should view the cathedral at St David's only from a wary distance that allows him to continue to view it as a sacred space: 'Here the cathedral's bubble of stone/ Is still unpricked by the mind's needle.' The image of the fragile bubble underlines the precariousness of the cathedral's claims to spiritual authority. Moreover, he can view the cathedral in this way only by setting it safely in the context of the anciently spiritual Pembroke-shire landscape. And the whole poem strongly implies that the safest guardian of Dewi's spiritual values is not the institution of the Church but rather the land that remains Dewi's land, despite the desecrations of the military. The true emblem of the spry saint is to be found, he concludes both in poem and in radio talk, not in the cathedral piously consecrated to the saint's memory, but in the tiny ferns that grow from local rock:

> the wall lettuce in the crevices
> Is as green now as when Giraldus
> Altered the colour of his thought
> By drinking from the Welsh fountain

Giraldus, it will be remembered, became more Welsh than Norman through his identification with St David's.

Let me reiterate: the poem pre-dates both the radio talk and the debates about St David's in the columns of *Y Llan* by several years, so there can be no question of the former being influenced by the latter. But I do feel that, taken as a whole, they represent consistent, long-standing concerns R.S. and other Welsh Anglicans of his cultural persuasion had about the disestablished Church in Wales generally and about St David's in particular.

Consequently 'A Line from St David's' can persuasively be read as a verse letter intended to awaken his fellow Welsh, and particularly the members of his own 'Welsh' Church, to what was at risk at St David's owing to the unenlightened and unreconstructed character of Wales's *soi-disant* national Church. It can be understood as a rescue mission; an implicit attempt to recover for Wales and its true national Church a foundational place and figure that had, through the defection of the nation's senior cathedral and its anglicised clergy, long fallen into the clutches of an invasive language and a foreign culture.

There's one little word in 'A Line from St David's' that has always fascinated me, because it stands out from the rest of the text. I refer to the word 'Plwmp': 'I came here by way of Plwmp'. Why that route? Why that word? There seems to me to be a note of defiance in its inclusion. After all, R.S. could have travelled to St David's by any number of routes. But 'by way of Plwmp' it had to be, because 'Plwmp' is a word that can't fail to sound vulgar and comical in English. Indeed a colleague of mine who visited the British Council offices in Malaysia just the other day actually found Plwmp singled out for mention in exactly such terms in a glossy brochure advertising the exotic culture of Wales. (Incidentally, that same brochure mentioned contemporary Wales's passion not only for rugby but for ferret racing – clearly I've still got a lot to learn about my own country.) To any monoglot English reader, 'Plwmp' is, then, a signifier of the exotic, and that's exactly how and why Thomas uses it. He uses it insidiously to smoke out prejudice and defiantly to reassert his right to use Welsh in any way, in any place, and in any context, he chooses, since it is the only rightful language of this particular neck of the woods. And, socially and culturally disempowered though Welsh might be – English-only though the road signs to St David's at that time we should remember still were, and English-only though were the public notices throughout the cathedral itself – Welsh continues in the poem to prove uniquely empowering. How? Because it alone can authentically name this land into being and into shape and into identity. Had Waldo also not famously written in 'Cymru a Chymraeg' of his Pembrokeshire Preseli, 'Dyma'r mynyddoedd. Ni fedr ond un iaith eu codi/ A'u rhoi yn eu rhyddid yn erbyn wybren cân' ('Here are the mountains. Only one language can raise them/ And set them in all their freedom against a sky of song')?[19]

R.S. might not then be able to reclaim the anglicised cathedral itself for his Wales and its Welsh. He could not restore Dewi's Church to its true, ancient, self. But through his poetry he could and did relocate it in a genuinely Welsh, because thoroughly Welsh-speaking landscape. It is that word 'Plwmp' that is the key. Once used it magically opens the door to a hidden Wales – hidden because overwritten by English, as indeed threatens to happen in the poem, and thus suppressed. But stick with it and, as the poem proceeds to show, 'Plwmp' is the open sesame that opens our eyes to the sacred, secret magic of this landscape:

> As I came here by way of Plwmp,
> There were hawkweeds in the hedges;
> Nature had invested all her gold
> In the industry of the soil.
> There were larks, too, like a fresh chorus
> Of dew

Had he come there by any way other than by way of Plwmp none of this, so the poem implies, would have been visible.[20] The truth is that R.S. is not really comfortable writing in the shadow of St David's Cathedral. When it comes to celebrating Dewi as the founder of everything that R.S. believed was authentic and valuable in the modern Church in Wales, he is much more attracted and attuned to the legends attaching Dewi to another spot that bears his name, Llanddewi Brefi. As early as 1948 he was addressing a poem – only recently recovered and safely collected – to what was for him a credibly hallowed spot:

> One day this summer I will go to Llanddewi,
> And buy a cottage and stand at the door
> In the long evenings, watching the moor[21]

It is not a strong poem but in its very weakness lies an alternative eloquence. That weakness is its obvious derivativeness. To read the opening lines (above) is immediately to realise that what we have here is a Welshified version of Yeats's celebrated 'Lake Isle of Innisfree', perhaps Welshified in part by the incorporation of echoes from Cynan's popular lyric 'Aberdaron', which imagines a retirement retreat to a cottage faced by nothing but the wild waves of the sea. And that process of cultural translation seems to me very telling. It suggests that, for Thomas the young Welsh churchman, Dewi's Llanddewi functions in much the same way as did Innisfree for the early Yeats: as the repository of yearning hope, of futile nostalgia. Already by 1948 it's thus obvious that R.S. had serious doubts about the practical possibility of re-establishing the Church in Wales on sound Welsh footings; about authentically reconnecting it with the tradition of

Dewi, and thus recalibrating it both spiritually and culturally; about recentring it at Llanddewibrefi.

However, both in this poem and in 'A Line from St David's' there is a determination of obstinate persistence in thus hoping. Because for R.S. it was this hope alone that could legitimise his Church's otherwise suspect claim to be the authentic, ancient, Church of Wales – *yr Hen Fam* ('the Old Mother'). Such a hope was, after all, his sole authority for dismissing that alternative designation of his Church by Welsh-speakers as *yr Hen Estrones* ('the Old Foreigner'), the dismissive epithet scornfully applied to her throughout the nineteenth century by her great rival and enemy, the socially, culturally and politically ascendant Nonconformist denominations.

At this point, then, we need to recall and understand what might be called the seminal Welsh Anglican myth of *yr Hen Fam*. It is as old as the establishment of the Anglican Church itself. And it was invoked by Glyn Simon in his inaugural 1968 address as Archbishop (considered above), challenging his Church to reconnect with the nation by recalling its ancient symbiotic connections with Welsh-language culture. Keenly aware of the stubborn addiction and adherence of the conservative Welsh *gwerin* to the Catholic Church they persisted in regarding as their very own, the Welsh Tudor bishops deliberately set out to destroy Welsh Catholicism's claims to direct descent from the original Celtic Church. They did so by devising and aggressively articulating a counter-claim. According to this alternative account, it was Anglicanism, by reforming and purifying a profoundly corrupt ecclesiastical order, that had enabled Wales to reconnect with its early, pristine, ascetic spiritual past. So important a polemical tool indeed was this new myth in the Anglicans' struggle for the popular Welsh mind during the Reformation that it was powerfully deployed by Bishop Richard Davies in his eloquent and seminal Epistle to the Welsh that prefaced the historic 1567 translation of the New Testament and Book of Common Prayer.

That translation itself was the first proof of this new, suspect Church of England's commitment to serve the spiritual needs of the Welsh people, which inescapably meant serving their language and culture. That Church's next great contribution was, of course, the publication in 1588 of the first Welsh Bible, overseen by Bishop William Morgan. R.S. never ceased to be awed by the way he had shaken 'The words from the great tree/ Of language'. Thereafter Welsh priests regularly continued to make seminal contributions to the maintenance and development of Welsh cultural identity throughout the subsequent centuries. Landmarks included Edmwnd Prys's first Welsh hymnal, the Vicar Prichard's popular homiletic verses, *Canwyll y Cymry*; Theophilus Evans's *Drych Y Prif Oesoedd*, in its day a masterpiece of Welsh historiography; Ellis Wynne's searing visionary satire *Gweledigaetheu y Bardd Cwsg*; the great eighteenth-century poems of the tragic priest Goronwy Owen; the landmark Sunday Schools of Gruffydd Jones, Vicar of Llanddowror, for the education of the Welsh peasantry; the heroic recovery by Evan Evans (Ieuan Brydydd Hir) of what survived in manuscript of the great Welsh bardic poetry of the earlier ages; and the collective work of cultural restoration accomplished by Yr Hen Bersoniaid Llengar, the old cultured parsons of the early nineteenth century.

At least for the intellectual elite of the newly disestablished Church in Wales, an elite that included R. S. Thomas, it was this proud historical tradition of cultural ministry that entitled their Church to the honorific 'Yr Hen Fam', even while they conceded that that Church, particularly in its alien, anglicised, colonialist nineteenth-century form, could not fail also to be stigmatised as *yr Hen Estrones*. Indeed, they felt that it continued to reveal itself all too frequently in these foreign aspects even in its new, disestablished, independent form. But it was the enticing vision of the disestablished Church as now poised to fulfil its potential as *yr Hen Fam* that persuaded a handful of prominent Welsh writers and intellectuals to abandon their Nonconformist background, during the interwar years, and to convert to the Church in Wales. Among these were two of the nation's most gifted poets, Gwenallt and Euros Bowen. The latter was to spend his life as a priest of the Church but the former was to become so disillusioned with the anglicised mentality of the disestablished Church that he eventually, and very publicly, reverted to the Welsh Presbyterianism of his childhood.[22] R. S. Thomas's own stormy relations with the Church in Wales need really to be placed in the context of the experiences of these key figures who were, of course, his exact contemporaries.

What seems clear to me is that those very early years in Manafon, when he was enthusiastically learning Welsh and simultaneously acquiring a Welsh cultural outlook, were years during which he hopefully cultivated what was then no doubt his new perception of the Church as *yr Hen Fam*. And such a vision seems to me to be present, although hitherto undetected, as at least the subtext of one of his very finest early poems 'Country Church (Manafon)'. All readers seem to be agreed as to the primary meaning of this poem. Very crudely summarised, it is a symbolic articulation of Thomas's central dilemma of how to reconcile the spiritual truths of religion with the cruel realities of a Darwinian natural order. But no reader, as far as I am aware, has registered the possibility of a secondary meaning, related to Thomas's awakening sense of the historical but threatened Welshness of his Church. Reading the poem in the light of my concerns in this discussion, what strikes me about it is how Thomas here chooses to see his church as, in what are perhaps the most beautiful and intense phrases in the poem, 'built from the river stone/ Brittle with light' (*CP*, 11). He elementalises it, making it seem a special outcrop, or stony excrescence, of the very landscape itself. This church is 'native' to its landscape: it is unmistakeably a *Welsh* church, a Llan rather than the routinely English parish church. Indeed, there is here no sense of this church being church of any parish – any more, of course, than in most of R.S.'s best poems, is there any sense of his being a parish priest.

Novice Welsh-learner as he was when he composed this poem, R.S. couldn't have failed to be fascinated by the name of his church – Manafon – and to notice its constituent elements: literally *man* ('place') and *afon* ('river'). And so there's a sense in which this poem is an onomastic poem – that is, a poem purporting to explain the name of a place and of that place's church. In the process it highlights that this church is built not only near water but actually out of 'river stone' – the ancient Celtic linkage of water with the sacred is surely obvious.

We know that it was by learning Welsh that R.S. became aware that one of his predecessors as rector of Manafon had been 'Gwallter Mechain', or Walter Davies, a celebrated member of that fraternity of Yr Hen Bersoniaid Llengar that has been mentioned already.[23] R.S. refers to this in *Neb*, immediately adding that his excitement at discovering such a congenial pedigree was quickly tempered by the realisation that already by the early nineteenth century of Davies's incumbency, the parish of Manafon had become predominantly English-speaking. One might, then, suggest that reinforcing the image of the thoroughly local, indigenous, elemental church at Manafon as increasingly threatened by its very own surroundings – 'the brimming tides of fescue' – is a sense of the Welshness of the Church as now being permanently and seriously at risk. And yet, hope defiantly counter-asserts, 'It stands'; and the young Thomas can already be here seen as preparing to stand for a lifetime by this tenuous spiritual and cultural hope.

Gwallter Mechain was to continue to fascinate the older Thomas as a point of reference and yardstick. When well into his seventies he dedicated a poem to him recently reprinted in *Uncollected Poems*. It makes it perfectly clear that Mechain was another of his intimate Welsh ecclesiastical kindred spirits: an alter ego. The poem specifically identifies the clerical Davies's contribution, as scholar, pioneering eisteddfodwr and poet, to the survival of Welsh-language culture. He may have died legally intestate, but we are his fortunate cultural legatees, inheritors of his work

> to light Welsh
> confidently on its way backward
> to an impending future. (*UP*, 133)

And Thomas's strong, but desolate, identification with this spiritually and culturally emblematic figure representative of the tradition of the Church in Wales is evident in his description of Davies's patient ministry of the word to a thankless people, involving

> The weekly climb
> into the crow's nest of his pulpit,
> telling them of the glimpsed land,
>
> trying to believe in it
> himself. The words digested
> the bell's notes more easily
>
> than his intellect his doctrine. (*UP*, 133–4)

It would be interesting to collect together the poems R.S. scattered in his collections over several decades paying tribute to some of the key figures from William Morgan to Gwenallt who had contributed so substantially to the establishing and maintenance of the tradition of the Church as *yr Hen Fam*. Included in this honourable lineage would be Ann Griffiths of Dolwar Fach. The blessed Ann, to whom R.S. addressed several memorable poems, is eligible for inclusion because until shortly after her brief lifetime the impassioned Methodism of her faith was still that of a reforming sect within the Anglican Church.

R.S.'s fascination – or rather identification – with Ann Griffiths is a particularly telling product of the terminal phase of his alienation from his church. He was well aware of his belatedness in recognising the spiritual genius of one whose spirit had, after all, been near neighbour to him at Manafon, which was only fifteen miles distant from her Llanfihangel-yng-Ngwynfa.

> Has she waited all these years
> for me to forget myself
> and do her homage? I begin
> now

he wrote in his 1987 'Fugue' in her memory: 'Ann Thomas, Ann Griffiths' (*CP*, 472). He thus pointedly addresses her first by her maiden name – which was 'Thomas', like his own.

Two factors seem to have contributed to his full 'discovery' of her a decade or so earlier. One, the celebration in 1976 of the tercentenary of her birth.[24] The other, the extraordinary public lecture in 1965, and subsequent 1972 essay, on her genius by R.S.'s great political and cultural hero, Saunders Lewis. Abhorring the embrace by Welsh Nonconformity of an Ann the chapels regarded as one of their own, soggy with sentimental intimacy with God, Lewis insisted instead that her true home was in the company of the great spiritually astringent mystics of the medieval Catholic tradition of Europe. R.S. takes his clue from his hero in focusing on the ecstatic sensual rapture of Ann's vision of God. And there is, of course, a tragic aspect to his celebration in Ann, in the form of a spiritual epithalamium, of that intimate encounter with God that he himself had sought all his life but had been denied:

> Down this path she set off
> for the earlier dancing
> of the body; but under the myrtle
> the Bridegroom was waiting
> for her on her way home. (*CP*, 470)

The allusion is to one of her greatest hymns.

But Thomas's underlying and unstated aim, it seems to me, is to celebrate Ann Griffiths as one of the great dissidents of the Anglican Church in Wales – like himself. Accordingly, he underlines the essential

Welshness of her language and, by implication, her genius. She becomes for him the Muse of the Church in its benign form of *yr Hen Fam*, and that Church's loss of sight of her – sadly instanced even by his younger self – is telling evidence of its alienation from the Welsh nation.

R. S. Thomas's conflicted relationship, both as poet and as priest, with the Church in Wales throughout his life invites extensive, sustained study way beyond the scope of this present discussion. There are so many aspects of it that intrigue me, such as that marked turn away from the Church and towards the ancient sacredness of the Llŷn landscape that followed, I feel, his slightly early retirement from the priesthood in 1978. This was a re-enactment, but forty years later and this time on a grand scale, of that turn we've already noticed, away from St David's Cathedral and towards the surrounding countryside. Llŷn was for him, during those final decades, a bough, suspended between sea and sky, so that to live there was to dwell in an uncanny, liminal region. As for the cottage of Sarn y Plas, dating back to at least the eighteenth century, it too seemed crudely fashioned, like Manafon Church, out of water-washed boulders, so that its walls resounded, re-sounded, with the ancient music of the nearby sea. Interestingly enough, R.S. had anticipated such a structure as well, in his radio talk on St David's a decade or so earlier, when he'd imagined the solitariness that had once characterised the precincts of the cathedral: 'A chyda'r nos, swn y môr, a'r muriau trwchus, fel esgyrn yng ngolau'r lloer' ('And by night, the sound of the sea, and the thick walls like bones in the light of the moon').

It was to Sarn y Plas (or Sarn Rhiw) that he removed with his wife upon his retirement from the Church in Wales, the Church he had for so long struggled to believe would allow him, by serving it, to serve his own nation as well. His concern, as priest in the Church in Wales, to serve his own nation permeates all of R.S.'s writing about his office. It makes itself apparent, for instance, in a poem like 'Service', a poem expressive of his chronic crisis of faith but also expressive of his chronic crisis of faith in his Church's connection with Wales:

> I call on God
> In the after silence, and my shadow
> Wrestles with him upon a wall
> Of plaster, that has all the nation's
> Hardness in it. (*CP*, 174)

Bearing in mind confessions like this to the isolating nature of his cultural as well as spiritual obsessions, and recalling R.S.'s last and famous period of service as rector of remote Aberdaron, I find poignancy as well as comedy in a snippet of news I came across in *Y Llan*. It concerned the recent installation in the great historic church of Llanbadarn Fawr, on the outskirts of Aberystwyth, of a microphone to ensure that the congregation throughout the body of the church could hear and follow every moment of the service. Previous to its installation, parishioners seated in the more remote reaches of this substantial church used, it seems, to refer to those parts as 'Aberdaron'.

What an allegory this is of R.S.'s chill, distant, polar relationship to the 'national' Church in Wales he served so faithfully, according to his idiosyncratic lights, for most of his life as poet and priest. And in noting it, I recall a wonderful story about him that still circulates in the Aberdaron region, about how, on the very day of his retirement from the Church, he lit a great bonfire on the beach in which he burned his cassock.[25] I do hope the story is true. Having been out in the cold all those many years he had been a priest in what he came to feel was still only the foreign Church of England in Wales, I feel he deserved to warm himself at the last. In one of his final interviews, R.S. even went on public record to confess, 'I wouldn't say that I'm an orthodox Christian at all'.[26]

And yet . . . What I believe was my very last encounter with him, at a David Jones Conference held in Lampeter a year or so before his passing, terminated with his excusing himself and turning in early, to be certain of making morning communion the next day. And Aled Jones Williams, R.S.'s own parish priest at the time of his death, has movingly recorded how he was always able to intuit from the hands held out by parishioners to receive the bread and the communion cup how deep they were in faith. R. S. Thomas's hands, he testifies, were always and unmistakeably those of a devout believer.[27] Like some animal returning instinctively to a salt lick, then, R.S. seems to have found, to the very end, some specific, special spiritual nourishment in *yr Hen Fam* that his wounded soul needed and craved, and that was not, for him, available anywhere else.

(Tucker Lecture Series 3, Trinity-St Davids, Lampeter [Lampeter: Trivium, 2013].)

Notes

[1] *Y Llan* (31 Mawrth 1972), 8, noticed the screening of Ormond's film profile of R. S. Thomas, and singled out his comments on poetry and religion.

[2] See his laconic account of the matter in Jason Walford Davies, trans., *R. S. Thomas: Autobiographies* (London: Dent, 1997), pp. 34–5: 'His mother lost her parents when she was six years old and was brought up by an aunt and her husband, who was a parish priest. She was sent to a boarding school in England which had an ecclesiastical atmosphere, and as a result she had some attachment to the church. So when she saw that her son had no strong objection to the idea of being a candidate for Holy Orders she secretly rejoiced and persuaded her husband to agree to the idea. And the son accepted that he would have to start learning Greek and go on to university'.

[3] The Welsh (Anglican) Church was disendowed and in effect disestablished by Act of Parliament in 1914, but the practical creation of a separate province of Wales within the Anglican communion was delayed until 1920 (31 March). See David Walker, *A History of the Church in Wales* (Cardiff: University of Wales Press, 1976); Revd D. T. W. Price, *A History of the Church in Wales in the Twentieth Century* (Penarth: Church in Wales Publications, 1990). This development is placed in wider, comparative contexts in several studies by Keith Robbins: see *England, Ireland, Scotland, Wales: The Christian Church 1900–2000*, Oxford History of the Christian Church (Oxford: Oxford University Press, 2008); *History, Religion and Identity in Modern Britain* (London and Rio de Janeiro: The Hambledon Press, 1993); 'Establishing Disestablishment: Some Reflections on Wales and Scotland', in Stewart J. Brown and George Newlands (eds), *Scottish Christianity in the Modern World* (Edinburgh: T. & T. Clark, 2000), pp. 231–54.

[4] 'Pensiynau', a letter in *Y Llan* (8 Mai 1970), 7, refers to the following clause in the Welsh Anglican statute book: 'If a clergyman who is in receipt of a pension from the Representative Body . . . be sentenced to imprisonment . . . the pension forthwith shall cease to be payable.'

[5] Quoted in Price, *History*, p. 12.

[6] R.S. had come to know Glyn Simon when the latter was the young Warden of the Church Hostel in Bangor that was home to Thomas while studying at the University College for his undergraduate degree in Classics. 'Although Glyn Simon was somewhat effeminate in his manner,' R. S. later recalled, 'he was firm enough in defence of his convictions' (*Autobiographies*, p. 40). Reliable report suggests that Simon was unsympathetic to the Welsh language when first he took up his post, but experienced a kind of cultural conversion through his encounter with the Welsh-language students of his hostel. The broad parallels with R. S. Thomas's experience at the very same time and in the very same location are intriguing and suggestive.

[7] *Y Llan* (27 Medi 1968), 7–8, includes the full text of Glyn Simon's inaugural address as Archbishop of Wales, that takes as theme the place of the Welsh language in the nation and in the Church. It takes its departure from a letter

Simon had received from a monoglot English priest arguing that Welsh had no relevance to his experience and profession of faith. Simon responds by tracing the origins of the Church in Wales back to the pre-Augustine British ('Celtic') Church, and then tracking the cultural history of the Church's subsequent development. He argues that the tragedy of the Church from the eighteenth to the twentieth century has been its steady alienation from the people it was supposed to serve. Drawing on Cranmer's statement that 'in these our doings' (i.e. in establishing a Church of England) 'we condemn no other nations, nor proscribe anything but for our own people only', Simon argues that fidelity to Wales is perfectly consistent with committed participation in the worldwide communion of believers. In warning against an incipient form of cultural apartheid within the Church communion, he proceeds to criticise both such Welsh-speaking Church members as are intolerant of monoglot English-speakers and such of the latter as treat Welsh as marginal and irrelevant. Ending with a plea for mutual respect and conciliation, he uses key passages from T. S. Eliot's *Notes Towards a Definition of Culture* to advance a blueprint of a meaningfully bilingual and actively bicultural Church in Wales.

8   'Golygyddol', *Y Llan* (14 Mehefin 1974), 4.

9   Letter, *Y Llan* (26 Mai 1967), 7: 'Yr Eglwys yng Nghymru yn rhoi cyfle i'w enllibwyr unwaith eto, "yr hen estrones." Pa hawl sydd gennym i gyfrif ein hunain yn Fam Eglwys, neu yn hen Eglwys y Cymry, neu i gyfrif fod gennym gyfrifoldeb ysbrydol dros Gymru gyfan?' ('The Church in Wales once again providing its traducers with an opening, "the old foreigner". What right have we to consider ourselves a Mother Church, or the Old Church of the Welsh, or to claim we have spiritual responsibility for the whole of Wales?')

10   See the letter from Revd John Davies, Wrexham vicarage, concluding with the remark 'Duw a'n gwaredo rhag colli ein ffordd fel Eglwys a throi'n gymdeithas diogelu iaith a dim mwy' ('God preserve us from losing our way as a Church and becoming a language-preservation society and no more') (*Y Llan*, 9 Mehefin 1967, 6). The Revd Terry Thomas's response to this in a subsequent number of *Y Llan* (16 Mehefin 1967, 7) is worth noting because it takes the form of a substantial quotation from *The Theology of Culture* by Paul Tillich, one of R. S. Thomas's favourite theologians: 'Every religious act, not only in organized religion, but also in the most intimate movement of the soul, is culturally formed. The fact that every act of man's spiritual life is carried by language, spoken or silent, is proof enough for this assertion. For language is the basic cultural creation.'

11   *Y Llan* (9 Mehefin 1967), 6; *Y Llan* (2 Mehefin 1967), 8.

12   The reverberations of this episode rumbled on and on. At the National Eisteddfod in Barry in 1968, both Bedwyr Lewis Jones and T. I. Ellis delivered passionate lectures on the rich cultural legacy of the Church in Wales (*Y Llan*, 16 Awst 1968, 6).

13   The Revd Bowen proceeded first to define the aims of the new society and then to advertise a meeting on 30 June 1967 in Llanegwad formally to establish this

new body (*Y Llan*, 21 Gorffennaf 1967, 6, 7). Subsequent issues of *Y Llan* carried notices about the development of this Cymdeithas.

[14] 'Tŷ Ddewi', *Y Llan* (28 Chwefror 1969), 7.

[15] 'A Line from St David's', *Collected Poems, 1945–1990* (London: J. M. Dent, 1993), p. 123. Hereafter *CP*. The poem was first published in *The Bread of Truth* (London: Hart-Davis, 1963).

[16] Waldo Williams, *Dail Pren* (Aberystwyth: Gwasg Aberystwyth, 1956), p. 68.

[17] Letter, *Y Llan* (10 Mai 1968), 6.

[18] For a full account of these feelings and their implications for his poetry, see 'The Leper of Abercuawg', in M. Wynn Thomas, *R. S. Thomas: Serial Obsessive* (Cardiff: University of Wales Press, 2013), pp. 147–70.

[19] *Dail Pren*, p. 100.

[20] Dr Jason Walford Davies has kindly drawn to my attention other possible implications of Thomas's choice of 'Plwmp'. The name is said to have derived from the English word 'Pump', and to refer specifically to the water pump in the village. As Dr Walford Davies has pointed out, the image of water recurs in Thomas's poem: 'Dewi/ The water-drinker', 'bubble', 'the Welsh fountain', 'sea', 'currents'. Furthermore, this imagery carries a strong political, as well as spiritual, charge, relating as it does to 'Welsh water' – a vexed resource, of course, in the context of twentieth-century Wales. And there is, moreover, more than a hint of 'reverse colonisation' in this relatively rare instance of adoption, and indeed absorption, by the Welsh language of an English word.

[21] Tony Brown and Jason Walford Davies (eds), *R. S. Thomas: Uncollected Poems* (Highgreen: Bloodaxe, 2013), p. 27. Hereafter *UP*.

[22] An obituary for Gwenallt was published in *Y Llan* (3 Ionawr 1969), 1. It specifically mentioned his disillusionment with the Englishness of the Church in Wales: 'Bu'n anffyddiwr, yn Ymneilltuwr, yn Eglwyswr, ac yna'n Ymneilltuwr drachefn am fod Seisnigrwydd yr Eglwys yn ei gadw draw' ('He had been an atheist, a Nonconformist, an Anglican, and then a Nonconformist once more because the Englishness of the Church alienated him').

[23] Walter Davies ('Gwallter Mechain') (1761–1849), poet, editor and antiquarian, was rector of Manafon from 1807 to 1837.

[24] There is a summary of the programme of celebration in *Y Llan* (16 Ionawr 1976), 1.

[25] An alternative, less colourful but no doubt more reliable, version has it that he burned the cassock in the back garden of his rectory.

[26] 'R. S. Thomas in conversation with Molly Price-Owen', *The David Jones Journal* (Summer/Autumn 1991), 97.

[27] Radio Cymru centenary profile of R. S. Thomas, broadcast Friday, 29 March 2013.

8

R. S. Thomas: 'A retired Christian'

I am retiring at Easter. I shall be 65. I could stay till 70, but I am glad to go from a Church I no longer believe in, sycophantic to the queen, iconoclastic with language, changing for the sake of change and regardless of beauty. The Christian structure is a meaningful structure, but in the hands of theologians or the common people it is a poor thing.[1]

When R.S. retired as priest of the Church in Wales in 1978, almost a quarter of a century of life, and half of his years as a writer, still remained to him. Although he himself repeatedly treated retirement as a watershed episode, no commentator (myself included) has hitherto considered its impact on his thinking and his poetry, preferring to refer indiscriminately instead to his late, Aberdaron, period. But in fact his writing testifies to the painful and pivotal nature of his break – for so in truth it was – with his church, and records a narrative of severance and reaction far more nuanced and complex and conflicted than I first supposed when my attention was first drawn to R.S.'s final years. I had assumed that break to have been simply liberating and creatively enabling. But while this was indeed straightforwardly the case with regard to the freedom he gained to act and to speak un-inhibitedly on those issues closest to his heart, such as environmental concerns, nuclear policy and the future of the Welsh language, the implications of retirement for his thinking and creative writing were altogether more mixed and ambivalent.

In this latter respect, it seems to me tentatively possible to distinguish between three different phases. The first (1978–85), immediately following his retirement, is characterised by a continuation of that process of spiritual exploration that had first found explosive expression in the first of his 'Aberdaron' volumes, *H'm* (1972). Central to the second (1985–92) are several seminal and radical exercises in retrospection, most notably *Neb* (1985), *Blwyddyn yn Llŷn* (1990), and that remarkable volume *The Echoes Return Slow* (1988). These include important sections that highlight the fraught circumstances of his retirement; and this second phase also features three volumes of mostly mediocre poetry (*Experiments with an Amen* (1986); *Counterpoint* (1990); *Mass for Hard Times* (1992)) which are the intermittently successful creative result of his efforts to work through the intellectual and spiritual crisis precipitated by the traumatic rupture he had experienced. The third, and concluding, phase (1992–5) sees him establishing a new equilibrium, as evidenced in an outstanding and in some ways summative, final volume, *No Truce With The Furies* (1995). What follows will primarily concentrate on the second of these phrases, since it seems to me to distil the crisis that determined Thomas to retire and dictated the whole tone and tenor of his last years.

* * *

Crisis indeed it was, judging by an intriguing, uncharacteristically full, letter he sent to his friend Raymond Garlick in 1979, the year following his retirement. He there confesses to having suffered from 'some sort of malaise lately; a nervous reaction or something which has given me to much thought'. 'Whenever I am unwell,' he continues, 'I fall to questioning various postures and tenets too easily and arrogantly held when one is well, both in one's life and in poetry.' And he then specifically connects his current psychically troubled condition to his worries about his relationship with his Church. It is a crucial passage, and therefore needs to be quoted in full:

> I am writing like this to you because of the difficulty both of us are having with our allegiance to a church which seems to be abandoning too lightly the wonderful traditions which have sustained [sic] over the centuries.[2] Many systems and structures tempt me from time to time, but I find, when I am unwell and nervously shaken, that I can't live by them. I can't bring myself to agree that Christianity is the only way, as so many dogmatists claim, but it is certainly one of the great ways and for one brought up in the European tradition, there is little point in turning to one of the other ways. So I am content to leave in such a

mysterious and wonderful universe the issues in God's hands, asking pardon for wilfulness and grace for humble trust and acceptance. The church is imperfect, God knows, but it has the scriptures and sacraments, if it only will have the grace to let those who prefer the old forms continue to enjoy them. So I shall still go along on Christmas morning. Perhaps you will? (LRG, 111)

To me, at least, this sounds like a *cri de coeur* from the brink of a breakdown prevented only by humble recourse to a makeshift credo. Gone is the proud defiance of a morally and spiritually bankrupt Church manifest in the earlier letter anticipating imminent retirement he'd sent to Garlick two years earlier and that serves as epigraph to this essay. Ten years later and Thomas would be claiming, in another letter to his friend, that his breakdown in 1979 – 'I had been feeling more and more on edge, until suddenly one night something snapped and I was seized with uncontrollable shivers. This was followed by a week of extreme depression and, as you mention, claustrophobia' (*LRG*, 138) – had been due to his having at that earlier time embarked on an unwise experiment with vegetarianism. Maybe. But my own instinct is still to suppose that the turmoil of soul attendant upon his break with his Church had more to do with it.

This crisis had certainly been a long time building. Long before his retirement, he had seen it looming, with a mixture of relief and dread. In his blither moments, he imagined a simple, clean break – 'Let retirement be retirement indeed', as he put it in *The Echoes Return Slow*.[3] But always shadowing that blitheness there were dark misgivings. 'Just when, after such long practice, he was beginning to approach spiritual health', he noted with characteristic wryness, 'life with that irony that is so dear to it announced that there is a time to retire even from a cure' (*CLP*, 62). He had always been whimsically drawn to the medical connotations of that traditional ecclesiastical term for a priest's duty of care to his parishioners and had been particularly appreciative of the irony of his own responsibility as a theologically challenged priest for the spiritual health of his flock (see *CLP*, 62). On the brink of retirement, he (correctly) anticipated that 'the problems he had concealed from his congregations' would have 'him now all to themselves' (*CLP*, 68). No longer would he have a round of duties to order his life by, or a fixed role within a community to ballast his solitary voyages through strange seas of thought. No longer either could he allow the Holy Sacrament to speak through him and for him, as it had done all those decades he had been the officiating priest. During those years he had come to appreciate how 'the simplicity of the Sacrament absolved him from the complexities of the Word' (*CLP*, 46). Now he was left face-to-face with those very complexities. If the prospect of having to move 'from a parsonage to a cottage' disheartened him – 'the poverty of the spirit must be extended to the flesh' as books, furniture and paintings had to be disposed of or placed in storage – much more dismaying was a downsizing of a wholly different kind: 'he was under compulsion to give away whatever assurances he possessed' (*CLP*, 70). There were therefore times when retirement even balefully seemed to him to be bathed in an apocalyptic light and he toyed with the conceit of millenarianism: 'Towards the end of one's life, towards the end of the century, worse still towards the end of the millennium, the tempter approaches us with desperation' (*CLP*, 67).

So concerned indeed was he about the practical as well as the psycho-spiritual consequences of retirement that, for all the bravado of that letter to Raymond Garlick at the end of 1977, he actually proposed a compromise arrangement to his bishop. He would, R.S. intimated, be willing to stay on for another five years as priest, provided that upon reaching the compulsory retirement age of seventy he then be allowed to remain in the vicarage 'and do voluntary work in the parish'.[4] His Church's rejection of this compromise may well have reinforced his bilious disillusionment with the direction in which it was heading. He hated the reformed services, and, while sympathetic to the aim of reconciling church and chapel in Wales, was suspicious of any concession to forms of Nonconformist service that seemed to drain worship of its numinousness (*A*, 89). Imagine the depths of his dismay, then, when his own Church seriously began to contemplate measures that in his eyes would fatally compromise its for him unique power to mediate the awe of the human encounter with the holy.

* * *

For over a decade before his retirement, the Church in Wales had been establishing committees and commissions to advise on the adaptation of its texts, liturgies and sacraments to suit modern needs. R.S. was particularly exercised by their recommendations on reforming the King James Bible and the Book of Common Prayer and by the modifications they proposed be made to the ministering of the Holy

Sacrament or Eucharist. A flavour of the controversies that swirled around the reform proposals of this period may be got by consulting the columns of *Y Llan* – the Welsh-language weekly of the Church that R.S. regularly read and to which he occasionally contributed.

Take the liturgy, for example. Notes in *Y Llan* to welcome in the new year of 1966 predicted a move within the Church to implement reforms even to the Communion Service and three weeks later the six members of the 'Liturgical Commission of the Church in Wales' were listed by name.[5] Indeed, every issue of *Y Llan* during the opening months of 1966 devoted space to discussing liturgical reform, culminating in an extensive report on debates on this subject at the Annual Meeting of the Church's Governing Body in April.[6] The moves afoot prompted considerable unease among some members of the clergy. Indeed, some (perhaps including R. S. Thomas) became rather demoralised by the whole process, because it seemed to them to diminish the sacerdotal power of the priesthood. For three weeks in the spring of 1969 *Y Llan* featured a series of powerful, highly articulate articles by a priest depressed by the prospective reduction of priestly authority – by which, as he explained, he meant not the authority of social status but the divinely bestowed authority to satisfy the deepest spiritual needs of his parishioners.[7] He confessed to a feeling of pointlessness because the proposed changes would, in his opinion, leave the priest with no duties to discharge save those that could equally well be discharged by the laity.[8] Traditionally, the central role of the priest – most completely fulfilled when serving the Eucharist at the altar – had been recognised and respected as that of bringing humanity unmistakeably face-to-face with the challenge and grace of the Gospel.[9] It was in performing this role that the spiritually privileged and unique status of the priest as 'Alter Christus' (the human surrogate of Christ Himself, thus, in classic Catholic terms, acting 'in persona Christi') had always been most fully revealed. In this resided the truly essential function of the priesthood, and if the priest was not essential then he could be nothing but an obstacle. That, indeed, was precisely what the priest was in danger of becoming, under the changes currently being seriously considered by the Church. These would reverse the traditional relationship between priest and people, by encouraging the congregation to participate in the liturgy on much the same level as the priest, and to turn the sermon into a forum for discussion.

Whether or not Thomas would have endorsed all the sentiments expressed in this series of articles, there were certainly striking affinities between them and his own position. But there were equally powerful voices raised in *Y Llan* in support of the proposed reforms, and the terms in which they argued their case also sharpen our understanding of R.S.'s stance. In early 1972, the Church weekly printed a summary of the preparation by the Liturgical Commission of the Church in Wales of its submission to the General Synod on the reforming of the Eucharist.[10] And a little later *Y Llan* noted that Communion in its proposed new form would now be trialled for a ten-year period, time enough for the Liturgical Commission to assess fully the practical implications of its prospective eventual adoption.[11]

This was the culmination of a process of review that *Y Llan* had been tracking for half a dozen years. In April 1967 it had approved the move to make the central thrust and divine purpose of the communion service clearer to all communicants, and had commended signs of an intention to increase the congregation's awareness of playing as active a role as the priest in the Eucharist service.[12] It approvingly quoted at length from an article on this subject by one of the leading Welsh Anglican laymen of the day, Aneirin Talfan Davies. He had recalled in an essay for the *Western Mail* how a Christian from another denomination had commented, after attending the traditional Eucharist service, that it had seemed odd for the priest to be doing everything, as if Communion were nothing but a priestly monologue. Three years earlier, an important editorial in *Y Llan* had warmly supported a proposal that in a new, reformed Eucharist service the altar should be so placed that the congregation could gather around it, with the priest facing the communicants rather than having his back to them and his face to the altar as hitherto.

This was precisely the proposed alteration to the sacrament that R. S. Thomas most deeply resented. And his own 'reactionary' view had been anticipated by *Y Llan* in its editorial, because it had anticipated objections to the reforms it was championing from those who sincerely believed that only an altar placed at a distance from the congregation could elicit the immense respect proper to the awesome mystery at the centre of the Eucharist, a mystery requiring communicants to approach it in fear and trembling. This, too, had been R.S.'s traumatic concern, as he made clear several years after retiring in *Blwyddyn yn Llŷn/A Year in Llŷn*:

> It pains me greatly, but ever since the Church reformed the Liturgy, I cannot partake of the Sacrament. The new order of the Church in Wales

has changed the whole atmosphere of Holy Communion for me. The pinnacle of the original service was when I, as a priest, would say the words of congregation over the bread and wine, with my back to the congregation as one who had the honour of leading them to the throne of God's grace. But now it is the congregation that the priest faces, inviting them to speak, as he breaks the synthetic wafer before them. It is to God that mystery belongs, and woe to man when he tries to interfere with that mystery. As T. S. Eliot said, 'Human kind cannot bear very much reality.' (*A*, 131)

So seminal a passage does this seem to me for any attempt to understand not only R.S.'s spiritual stance in retirement but the very character of the remarkable body of poetry he produced during that period, that I remain astonished its implications seem never to have been properly considered.

In *Blwyddyn yn Llŷn* he even proceeded to gloss his anguished comments about the Eucharist by drawing a distinction between the two sides of existence – 'the transcendental and the subordinate, as it were'. 'It is', he explained, 'an abysmal rift that exists between those who seek to exalt life and those who want to reduce it to the "bare facts", as they term them. "Life is nothing but" . . . they say.' And most tellingly of all, he turned, when seeking to lay this fundamental fallacy to rest, not to the central sacrament of his Church, which, in its traditional but now tragically 'superseded' form had been the irreplaceable symbolically expressive mainstay of his belief in the sacred source of all life, but to the life of Nature in which alone he could now find consolatory reassuring evidence of a belief essential to him both as a human being and as a creative artist. After all, Jesus himself, he became fond of stressing, had been a poet of nature. As a natural phenomenon, the Northern Lights, he affirmed, 'is in the same class as thunder and lightning and earthquakes. If it doesn't frighten you in the same way, it nevertheless sends a shiver through your being like something *tremendum et fascinans*.' 'It is likely', he tellingly added, 'that Jacob was too far south to see it, and yet it isn't unlike a huge ladder between earth and heaven, and "behold the angels of God ascending and descending on it"' (*A*, 133).

In that culminating fusion of a phenomenon of Nature with the imagery of the Old Testament, R.S. implicitly anticipates the crucial turn away from the Church and towards the natural world his creative mind was to take in his last decades, following his tragic estrangement.

It was his attempt to recuperate the authentic imagery of the sacred he felt had been so culpably abandoned by the Church in Wales in favour of what it misguidedly supposed, under the influence of the powerful modern secular, purportedly 'scientific', outlook, to be the 'bare facts' of the Christian faith.

* * *

But in order fully to appreciate the nature and depth of R. S. Thomas's late alienation from 'his' Church, and its implications for his great religious poetry, it is necessary to consider not only the crucial alter-ations to the Eucharist outlined above but the simultaneous movement to modernise the language of both the Bible and the Book of Common Prayer. 'Revision was in the air', he noted acidly in *The Echoes Return Slow*, 'Language was out of date; too formal. God was available for conversation' (*CLP*, 60). And as with the movement to reform Holy Communion, *Y Llan* scrupulously recorded the developing debate. In March, 1969, for instance, it summarised the history of the preparation of a New English Bible, beginning with the establishing of an Inter-denominational Committee by the Church of England in 1947 and culminating with the publication of the modernised New Testament in 1961.[13] (In 1963 the Welsh Free Church Council had likewise sponsored a new translation of the Bible into Welsh.) Four years earlier, in May, 1965, the weekly had reported a proposal to produce a simplified form of the Book of Common Prayer.[14] Sympathetically noting that the intention was to reach the ninety per cent of people who were baffled by the traditional forms of worship of the Church, it nevertheless warned against simplification to a point that would dilute the richness and maturity of spiritual experience embodied in the existing, traditional form of the Prayer Book, and the following month it published a critique of an attempt to reform the text in order to bring it more into line with the views of the modern age.[15] A year or so later it recorded similar reservations about the reforms in train, approvingly quoting the comment of Stephen Bayne that the Book of Common Prayer was 'our best watchman of the supernatural and the holy'.[16]

   That neat, pithy, phrase captures the very essence of R. S. Thomas's profound objections to the reform of sacred texts being not only contemplated but actively pursued by his Church. Such seemed to him appallingly consistent with the reforms to the Eucharist, and all

were symptomatic of the fatal misconception that the symbolic language of both ritual and text was a mere expendable form of expression
rather than the very substance of religious experience and the *sine
qua non* of the sacred. In *Neb* he gave measured expression to his
objections. Referring to the new English translations he commented,
speaking of himself in the third person:

> For good or ill, this was his mother tongue and the language he had to
> write his poetry in. He wasn't content at all. He therefore clung to the
> King James Bible and to the 1662 Book of Common Prayer, considering
> the language of both to be indescribably superior. (*A*, 88–9)

The remark about the language of the Prayer Book and the Bible being
'the language he had to write his poetry in' is very revealing. It under-
scores the intimate connection R.S. saw between the 'poetry' of the
religious texts and the religious poetry he himself wrote. 'Poetry' was,
for him, a word subtle and capacious enough to comprehend both
forms of spiritual expression. 'Bishops were overawed by theologians',
he caustically noted of the modish contemporary craze for reform,
before enquiring 'What committee ever composed a poem?' (*CLP*, 60).
  Some six years before R.S. retired, the distinguished film-maker
John Ormond produced a documentary during which the poet shocked
viewers by casually remarking that 'Christ was a poet'. It was in the
context of explaining that 'poetry is religion, religion is poetry . . .
the New Testament is a metaphor, the Resurrection is a metaphor'.
The core of both poetry and Christianity, he added, 'are imagination
as far as I'm concerned'. And then he proceeded to make explicit,
intimate, connection between 'the ministry of the word and the ministry
of the sacraments':

> Well, word is metaphor, language is sacrament, sacrament is language,
> the combination is perfectly simple. In presenting the Bible to my congre-
> gation I am presenting imaginative interpretation of reality. In presenting
> the sacrament, administering the sacrament of bread and wine to the
> congregation I am again conveying, I'm using a means, a medium of
> contact with reality (in a slightly different medium from language).[17]

Such thoughts had been haunting Thomas's mind for some time –
in reaction, perhaps, against his Church's seemingly inexorable repudiation of the poetry of Bible and Prayer Book. As early as 1966, he

was defiantly insisting that 'Religion has to do first of all with vision, revelation, and these are best told in poetry', and speaking of 'the poetic nature' of the 'original [Christian] message, which allows itself to be interpreted and expressed in an infinite number of new ways'. 'Jesus', he bluntly continued,

> was a poet, and he changes and grows as each new epoch explores and develops the resources of that living poetry. In another sense, he is God's metaphor, and speaks to us so . . . How can anyone who is not a poet ever fully understand the gospels in their accumulation of metaphor.

And then he reached the very heart of his credo as poet and as Anglican priest: 'how shall we attempt to describe or express ultimate reality except through metaphor or symbol?'[18] Such sentiments seemed obvious to a Thomas steeped in the poetry of great English Romantics such as Blake and Coleridge, both of whom tended to equate poetry with pristine spiritual apprehension. And intriguingly, at the very time Thomas was making his controversial remarks, the kind of poetic favoured by Blake and Coleridge was being revisited, and reformulated under the title of 'theopoetics', by a number of intellectuals.[19]

Of relevance in this connection is Thomas's particular interest, a few years into his retirement, in the later writings of the remarkable polymath George Steiner, whose championing of the rich diversity of languages in his classic study of translation, *After Babel*, had naturally appealed to a champion of the Welsh language. In the aftermath of the crisis he'd experienced with his inexorably reforming Church, Thomas turned to another of Steiner's books, *Real Presences* (1989), a study that includes one of the most pithy accounts of the theology of the *deus absconditus* that he was so preoccupied with in his poetry.[20] But even more pertinent to Thomas's condition was Steiner's central insistence that 'it is, I believe, poetry, art and music which relate us most directly to that in being which is not ours' (*RP*, 226). 'It is', Steiner added,

> the enterprise and the privilege of the aesthetic to quicken into lit presence the continuum between temporality and eternity, between matter and spirit, between man and 'the other.' It is this common and exact sense that *poiesis* opens on to, is underwritten by, the religious and metaphysical. (*RP*, 227)

In his unchurched state, this was the credo upon which Thomas depended.

At the end of the talk in which he made his comments about Jesus the poet, R. S. Thomas quoted words by Geoffrey Hill, the contemporary poet he most admired not least because there were striking similarities between Hill's obsessive preoccupation with the 'fallen language' of the present age and his own.[21] And Hill is a poet prominently featured in a recent important study of Eucharistic Poetry by Eleanor McNees which reflects on the complexities – greatly exacerbated, of course, by modern linguistic studies stressing the closed, self-referential, purely artificial and conventional character of all signifying systems. Still, the human desire for divine verbal 'presence' is, she argues, evidenced in religious poetry's core desire to 'bridge the linguistic gap between the ordinary word and its extraordinary implications'.[22] 'The relentless paradox at the centre of Hill's work', she quotes E. D. Hirsch as piercingly observing, 'is the sense of a linguistic responsibility to a reality that evades language' (*EP*, 152). And she singles out a comment from Hill's essay collection *The Lords of Limit* that has a direct bearing on R. S. Thomas's profound anxiety about the heedless discarding by his Church of the traditional texts of Scripture and the Prayer Book: 'If language is more than a vehicle for the transmission of axioms and concepts, rhythm is correspondingly more than a physiological motor or a paradise of dainty devices. It is capable of registering, mimetically, deep shocks of recognition' (quoted in *EP*, 87). If R. S. Thomas's Church itself was hell-bent, so to speak, on ridding itself of the poetry that alone endowed it with the sacred power to awaken in its faithful the 'deep shocks of recognition' of an ultimate, transcendent reality, then it was left to poetry, or so R. S. Thomas seems increasingly to have felt in his early retirement, to try to remedy that fateful deficit. But would he, as a poet, be up to the awesome demands of such an alternative post-retirement 'calling'?

* * *

The works of his concluding decades seem to me dominated by the several rhetorical strategies he devised to deal with this late crisis. The first we might consider is his search for alternative liturgies – a rich symbolic vocabulary of religious ritual he could substitute for those hallowed rites of the Church of which he had effectively been deprived. It was an on-going, open-ended process of invention, and its ambiguous character was well caught in the title poem from his 1988 collection, *Mass for Hard Times*. This parodied both the ignorant modern worship of a debased version of 'science' and the sentimental platitudes of traditional Christian faith that had become manifestly untenable in the light of the disclosures of authentic scientific discoveries. The ritual obeisances both of the modern worship of a vulgar technologised science and of a Church barren of spiritual imagination were mercilessly exposed in this volume. But through the desolate debris of this modernity there shyly peeped sprigs of the growth of a new kind of sacramental experience. Thomas believed that in destroying the originating and sustaining poetry of its language of faith, the Church had abandoned the Gospel itself. Whereas in the old traditional forms of service, words had been mysteriously rooted in the Word, in the new reformed texts the debased words had become 'the kiss of Judas/ that must betray [Christ]' (*CLP*, 137). In response, Thomas proceeded to fashion his own interim 'Credo' out of petitionary prayer:

> Almighty
> pseudonym, grant me at last,
> as the token of my belief,
> such ability to remain
> silent, as is the nearest to a reflection
> of your silence to which
> the human looking-glass may attain. (*CLP*, 137)

Elsewhere in the same collection, Thomas found powerful ways of registering his indictment of a Church that, in supposedly privileging 'plain talking' had, in fact, embraced the modern, secular, reductive vision of human existence. This abdication of its core responsibility, he argued in 'Christmas', had turned that key sacramental festival into a parody of the poetry of incarnation. While 'five hundred poets,' pen in hand, awaited to record the miraculous event, the 'poem passed them/ by on its way out/ into oblivion', because 'they had ceased to believe'. All that was left on the bare doorstep was the orphaned figure of 'the sky-rhyming/ child to whom later/ on they would teach prose' (*CLP*, 145). In 'The God', he contrasted the God of Theologians – whom he blamed, along with the scientists, for the devaluing and ultimate defacing of his Church's sacred texts – with the God of Poets. For the former, the word was simply 'an idea' that they proceeded to embalm in 'the long sentences/ of their chapters', resulting in an arid 'sacrament that,/ if not soon swallowed, sticks in the throat' (*CLP*, 150). While for the latter, God was, he noted in an interlocking chain of luminous conceits reminiscent of George Herbert's coruscating sonnet on 'Prayer',

> made of rhyme and metre,
> the ability to scan
> disordered lines; an imposed
> syntax; the word like a sword
>
> turning both ways
> to keep the gates of vocabulary. (*CLP*, 149)

In a world such as he now faced, R.S. could naturally identify with the William Blake who, in *The Marriage of Heaven and Hell*, had found that since 'heaven' had been shanghaied by rational materialists, the only safe place left for a visionary poet was hell. 'Questions to the Prophet' are accordingly Thomas's version of Blake's Proverbs of Hell, a kind of anti-liturgy fashioned out of an inverted litany of 'perverse' questions, such as 'Where will the little child lead them/ who has not been there before?' and 'How shall the hare know it has not won, dying before the tortoise arrive?' (*CLP*, 146). But there was also another William, apart from Blake, with whom he strongly identified in this hour of crisis – William Morgan, the renowned bishop who, in 1588, authored the first, majestically poetic, translation of the Bible into Welsh. Commemorating him in 'RIP, 1588–1988', Thomas begins by noting that the name of the place forever associated with Morgan's great enterprise – Llanrhaeadr-ym-Mochnant – can seem barbarically unpronounceable to fastidious English ears. The implication clearly is that such ears remain as deaf to the poetry of the place name as to the poetry of the great text Morgan produced. The analogy with the tone-deafness to poetry of the modern Church in Wales is unmistakeable. Morgan thus serves Thomas as another of his alter egos from the past of his Welsh Church.[23] And so his poem naturally gravitates towards a preoccupation with his own current predicament – 'Is an obsession with language/ an acknowledgement we are too late/ to save it?' he wonders. 'It has been infiltrated/ already by daub and symbol' (*CLP*, 161).

His elegy for Morgan ends with a strikingly apt trope for Thomas's stance as a voluntarily defrocked priest. Speaking of Morgan's great

Bible of 1588 – whose language had for four centuries been as powerfully creative an influence on Welsh creative writing as had the resonant
language of the King James Bible been on English writers – R.S.
deplores the 'hubris' of a modernity that had reduced such miracles
of sacred discourse to dust. 'Out of breath/ with our hurry', he
caustically adds, 'we dare not blow off' the dust

> in a cloud, lest out
> of that cloud should
> be resurrected the one
> spoken figure we have grown
> too clever to believe in. (*CLP*, 161)

Through the device of a pun – the antithesis of course of the plain
speaking now favoured by his dis-graced Church – these lines conflate
the poetry of Christ's Resurrection with the resurrection of Poetry
itself. The 'spoken figure' of whom the poem speaks is at once the
figure of the Risen Christ, and also the 'figure of speech' itself – a speech
that values the 'figures' (or tropes) out of which it is essentially fashioned.

Mass for Hard Times even includes Thomas's very own 'Bleak
Liturgies', a savagely imagined commentary on a Church that, in
rejecting the poetry of its faith had ejected the sacred itself. The
opening rhetorical question implies that 'in revising the language . . ./
we alter the doctrine' (*CLP*, 183). Past witnesses had 'commended
their metaphors// to our notice' as they departed this life, but 'We
devise/ an idiom more compatible with/ the furniture departments of
our churches' (*CLP*, 183). And so the poem proceeds through a series
of cleansingly cynical apothegms: 'Frowning/ upon divorce, they
divorce/ art and religion' (*CLP*, 183). Several of these epigrams are
piercingly well phrased. The only Amens left to him, he desolatingly
declares, 'are rents in the worn fabric/ of meaning' (*CLP*, 184); and
he mocks the vulgar modern supposition that to grow up is

> to destroy
> childhood's painting of one
> who was nothing but vocabulary's
> shadow (*CLP*, 184–5)

The Eucharist has been replaced by the Black Mass – 'Crosses/ are
mass-produced [the pun is arrestingly just] to be worn/ on punk chests'

(*CLP*, 185). And the new reformed Eucharist continues to disappoint him: 'Instead/ of the bread the fraction/ of the language' (*CLP*, 183). But so overladen with despair is his discourse in this poem that the poetry is frequently compressed into turgidity, and the bathetic prose he so derides and deplores seems to infiltrate even his highly charged repudiation of it. The poem thus unintentionally instances and even enacts the tragedy of the dispossession that it mourns.

Given that *Mass for Hard Times* is repeatedly and elegiacally ghosted by concerns such as these – its poetry being what Freud would term a work of mourning for what Thomas has lost along with his Church – it is appropriate that it should include one poem specifically about retirement. And that poem – 'Retired' – reminds us that his alienated state could result in gains in imaginative originality and spiritual intensity that at times more than offset his losses. In being deprived of the traditional spiritual discipline of liturgical expression he was authorised to explore the sacramental potentialities of the natural world with a new creative freedom. He was now free to discover a new order of service, mediated not in church meetings and services but, for example, through encounters with the great overarching sky of stars,

> those nocturnal
> gatherings, whose luminaries
> fell silent millennia ago (*CLP*, 147)

Some of the most powerful 'liturgically inclined' poems in this vein can be found in *The Echoes Return Slow*, sometimes appearing in a context revealing of the process of 'translation' involved each case. In one of the beautifully crafted prose poems in that volume, Thomas decries the modern fashion 'for a revised liturgy, for bathetic renderings of the scriptures[.] The Cross always is avant-garde' (*CLP*, 53). Then in the next passage of poetically condensed prose he approvingly notes that 'one can celebrate the coming of three waves from afar, who fall down, offering their gifts to what they don't understand' (*CLP*, 54). Paired with this prose passage is a poem illustrative of the proposition just recorded, in which nature supplies what is missing in the revised Christmas liturgy of the modern Church and its infernal twin or shadow self, the heavily commercialised Christmas of the secular world. The natural world provides

>   mistletoe
>   water there is no kissing
>   under, the soused holly
>
>   of the wrack, and birds coming
>   to the bird-table with
>   no red on their breast.

Although 'All night it has snowed// foam on the splintering/ beaches',
these drifts disappear at dawn, leaving sand as pristine clean as 'young
flesh/ in a green crib, product/ of an immaculate conception' (*CLP*,
54). The translation of the banal staple emblems, products and acces-
sories of a modern, largely secularised, 'Church' Christmas into the
alternative liturgical terms provided by the natural world here results
in a redemptive re-sacralisation of what has become a paganised
religious festival. And it is poetry alone that has possessed the power
to effect this miracle of transfiguration, not least through the reinvigoration of tired figures of speech.

In another significant pairing from *The Echoes Return Slow*, the
prose fronts up to Thomas's post-clerical status: 'Let retirement be
retirement indeed', he exclaims as he contemplates avoiding a con-
frontation with the incoming changes to the liturgy of the Church.
'But', he adds, 'the sea revises itself over and over. When he arose in the
morning or looked at it at night, it was always a new version of it' (*CLP*,
63). There are, then, revisions and revisions – or rather re-visions that
are re-cognitions: new ways of viewing the wonders of a divine creation;
new revelations of sacred presence. Such ways are akin not to the
substitution of prose for poetry but rather to poetry's inexhaustible
powers of self-renewal. And this can find expression through its power
of paradox – its ability for instance to suggest the power of silence
through utterance. 'I am left', Thomas reflects in the poem that
accompanies the above passage of prose and that allows its pregnant
meanings to reach their full term, 'with the look// on the sky I need
not/ try turning into an expression' (*CLP*, 63). Another pun, then,
that leads into the reflection that he might after all have been led here
– beyond the sheltering but also imprisoning world of his Church –

>   to repent of my sermons,
>   to erect silence's stone over
>   my remains, and to learn

> from the lichen's slowness
> at work something of the slowness
> of the illumination of the self. (*CLP*, 63)

The erasures of language implicit in these images signify both the slow erosion of the ego-identity of mundane existential selfhood and the extinction of poetry – poetry empowered to imagine its own erasure and to identify the limits of its capacities. In text like this, Thomas seems to have been able, through naked exposure to the cosmos, to re-ground sacramental experience and expression in the eternal silence that underlies and underpins all the animation of life.

* * *

R. S. Thomas's late works may, then, be understood as the vindication of poetry as a *fons et origo* of the human experience of the sacred in the wake of his Church's repudiation of it. But there are other aspects too of his post-retirement writing that stemmed directly from his disillusionment with his Church. In rejecting the Prayer Book and the Holy Scriptures in their traditional, inherited, forms, the Church in Wales seemed to Thomas to have effectively disinherited itself spiritually and culturally by severing all links with its past. And his response took two forms in particular. First, he sought alternative means of reconnecting himself locally in Llŷn with the peninsula's ancient history of religious belief and practice; and second, he set out to review the mysterious continuities in his own life between his present and past self. This last resulted in a series of strikingly original experiments in autobiography, including *Neb*, *The Echoes Return Slow* and *Blwyddyn yn Llŷn*.

The first two of these texts have already received extensive attention from me and others elsewhere, and therefore do not need to be revisited in detail here.[24] But one very important feature of them remains to be briefly noticed. 'For some there is no future but the one that is safeguarded by a return to the past' (*CLP*, 45): the remark occurs at the point in *The Echoes Return Slow* where Thomas notices the uncanny similarity between the Llŷn peninsula he had reached in his old age and the environs of Holyhead where he'd grown up as a boy. The two locations were the same and yet different, so that for Thomas there was indeed re-vision in the air in Llŷn –the double vision caused by the intrusion of childhood recollections on to his perception of the peninsula in his old age.

In his last decades, Thomas's fascination with such asymmetrical symmetries steadily grew. For him, they were the sites of telling slippages, instances of the unpredictable disruption of the flow of the space–time continuum that was the trace of the eruption of the metaphysical into an otherwise deterministically regulated physical universe. These locations could be found throughout the cosmos, from the immensities of space to the quarks and quirks of the sub-atomic level. And it was along similar fracture lines in human discourse that poetry and hence religion appeared – at those points of slippage in ordinary language use where the bland prose of our everyday life suddenly revealed its inadequacy to account for the whole of our existence. It was at exactly such mysterious points of hiatus that the Church had traditionally positioned itself – until, that is, it had lost its nerve, seeking refuge in everyday language and placing its trust in everyday experience. Now, in his retired, 'extra-mural', state R.S. suddenly discovered he could after all be redemptively reconnected to the sacred eccentricities of human being through immersion in the sacred landscape of Llŷn. Such spiritual encounters had been tragically denied to him during his last, increasingly disillusioned, years as a priest of the 'reformed' Church in Wales.

Thomas's most powerful testament to these encounters is *Blwyddyn yn Llŷn*, a text that, in my opinion, has hitherto received insufficient attention. It includes some of the most ecstatic lyrical writing Thomas ever produced. And it also includes some of the darkest jeremiads of his whole career. It therefore registers the traces of a riven sensibility; of a fractured psyche. Like the episode of clinical depression of which Thomas had spoken in his remarkable confessional letter to Garlick, the symptoms inscribed in the rhythmical alternation between light and dark in this text are related to the trauma attendant upon his split from his Church. Taken at its face value, *Blwyddyn yn Llŷn* is a nature journal, lovingly tracing the cycle of the seasons on a peninsula suspended in time, like a great bough suspended between sea and sky and smothered with white flowers of cloud. As such, it is another example of Thomas's attempt to substitute rituals of his own poetic devising for those he had lost in turning his back on his Church. In the absence of the great Church calendar of feasts and festivals, Thomas sets out to turn time sacred – that is, to invest its passage with meaningful spiritual pattern and order – by chronicling the monthly changes that constitute the mysterious rhythm of a natural year, with particularly loving attention to the constantly changing bird population.[25]

In a humorous aside in the text, Thomas indicates how, on leaving the Church, he has in effect gone native. Wryly noting how the cats from a neighbouring farm seem to seek out the garden of Sarn Rhiw for courting and mating he deplores their incestuous tendencies in tones of mock horror, professing comic outrage at their disregard for his status as retired priest (*A*, 23). It is a neat comic parable of his new status as ex-vicar now free to walk on the wild side. And walk there he joyously does, uninhibitedly indulging in what – with a frankness he had previously tended to avoid – he now openly labels as 'nature mysticism' (*A*, 19). The complex relationship between his present state and his past life as priest is interestingly revealed in several key passages in the text. April, he recalls, is the month of the Christian Easter when the Church overflowing with flowers reminds him – and here he quotes from a great sacramental poem by the Welsh Catholic Saunders Lewis – of 'the Father kissing the Son in the white dew' (*A*, 131).[26] Then comes, he adds, 'the moment of pure pleasure, when the sun strikes warm on some recess sheltered from the wind, and the willow warbler showers its silver note on you from the arbour above your head'. But next there is an abrupt alteration of tone, as Thomas now confesses with pain that 'ever since the Church in Wales reformed the Liturgy, I cannot partake of the Sacrament'. The reason he gives has already been quoted above – since the priest now turns to face the congregation at the point of consecration of the wafer, the reformed service violates the mystery that is an inalienable aspect of divine worship.

Here, in miniature, we can see how the nature mysticism of Thomas's last years, of which *Blwyddyn yn Llŷn* is the most lyrical record, was rooted in what he did not shrink from terming pain. And it is this psycho-spiritual pain that surfaces frequently as bitter anger – at the condition of Wales and the state of the modern – whenever he reluctantly forces himself in the text to turn from the natural to the human world. The serene, often rapturous, main text of his nature journal is punctuated by angry interjections and splenetic outbursts as he rails alike against the influx of heedlessly anglophone visitors into his peninsula and the apathy and docility displayed by its culturally servile inhabitants, deplores modern materialism, champions anti-nuclear activities, and struggles to organise environmental groups. Such causes and complaints as these had long antedated his departure from his Church, of course, but they are now imbued with a new intensity of anguish, occasioned, I would suggest, by his feeling that the Church in Wales itself has capitulated to these malign manifestations of modernity, leaving him spiritually unhoused and exposed. A halfway house nevertheless seemed to suggest itself as refuge to him from time to time, alluded to in a strikingly enigmatic phrase in one of his letters to Garlick. We are living, he informed his friend, in a 'post-Davidum wilderness' (*LRG*, 112). What could this possibly mean?[27] As I have endeavoured to explain at length in a 'prequel' to this present essay,[28] throughout his long career in the clergy R.S. had entertained the increasingly faint hope that his disestablished Church would eventually come to admit its obligations to Wales by realising it was heir to the 'indigenous' Church of the nation – the Celtic Church of the early Christian centuries, whose semi-legendary 'primate' had been St David. In bleakly labelling the present age 'post-Davidum' he was thus acknowledging the final extinction of a hope that had sustained him as a priest from first virtually to last. Both before retirement and after he would nevertheless wistfully revert to his dream of a spiritual revival of the 'Celtic' spirit, but now without any of his early illusions of a rapprochement between it and the modern Church in Wales. As he confessed in *The Echoes Return Slow*, he sought out unfrequented churches well off the beaten track, 'Celtic foundations down lanes that one entered with a lifting of the spirit' (*CLP*, 53). These were comforting proof that God was not to be 'worshipped only in cathedrals, where blood drips from regimental standards as from the crucified body of love'. In the stubborn integrity of their silent witness to the ancient past of Christian faith in Wales, such small, plain churches confirmed there was 'no need for a revised liturgy, for bathetic renderings of the scriptures'. His journeys to such sites were for him the modern day equivalent of medieval pilgrimages through Llŷn to the holy island of Enlli (Bardsey), the fabled resting place of 20,000 saints.

These simple old churches also spoke to him of the many far older prompts to awe and reverence surrounding him in Llŷn, most notably the pre-Cambrian rocks of unimaginable age. Moving the mind to 'vertigo . . . from the abyss of time' (*CLP*, 55), these were already 'immemorially old' in the time of the great poet Dafydd Nanmor, who had commemorated them in a love poem from which Thomas never tired of repeating the celebrated couplet: 'Mewn moled main a melyn/ Mae'n un lliw â'r maen yn Llŷn' ('In a fine kerchief of golden sheen/

She's of the same hue as the rock in Llŷn') (*A*, 133). Dafydd Nanmor,
he further recalled, antedated the dissolution of the monasteries, and
so the poet would have been aware of monks – the spiritual descendants
of the Celtic saints – residing on Enlli (Bardsey), directly opposite
those ancient yellow rocks, at the very time he was composing his
couplet. Such conjunctions resonantly confirmed Thomas in his belief
that there had always been an intimate, indissoluble connection between
poetry and the sacred.

* * *

But with the house of God now effectively closed to him, Thomas
increasingly looked for sanctuary of a kind to the old cottage of Sarn
Rhiw, the grace-and-favour retirement home of his wife and himself.[29]
Built, or rather quarried, from the ancient boulders of the Llŷn
peninsula and dating back to at least the eighteenth century, the low-
lying cottage cleaves to the contours of its landscape. It nestles self-
protectively into a gentle, but exposed, slope above the dramatic shingle
of Porth Neigwl, a bay whose shallows used to prove so treacherous
in the days of sailing ships that the locals in this isolated spot acquired
a reputation for being excellent wreckers. 'I inhabit a house', he could
there write, 'whose stone is the language of its builders.'[30] For him,
the massive boulders of Sarn Rhiw became psychically reassuring
guarantors of the long-term survival of the language and faith of its
builders. Thomas was deeply aware of 'cadw tŷ mewn cwmwl tystion',[31]
of keeping house in a mystic company at Sarn Rhiw: 'In the fire/ Of
an evening I catch faces/ Staring at me', he wrote, recalling the impression of 'Thin, boneless presences' flitting through his room (*CP*,
460). He felt himself to be answerable to these companionable but
exacting ghosts and wondered whether he would eventually be judged
to have been equal to their implicit challenge.

For R. S. Thomas, Sarn Rhiw was much more than an old cottage.
As Gaston Bachelard resonantly suggested in *The Poetics of Space*,
poetry offers us abundant evidence that dwellings have the habit of
inhabiting our imaginations, of becoming 'the topography of our
intimate being'.[32] And it is by bearing this in mind that we may come
to see how much Thomas's cottage resembles a famous tower. The
tower in question is that of his favourite poet, W. B. Yeats, through
the magic medium of whose poetry the semi-derelict Norman tower
he bought in Gort, in the far west of Ireland, and painstakingly

restored was turned into a remarkable storehouse of emblems seminal
to his extraordinary imaginative existence. For him, Thoor Ballylee,
a multi-storied tower with a winding stair, represented the spirit's
ascent to exalted, esoteric knowledge, while in the stubborn persistence
of its massive stone walls Yeats discerned signs of the stubborn
endurance throughout the centuries of the superior, aristocratic
Anglo-Norman cultural tradition of Ireland with which he was so
anxious to associate his own thoroughly bourgeois family pedigree.
Yeats thus turned his tower into a primary enabling myth of his mature
poetry, and R. S. Thomas likewise turned Sarn Rhiw into one of the
primary enabling myths of his own late, great period of spiritual
search.

Very much against the odds – the Thomases had at first been resistant
to the Keating sisters' offer of refuge at Sarn y Plas – the move to a
home 'on a wooded slope above Porth Neigwl' turned out to be
profoundly auspicious:

> The local stone is called dolerite, and a single small piece of it is
> surprisingly heavy. Some of the stones of the house itself are huge.
> How the builders managed to get them into place to begin with, no-
> one knows. They certainly had a talent that has by now disappeared.
> (*A*, 91)

How expressive of his own creative temperament that his home should
have been made of volcanic rock that had hardened as it cooled. How
reassuring that his spiritual fastness was itself fashioned out of the
primordial rocks of a liminal peninsula whose landscape had from
time immemorial been saturated with the sacred. Llŷn's seascape, too,
was charged with the numinous. 'From this cottage', he noted,

> one can always hear the sound of the sea, as it is only about a hundred
> and fifty years away. And sometimes on a still night there comes a sudden
> tumult from the beach, as the surge from the far Atlantic reaches the
> end of its journey. (*A*, 91)

As he repeatedly emphasised in the poetry and prose of his final
decades, it was the sea that, from boyhood to old age, had succoured
his spiritual needs, repeatedly offering his soul mysterious passage.
Not so much retired from his Church as, or so he felt, effectively
expelled from it, Thomas turned repeatedly to the ocean for comfort.

A house, Bachelard observed, can serve humans as 'an instrument with which to confront the cosmos' (*PS*, 46). 'A house that is as dynamic as this', he writes elsewhere, 'allows the poet to inhabit the universe. Or, to put it differently, the universe comes to inhabit his house' (*PS*, 51). It is for precisely this quality that R.S. came most to appreciate Sarn y Plas. It literally 'placed' him in a special relationship to nature, and indeed to the whole cosmos. Thus, in *Blwyddyn yn Llŷn/A Year in Llŷn*, he recalls how on occasions the cottage seemed almost porous, as tiny bats (*Pipistrellus pipistrellus*) exercised their ancient right to zigzag at twilight through the house (*A*, 51). They entered, as they had done for at least three centuries, through the large central chimney.

And then there was light's miraculous penetration of the cottage's dark interiors. Every time R.S. saw its shaft strike a boulder that had for so long stood in place, he felt like a prisoner briefly released from the confines of his narrow cell (*B*, 17). Most importantly of all, for the son of a sailor who had been raised in Holyhead and had sea salt in his veins, the cottage 'was a sounding-box in which the sea's moods made themselves felt' (*A*, 54). 'The blessing of Sarn Rhiw', he noted, 'is that I can look out over Porth Neigwl and spy out what's happening, what kind of weather it's making and what is the state of the sea' (*A*, 60). That very moment, he added, he had happened to look up and caught the plunge of a gannet just before it hit the water (*A*, 91). As a result, his late period is notable for its serial meditations on the great waters that, at Sarn Rhiw, constantly met his eyes and haunted his ears. 'The sea at his window was a shallow sea; a thin counterpane over a buried cantref. There were deeper fathoms to plumb, "les délires des grandes profondeurs", in which he was under compulsion to give away whatever assurances he possessed' (*CLP*, 70).

The French phrase is worth exploring, because it leads us to the fear that was another facet of Thomas's fascination with the sea. In stanza 33 of 'Homage to Mistress Bradstreet' – a poem known to Thomas – Berryman writes of 'A delirium of the depths',[33] which commentators have traced to accounts by divers (such as Jacques Cousteau) of suffering from euphoria, and associated hallucination, which can sometimes be fatal. In the context of the poem, the phrase is used by Berryman to express his fear of fatal loss of contact with his own 'reality principle', the seventeenth-century American poet Ann Bradstreet. Thomas may have conflated this arresting image of the dangerously seductive power of the sea with the similar treatment of the ocean in one of his favourite French poems, Paul Valéry's 'Le Cimitière Marin', where at the poem's outset Valèry is hypnotised by the seascape he views from the seaside graveyard:

> When thought has had its hour, oh how rewarding
> Are the long vistas of celestial calm!
>
> What grace of light, what pure toil goes to form
> The manifold diamond of the elusive foam!
> What peace I feel begotten at that source!
> When sunlight rests upon a profound sea,
> Time's air is sparkling, dream is certainty –
> Pure artifice both of an eternal Cause.[34]

He is saved from this dangerous illusion of complete serene transcendence by the graveyard, which literally brings him back to earth, to the time-bound existence that links him to the bodies buried there.[35] What 'les délires des grandes profondeurs' therefore seems to suggest, as used by Thomas, is how aware he was, after slipping the anchor of his Church, of the dangers of 'the deeper fathoms' that lured him away even from such tentative spiritual 'certainties' as had hitherto sustained him.

One of the most important countervailing forces at work within and upon him, he came to realise, was the strong tie of affection between him and his wife. It was living at Sarn Rhiw that helped him appreciate, for one final, conclusive time, how much he owed Elsie, and how deeply indebted he was to her quiet, self-effacing, cherishing, and nurturing love; to the steadying constancy of her fidelities. To him she was what Bradstreet was to Berryman; his Muse, the better angel of his nature, his guardian spirit, protecting him from himself. 'I look out over the timeless sea', he wrote:

> over the head of one, calendar
> to time's passing, who is now open
> at the last month, her hair wintry. (*CLP*, 71)

Even as he wrote this poem, he must have been painfully aware that the time remaining to them together would be very short. Elsie passed away in 1991, and with her passing, Sarn Rhiw came, for R.S., to assume one final complexion.

From the beginning, one of his images of the cottage had been that of a hermitage, with himself as hermit.[36] 'The poverty of the spirit must be extended to the flesh, too; books given away, furniture dispensed with; paintings that give colour to expanses of white wall, stored away in the loft' (*CLP*, 64). After his wife's death, he returned to this image with a haunting intensity, turning his bare, tiny bedroom into a monk's cell:

> Few possessions: a chair,
> a table, a bed
> to say my prayers by,
> and, gathered from the shore,
> the bone-like, crossed sticks
> proving that nature
> acknowledges the Crucifixion. (*CLP*, 246)

Back in 1967, he had congratulated his friend, Raymond Garlick, for adjusting to a small room whose window 'opens on eternity'. 'An eternity of what', he'd mordantly added, 'is the question' (*LRG*, 70). Now his physically and emotionally straitened surroundings at Sarn y Plas prompted his imagination to range far and wide throughout the wide, diverse, world of the spirit, freed from any obligation to confine itself within the bounds of 'his' Church's beliefs. The great poetry of his final years are a record of these speculative excursions. By now, he regarded himself as a thoroughly 'retired Christian', as he'd provocatively phrased it to Garlick on his departure from the Church in 1978 (*LRG*, 102). He had, we'll remember, later glossed his remark by explaining that he couldn't 'bring myself to agree that Christianity is the only way, as so many dogmatists claim'. But he'd also admitted that 'it is certainly one of the great ways and for one brought up in the European tradition, there is little point in turning to one of the other ways'. In moving from Aberdaron to Sarn Rhiw, he may have exchanged the grand body of the Church for a 'cell' but, for him as a poet at least, the view had improved as a result, and as a 'pilgrim' of the spirit, he was convinced his outlook had been immeasurably extended.

(Essay commissioned by R. S. Thomas Centre, Bangor University.)

Notes

[1] Jason Walford Davies (ed.), *R. S. Thomas: Letters to Raymond Garlick,
     1951–1999* (Llandysul: Gomer, 2009), p. 101. Hereafter *LRG*.

[2] Raymond Garlick, poet, critic and educationalist, was at this time experiencing
     a crisis of faith in the Catholic Church to which he had converted as an adult
     and about some of whose neglected Welsh martyrs he wrote some fine poems.
     The crisis eventually resulted in his leaving the Church.

[3] R. S. Thomas, *Collected Later Poems, 1988–2000* (Tarset: Bloodaxe Books,
     2004), p. 63. Hereafter *CLP*.

[4] Jason Walford Davies, trans., R. S. Thomas, *Autobiographies: Y Llwybrau Gynt/
     Former Paths; Hunanladdiad y Llenor/The Creative Writer's Suicide; Neb/No-
     One; Blwyddyn yn Llŷn/A Year in Llŷn* (London: Dent, 1997), 89. Hereafter *A*.

[5] *Y Llan* (7 Ionawr 1966), 5; and *Y Llan* (28 Ionawr 1966), 4.

[6] *Y Llan* (29 Ebrill 1966), 6–7.

[7] *Y Llan* (7 Mawrth 1966), 1.

[8] *Y Llan* (21 Mawrth 1966), 1.

[9] *Y Llan* (21 Mawrth 1966), 8.

[10] *Y Llan* (18 Chwefror 1972), 4.

[11] *Y Llan* (6 Mai 1972), 4.

[12] *Y Llan* (21 Ebrill 1967), 7–8.

[13] *Y Llan* (Mawrth 1969), 4.

[14] *Y Llan* (7 Mai 1965), 2.

[15] *Y Llan* (25 Mehefin 1965), 4.

[16] *Y Llan* (Ebrill 1966), 7.

[17] John Ormond, 'Priest and Poet', a transcript of his film for BBC TV, broadcast on
     2 April 1972, *Poetry Wales: Special R. S. Thomas Number* (Spring 1972), 52–4.

[18] Sandra Anstey (ed.), *R. S. Thomas: Selected Prose* (Bridgend: Poetry Wales
     Press, 1983), p. 90.

[19] See, for instance, Paul Ricoeur, *Interpretation Theory* (Fort Worth: Christian
     Press, 1976); Stanley Romaino Hopper, R. Melvin Kaiser, and Tony Stoneburner
     (eds), *The Way of Imagination: Religious Imagination as Theopoetics* (West-
     minster: John Knox Press, 1992).

[20] George Steiner, *Real Presences: Is there Anything in What we Say?* (London:
     Faber and Faber, 1989), pp. 228–9. Hereafter *RP*.

[21] 'Let me commend to your notice *Tenebrae*, Geoffrey Hill's new book', he wrote
     to Raymond Garlick at Christmas, 1978, the year of his retirement: 'He is a
     fine poet, certainly the best now writing in English. I wish I wrote with his
     economy and intelligence' (*LRG*, 110).

[22] Eleanor J. McNees, *Eucharistic Poetry: The Search for Presence in the Writings
     of John Donne, Gerard Manley Hopkins, Dylan Thomas and Geoffrey Hill*
     (Lewisburg: Bucknell University Press, 1992), p. 17. Hereafter *EP*.

[23] See the preceding chapter.

[24] See, for instance, 'Time's Changeling', ch. 8 in M. Wynn Thomas, *R. S. Thomas:
     Serial Obsessive* (Cardiff: University of Wales Press, 2013), pp. 193–218;

Barbara Prys-Williams, '"A Consciousness in Search of its Own Truth": Some Aspects of R. S. Thomas's *The Echoes Return Slow* as Autobiography', *Welsh Writing in English*, 2 (1996), 98–125.

[25] There is here an analogy with Henry Vaughan. It was after, and I suspect because of, his effective 'expulsion' from his beloved Church in the valley of the Usk by the militant Puritan ascendancy of the Cromwellian period that the Silurist turned to producing the two volumes of *Silex Scintillans*.

[26] 'Ascension Thursday', in Joseph P. Clancy, trans., *Saunders Lewis, Selected Poems* (Cardiff: University of Wales Press, 1993), p. 35. The poem infuses the wonders of a May morning with sacramental import: 'Look at them, at the gold of the bloom and the laburnum./ The glowing surplice on the hawthorn's shoulders/ The alert emerald of the grass, and the tranquil calves;// See the chestnut-tree's candelabra alight'.

[27] The context is as follows: 'A neighbouring vicar was here yesterday asking me to give a Lenten talk. Enid Pierce Roberts on March 1 on Dewi Sant. And I on the 18th. What would my title be? Ar ôl Dewi. I said.' The Welsh phrase translates as 'After Dewi', but may be also understood as 'Following Dewi', where 'following' refers both to mere succession and to active discipleship. While 'post Davidum wilderness' builds on the former sense, the context alerts us to the second, which would obviously apply to the state of a Thomas who had refused to become lost, along with his Church, in a cultural and spiritual wilderness.

[28] In 'Yr Hen Fam' (previous chapter, I make extensive reference to Thomas's identification with Dewi Sant in the context of his disgust with the lack of Welshness of his supposedly disestablished Church.

[29] What follows draws in parts on materials of mine that have already appeared in print elsewhere.

[30] R. S. Thomas, *Collected Poems, 1945–1990* (London: Dent, Phoenix, 1993), p. 460. Hereafter *CP*.

[31] The celebrated phrase is from Waldo Williams, 'Pa Beth yw Dyn?', in *Dail Pren* (Aberystwyth: Gwasg Aberystwyth, 1971), p. 67. It captures what it means to live consciously as part of a national collective of long, stubborn, persistence.

[32] Maria Jolas, trans., Gaston Bachelard, *The Poetics of Space* (Boston: Beacon Press, 1994), p. xxxvi. Hereafter *PS*.

[33] John Berryman, 'Homage to Mistress Bradstreet', in *Selected Poems, 1938–1968* (London: Faber, 1972), pp. 45–66, Stanza 33, 57.

[34] Paul Valéry, 'Le Cimitière Marin', translated by C. Day Lewis as 'The Graveyard by the Sea', *http://unix.cc.wmich.edu/~cooneys/poems/fr/valery.daylewis.html* (accessed 30 September 2013). Towards the end of the poem, Valéry invokes the sea as '[la] grande mer de delires douée' ('mighty sea with . . . wild frenzies gifted').

[35] In his early essay (1946) 'Some Contemporary Scottish Writing', Thomas enthuses over 'Douglas Young's magnificent rendering of Valéry's "Le Cimitière Marin" and interestingly, at that point in his career, singles out not a passage about the sea but one about the cemetery in which the dead are interred: 'But

i' their nicht, wechtit wi marble stane,/ A drowsie fowk, down at the tree ruits lain,/ hae sideit si you i slaw solemnitie' (Anstey, *Selected Prose*, p. 30). He later included Young's translation in his *Penguin Book of Religious Verse*.

36   One of the many things he admired about his great hero, Saunders Lewis, was how in his later years he had become a 'recluse . . . himself his hermitage' (*CP*, 466).

9

VERNON WATKINS: TALIESIN IN GOWER

I have an interest to declare: Vernon Watkins has, on two occasions, been a very close neighbour of mine. His room was little distant from mine in 1966, the year in which I took up my first appointment as a very young, and very callow, Assistant Lecturer at University College of Swansea. It was the year before he was to pass away, in his early sixties, on a tennis court in distant Seattle: and in many ways his international reputation as a substantial poet, envied by his great friend Dylan Thomas, and admired by Yeats and Eliot, passed away with him. At Swansea his absent-mindedness became as much of a campus legend as his unselfconsciously bardic bearing. He was rumoured not only to wear his room key around his neck but to kneel down to open the door, because he couldn't risk losing the key by removing it. And from his year's residency as writer in the Department of English I warmly remember the occasion when, gentle, generous and courteous as ever, he accepted the invitation to come and talk, in a characteristically rapt and intense manner, to a very small group of us about his cherished acquaintance with Eliot and the insights that had given him into *Four Quartets*. In 1997 he again became my neighbour, after a fashion, when my wife and I moved to live in our present home, just three doors away from 'Y Garth', Watkins's home on the magnificent dramatically striated limestone cliffs of south Gower. On my daily walks there I continue to sense his sinewy presence, long-striding across the cliffs, gazing seaward or beachcombing in stunning Three Cliffs bay; I hear his voice raised in argument with his great friend Dylan Thomas, or as he plays cricket boisterously with his children in the back garden.

This is unmistakably his patch; the native territory of his imagination.
He is, in quite an important sense, a Gower poet. It was on those
'curved cliffs' that, during the Second World War, he felt it fitting to

> remember the drowned,
> To imagine them clearly for whom the sea no longer cares,
> To deny the language of the thistle, to meet their foot-firm tread
> Across the dark-sown tares, (*CP*, 7)[1]

And it was on these cliff-tops he realised that 'Art holds in wind the
way the ravens build' (*CP*, 183) and where he tried to mortise his vision
if not in granite, like Whitman, then in Gower limestone:

> Stand to time now, my Muse,
> Unwavering, like this rock
> The mated ravens use,
> Building against the shock
> Of dawn, a throne in the air
> Above the labouring sea,
> Yet fine as a child's hair
> Because great industry
> Accomplishes no art
> To match the widespread wing
> Riding the heavens apart,
> A lost, yet living thing. (*CP*, 182)

The beautiful Gower peninsula, sticking out its scrawny neck to the
west of blitzed Swansea, was to him what Shoreham was to Samuel
Palmer; or Cookham to Stanley Spencer – it was the visible form of
his visionary imagination, where 'All that I see with my sea-changed
eyes is a vision too great for the brain' (*CP*, 185). Here he loosened
his 'music to the listening, eavesdropping sea'. In his poetry he created
a textual map of this soulscape, finding Yeatsian emblems everywhere
– in the sudden autumn reappearance of Bishopston Stream where
it trickled into Pwlldu; in the stories of smugglers in Hunt's Bay,
successfully evading the excise men; and in the Bristol Channel shipwrecks and the debris washed ashore. Everywhere he found dramatic
symbolic expression of the timeless, eternal, dimension of the tem-
pestuously changeful temporal order. It was there in the collision
between 'flying, flagellant waves' and intransigent rock; it was there

in Paviland Cave, where the oldest skeleton in Britain was discovered, reminder of the ancientness of this peninsula, some of whose earliest inhabitants were coeval with those who produced the great cave drawings of Europe; and it was there at incomparable Rhossili and Worm's Head, where Gower, become 'the world's very verge', turned into a finger of land pointed dramatically not only across the Atlantic towards America, but, for Watkins, into infinity itself:

> Pushed out from the rocks, pushed far by old thought, long into night,
>   into starlight, . . .
> Rhossili! Spindle of the moon! Turning-place of winds, end of Earth,
>   and of Gower! (*CP*, 119)

Watkins was nothing if not a visionary poet, keeping proud aloof company with those Immortals whom he regarded as the elect of the ages, those 'poets, in whom truth lives' – from Dante through Blake to Hölderlin and Heine and the other great German Romantics, and from the French Symbolists to George, Rilke – and, above all, the incomparable Yeats. In becoming a poet, Watkins chose to be reborn as Taliesin in Gower. For him, poetry had to be exalted, rapt, time-defying, fixated on eternity; rhythmically it had to be ritualistic, incantatory and consciousness-altering; sonically it had to become the echo-chamber of the Soul – a word Watkins was not shy of using; and, of course, the native language of soul poetry was symbolism, since he was convinced that the ultimate, eternal truths cannot be rationally known, they can only be imaginatively symbolised. And whereas Dylan Thomas, that serpent in Watkins's bosom, was a Freudian symbolist, Watkins was incorrigibly Jungian, believing in the persistence, the recurrence, in every person's unconscious, of archaic images embodying eternal, universal truths. Indeed, for all its emphasis on process, metamorphosis and allied forms of reproduction, Watkins's poetry is essentially a sex-free zone. Which is, perhaps, one of its many significant limitations. Except when couched in the circumspect language of myth, there is no acknowledgement of the sexual dynamic of what Walt Whitman famously called 'the procreant urge of the world'.

Contemporary with Watkins was another great Gower artist – the painter Ceri Richards, from Dunvant. He, too, was obsessed with the mysterious metamorphosis of forms that constituted the living universe; his great subject, too, was the Cycle of Life; he, too, was haunted by

Jung's disclosure of the ancient symbols of permanent truths lodged deep in every human psyche at every time and in every place.[2] Early a friend of Dylan Thomas, like Watkins, Richards eventually became a close friend of Watkins too, and produced an important series of late images in homage to his work.[3] As there were very deep affinities between the creative imaginations of these two remarkable Gower artists, this essay will be punctuated by references to some of Richards's most celebrated images.

Watkins's poetry is sadly no longer highly rated by the cognoscenti. It's as if he'd tried his very darnedest to be totally resistant to present-day taste. It may be possible to squeeze out some sympathy for him as a poet of his time – a Neo-Romantic, or New Apocalypse writer, say, who was totally unable to redeem himself by reinvention when the Movement swept all that old nonsense away, installing Larkin, Watkins's one-time admirer, as its great poet. But there isn't much I can do to make him look really respectable, let alone cool, from today's streetwise, self-conscious, postmodernist, radically ironic and ruthlessly deconstructive point of view, when poets and poetry I very much like prefer to dress casual and serve verbal takeaways in disposable textual trays. In his white Druidic singing robes Watkins offers himself up as a lamb to the slaughter – and indeed, if his core innocence protects him from the obvious charge of pretentiousness, it is also provocative: it can bring out the devil in even a well-disposed reader such as myself.

Dylan Thomas remains far and away the best of Watkins's critics, once necessary allowance has been made for the self-interested and self-serving nature of some of his remarks. Watkins was, Thomas cruelly but correctly noted, prone to 'elongate a thin nothing; a long, grey, weeping sausage'; 'All the words are lovely', he remarked to Watkins of one poem,

> but they *seem* so *chosen*, not struck out. I can see the sensitive picking of words, but none of the strong, inevitable pulling that makes a poem an event, a happening, an action perhaps, not a still life . . . They seem . . . to come out of the nostalgia of literature.[4]

That last phrase is devastatingly accurate. And yet, as Thomas also acknowledged, there are in Watkins dazzling passages that suggest an undeveloped gift for sensuousness: 'Lizards on the dry stone; gipsy-bright nasturtiums/ Burning through round leaves, twining out in torch-buds' (*CP*, 323).

I must myself come clean. I would strongly advise against trying to read Watkins in bulk – his *Collected Poems* runs to almost 500 pages. To overdose on Watkins is not a pleasant experience – the symptoms, I find, are first irritation and then numbness. When he trundles up the Big Bertha of his rhetoric once again, you know he's about to vaporise the sensuous, material world. Meant to be spellbinding, his rhythms are not so much mesmeric as narcotic. And as for his symbols, well, the mind ends up feeling it has been force-fed with candy-floss. Addicted to a self-enfeebling rhetoric and besotted with the ineffable, Watkins sometimes seems to be an ostrich burying its head in Gower sands. He could have done with meeting Marianne Moore's famous creature, the ostrich that 'digesteth harde yron'. I say all this somewhat reluctantly, aware of sounding like a Grumpy Old Man; of appearing to be the Victor Meldrew of critics. With friends like me, what enemies could Watkins possibly need? But irritability is the mood in which I am able to get closest to the root of my mixed feelings about Watkins. What I'm irritated by is his failure, not to be a different kind of poet, but to be consistently his own best self, as that is prefigured in a handful of poems that seem to me not negligible in quality or character.

For me, Watkins is at his best when one senses an undercurrent of anxiety, of fear underlying his luminous affirmations of trust in a constancy of spiritual truth at the core of all life's headlong chaotic change. I find his poetry most compelling when I feel it functions as an urgent coping mechanism, as a stabiliser of a mind forever on the point of tipping over into horror at the mere nihilism of existence. That, it seems, was what occasioned the terrible breakdown Vernon Watkins experienced in early manhood, shortly after leaving Repton, the public school where he'd been a pupil. And it is to that breakdown that I would look for the source of his subsequent lifelong devotion to poetry, his trust to its restorative, psychically redemptive powers. 'Always it is from joy my music comes', he wrote, 'And always it is sorrow keeps it true' (*CP*, 285).

During the Second World War, Watkins wrote several poems that endeavoured to address the horrors of war directly, and was intensely distressed by the bombing of Swansea in 1941, recalling those three nights' Blitz (February 19–21) 'when memory was shattered' (*CP*, 87) and he witnessed 'All the villainies of the fire-and-brimstone-visited town' (*CP*, 86).

> Here, like Andersen's tailor, I weave the invisible thread,
> The burnt-out clock of St Mary's has come to a stop,
> And the hand still points to the figure that beckons the
>   house-stoned dead. (*CP*, 86)

Addressing his little god-daughter, born in Paris at that very time, he notes how

> Through the criminal thumb-prints of soot, in the
>   swaddling-bands of a shroud,
> I pace the familiar street, and the wall repeats my pace,
> Alone in the blown-up city, lost in a bird-voiced crowd
> Murdered where shattering breakers at your pillow's head
>   leave lace. (*CP*, 86)

These are lines from a twenty-page poem Watkins wrote in an unsuccessful attempt to come to terms with the destruction of his home town. But, like his compatriot Henry Vaughan, he was really at his best when dealing obliquely and figuratively with devastating experiences. I am particularly fond of 'The Ballad of the Mari Lwyd'. The poem was first drafted in 1938, but actually published shortly after Watkins's beloved Swansea had been razed to the ground over three nights of German Blitz, an experience that hurried him again to the edge of a nervous breakdown. With its liminal experiences, this ghost-haunted poem with its premonitions of war is, then, Watkins's equivalent of 'Little Gidding'. In the 'Ballad' he, too, in his anticipatory imagination is desolately wandering the disfigured streets of Swansea, treading the pavement in a dead patrol: the work deserves to be recognised as one of the powerful war poems of the Second World War. The Mari Lwyd is a mysterious disturber of the peace, invader of homes, intercessor for ghosts, would-be mediator between the disquieted living and the unquiet dead. It is we who live who have need of protection, because

> Out in the night the nightmares ride;
> And the nightmares' hooves draw near.
> Dead men pummel the panes outside,
> And the living quake with fear.

> Quietness stretches the pendulum's chain
> To the limit where terrors start,
> Where the dead and the living find again
> They beat with the selfsame heart. (*CP*, 47)

Such lines exactly capture the potent, ambivalent character of dangerous traffic with the ghosts of one's own past, even as they capture the uncanny atmosphere of wartime. 'The Ballad of the Mari Lwyd' is one of the very few of Watkins's poems – and those are among his very best – where one seems directly to feel the after-tremor of the mental catastrophe that had befallen him in his youth. 'I, a man walking, alive to fear' (*CP*, 149), Watkins once memorably wrote, accurately identifying the surest source of his own poetic power.

Very occasionally, indeed, the underlying fear of the nihilistic annihilations of time is even allowed still to peep starkly through, as in these lines that turn the kestrel into the bleak antithesis of Hopkins's windhover:

> A gloom you make
> Hang from one point in changing time
> On grass. Below you seawaves break
>
> Rebellious, casting rhyme on rhyme
> Vainly against the craggy world
> From whose black death the ravens climb. (*CP*, 244)

There's a sombre magnificence to these lines, and a tragic overtone, too, since Watkins seems here to be casting the sea in the role of a futile rhymester, attempting in vain to turn the dark destructive matter of the craggy mortal world to harmonious order. And it is the permanently unexorcised fear of that failure that surely lies at the heart of Watkins's own compulsive repetitive actions as poet, his lifelong casting of rhyme on rhyme against 'black death' like some charlatan sorcerer.

And that's where his key image of himself as the Taliesin of Gower comes in. Who then was Taliesin? Well, there are two Taliesins in Welsh legend. The first is indisputably a historical figure – the great sixth-century poet, who stands alongside Aneirin as one of the two founding figures of the ancient, majestic Welsh tradition of strict-metre poetry. And the second Taliesin? Well, he is a figure of folklore and legend, a magician, a shape-changer, a shaman. The most famous mythic account of his birth is that in the *Mabinogion* which concerns the witch Ceridwen, who assigns to her little serving-boy, Gwion Bach, the task of stirring a cauldron brimful of a potion that will bestow magical powers on whoever imbibes it. Gwion slyly takes a drop for himself and is instantly endowed with remarkable powers. Pursued by a furious Ceridwen, he changes himself into a goose and she becomes a fox; then he metamorphoses into a sparrow and she into a hawk; and finally he transforms himself into a grain of wheat, whereupon she becomes a hen and gobbles him up. Nine months later she gives birth to an extraordinarily graceful little boy, whom she names Taliesin – or beauteous-browed. She immediately sets him adrift at sea, but he is rescued by Prince Elphin and raised as his own son.

Taliesin the poet; Taliesin the shape-changer; Taliesin the beautiful – these merge over time, because in ancient society the poet, the *bardd* (whence 'bard'), was after all regarded as endowed with magical powers to transform language and through it the world. And given the pathology of his own imagination, Watkins became understandably fascinated by a legendary creature in whose miraculous tale was figured his dream of the unique power granted to the artist to track every twist and turn and transformation of the changeful world, yet to recognise that in its spiritual essence that world remained ever the same. This was the core of the vision that had rescued him from his breakdown and it was this vision that made him a Christian Platonist artist for the rest of his life:

> Come, buried light, and honour time
> With your dear gift, your constancy,
> That the known world be made sublime
> Through visions that closed eyelids see. (*CP*, 260)

As is known, Watkins identified strongly with the figure of Taliesin. He wrote no fewer than six poems on that subject over a period of fifteen years.[5] And it's pertinent to remember that there was a curious mini-cult of Taliesin in English poetry before and after the Second World War. Did time permit, it would be interesting to explore the wildly eccentric, if not mad, use that Robert Graves makes of him and of Welsh materials in *The White Goddess*. And in her fascinating correspondence with Graves the Argentinian-Welsh experimental modernist Lynette Roberts assures him that his treatment of the Taliesin figure has real scholarly weight compared with the facile attempts of that hapless ignoramus Charles Williams.[6] The reference is, of course, to the eminent Oxford University Press editor who was a bosom buddy of J. R. R. Tolkien and of C. S. Lewis at Magdalene College, Oxford and who in 1938 had published his *Taliessin through Logres*, later followed in 1950 by *The Region of the Summer Stars*.[7] And in *Affinities* (1962), the Anglican Watkins included Three Sonnets for his fellow Anglican Charles Williams (*CP*, 291–3), whose verse he admired because it, too, was dedicated to the Christian mysteries of the incarnation and the Second Coming.

Like the lyrics of Watkins, Williams's time-consuming poetry is spiritually and symbolically concerned to reconcile mortal pain with immortal healing. But to a modern Welsh reader *Taliessin through Logres* may seem less compelling as religious allegory than as a fascinating example of the age-old English self-serving cultural practice of appropriating Welsh myth for the manufacture of an Anglo-Britain. For Williams, the Taliesin of Celtic and Welsh legend needs to be removed from his wild, Druidic, pre-Christian Welsh tribal background and to be sent to Byzantium to become a true Christian. As C. S. Lewis's commentary blithely puts it, 'He comes out of Wales and legend and old Druidic poetry into the geometric world of Byzantium and only by so doing becomes useful to Logres.'

Lewis, like Williams, glosses Logres as Arthurian Britain. But I'd prefer to trust to my own Welsh ears, and to them Logres sounds perilously like *Lloegr*, which is of course the Welsh world for England. In other words, a provocative case could be made that in relation to Wales *Taliessin through Logres* is a colonial poem. And Watkins's own ambivalent relationship to Welsh tradition is reflected in his at once identifying with Williams's Taliesin and Arthur while also creating an alternative Taliesin of his own, whose grounding in specifically Welsh soil and legendary matter is much firmer and more specific. So if there are colonial aspects to Watkins's Taliesin, too, they coexist with ambivalently post-colonial, or anti-colonial aspects of the same figure, as if Watkins did, if only in uncertain part, want to reclaim legendary native ground lost to the English. But it is also useful to think of both Williams and Watkins as, in essence, war poets – members of that generation of artists who, faced with the real threat of the invasion of England (and I use England advisedly), sought reassurance and refuge in the concept of an ancient, and therefore invincible, Britishness. And from Graham Sutherland to David Jones, such wartime artists and writers were, under these conditions, irresistibly attracted to the idea of safely 'grounding' their Britishness in the ancient land of Wales, to whose mythical landscape they therefore entrusted the survival of their English national identity.

And what, in all of this, of little old Wales itself? Well, it's worth briefly noting that the Celtic antiquity of Wales was an imaginary construct actively operative in Welsh literary culture during the first half of the twentieth century. Watkins's Celticism may fruitfully be set in the context of the calculated Celtic paganism of his friend Dylan Thomas's surreal Jarvis Hills stories of the 1930s and of the writings of Rhys Davies in the same period. This Anglo-Welsh Celticism served several historically specific functions, including offering an alternative to the contemporary, accurate image of modern Wales as home to one of the great early cosmopolitan industrial cultures of the world and the image of recent Wales as the preserve of a supposedly anti-life Nonconformist religion. And to see Watkins in this bifocal vision – as intimately related at once to Charles Williams's English Celticism and to the distinctively Welsh Celticism of the early Dylan Thomas – is to appreciate the ambivalent character of Watkins's poetry, culturally considered.

There is no mention of Gower in any of the legends attached to Taliesin. But for Watkins it was here that his Taliesin – the Taliesin of his own imagination – had been washed ashore. That was because it was his experience of Gower, I feel, that had enabled Watkins to recover full mental equilibrium. Here it was that he'd been able to compose his mind – and by that I mean two things: he had been enabled to recover mental composure, and he had been enabled to do so specifically by the act of 'composition', that is by writing poetry, 'magically conjuring words against chaos', weaving sound and texture and rhythm and sense into singular verbal icons, emblematic of endurance. There is in Watkins's work a powerful sense of the sacramental dimensions of poems and a corresponding sensitivity to the sacred aura of place.

What had Gower to offer him? Well, it provided him with the exact configuration of contrasting elements out of which his imagination could fashion a new, precarious balance. Here enduring rock survived the raging ebb and flow and concussion of water. Here, stone had been worn down over aeons yet still survived as sand. Here raucous ravens built their spindly yet wiry nests in the very teeth of gales – 'Art holds in wind', he was to write, 'the way the ravens build.' Gower was for him a magical, liminal space, a mysterious zone between time and eternity, and he felt that nowhere more strongly than at Rhossili, 'Turning-place of winds, end of Earth, and of Gower'. For him Worm's Head was 'the rock of Tiresias' eyes' – Tiresias being, of course, the ancient, blind prophet of Thebes endowed with the power to penetrate the secrets of time and space. And on Rhossili's cliffs he prostrated himself – 'Flat on my face I lie, near the needle around which the wide-world spins' (*CP*, 118). Because here was the very axis of the world, the very navel of the universe.

Gower cliffs are limestone and, like W. H. Auden, Watkins was a passionate lover of limestone landscapes. They were the veritable landscapes of the soul, honeycombed by secret caves and cavities, and carrying deep within themselves underground pools and streams that occasionally glinted unpredictably and mysteriously to the surface. The map of such a landscape's deep interior was nothing like its familiar geographical surface appearance. Limestone landscape thus emblematised temporal mortal existence, which also carried in its secret depths perennial truths that occasionally manifested themselves to the initiate and could be expressed only through the esoteric vocabulary of image uniquely available to art. This vocabulary was the great carrier of a perennial philosophy, universal to all civilisations, surviving by metamorphosing anew from millennium to millennium. These myths, symbols and images belonged to the deep grammar of the human soul. Watkins therefore felt that the ancients of all ages and cultures were his closest contemporaries. And Gower helped him to feel this – after all, wasn't it in Paviland Cave that the bones of the supposed 'Red Lady' (the oldest skeleton to be unearthed in the British Isles) were discovered?[8] And wasn't there an ancient drowned plain beneath the Bristol Channel, just as there was an ancient spiritual wisdom permanently lurking deep within the human unconscious? Ceri Richards was likewise famously attracted by legends of drowned lands, producing a great suite of paintings on the theme of *La Cathédrale Engloutie*. Here we see the submerged forms of ecclesiastical columns and pillars. While Richards was drawing on a Breton legend, he couldn't have failed to have been reminded of the parallel Welsh legend of Cantre'r Gwaelod in Cardigan Bay, nor could he have forgotten the drowned land off the coast of south Gower. After all, towards the end of his life he spent most of his summers at the house he'd rented on Pennard Cliffs, near Watkins's home.

And then for Watkins there was the bicultural character of Gower. For almost a thousand years, the ridge of Cefn Bryn had constituted a local landsker, a boundary dividing a Welsh-speaking north Gower from the Englishry of south Gower. Strictly speaking, Watkins was not a Gower poet: he was a south Gower poet. Like so many Welsh-speaking families of the day, the Watkins family had achieved upward social mobility by abandoning the Welsh language that had been native to it in favour of the cosmopolitan language of English. More-over, Watkins had been educated at thoroughly English prep and public schools specifically intended to anglicise him. And anglicised to a highly significant degree he had duly become – indeed he had been deliberately fashioned into a genteel member of the influential English lower-upper middle class. And as such he may have felt completely at home in some south Gower circles. But his was a complex cultural inheritance, and to some extent he seems to have been a psychically dislocated and culturally displaced person. He knew little, if anything, about contemporary Welsh-language culture. Instead, in his work he seems to have viewed that world stretching north and west of Cefn Bryn through the eyes of English neo-Romanticism and regarded it as ancient and Celtic. And it was on those terms he felt strong affinities with it – so much so, as we have seen, that in imagin-ation he chose to bring Taliesin himself ashore on a Gower beach:

> Ceridwen's prey,
> Child of the sea,
> I was cast that day
> On wild Pwlldu. (*CP*, 317)

> Late I return, O violent, colossal, reverberant,
>   eavesdropping sea.
> My country is here. I am foal and violet. Hawthorn breaks
>   from my hands.
> I watch the inquisitive cormorant pry
>   from the praying rocks of Pwlldu.
> Then skim to the gulls' white colony,
>   to Oxwich's cockle-strewn sands. (*CP*, 184)

And the lines in which he describes Taliesin's actual birth provide us with a conveniently short and simple example of the richly syncretic character of his imagination, his love of fusing together myths and images from a wide range of ancient civilisations.

> Music flows through me as through a shell . . .
> My master from the rainbow on the sea
> Launched my round bark. (*CP*, 353)

The shell is the coracle in which the legendary Welsh Taliesin was set adrift and Watkins was very aware that his own family had hailed from Carmarthen, where once coracles had plied on the Towy, as they famously continued to do at Cenarth on the Teifi. But the shell is also the shell in which Venus/Aphrodite floats ashore in the Platonist Botticelli's world-famous image.[9] Aphrodite is, for Platonists, the goddess of all this world's beauty, and what is Taliesin the poet but the 'beauteous-browed' one, magically endowed with sensitivity to the spiritual beauty miraculously incarnate in this world of matter? As for the sea, well in addition to all its biblical associations, it is clearly the Platonist William Blake's potentially destructive sea of space and time into which our immortal souls are plunged at birth. But over that sea hovers a reminder, in the rainbow, of God's special covenant with man, an emblem of the otherworldly beauties that continue to shimmer within our fallen world. And of course, behind this use of the rainbow image is Watkins's memory of the most celebrated passage on the subject by yet another Platonist, Shelley. 'Life, like a dome of many-coloured glass,/ Stains the white radiance of Eternity.' And it is on this great, famous passage that Watkins so powerfully muses in his majestic 'Music of Colours' suite of poems, as we'll see, which is dedicated to pondering the paradox of the Fortunate Fall – the human soul's Fall from the white radiance of eternity into the many-splendoured colour of Life.

It is at Pwlldu that Bishopston Stream reaches the sea, and that stream fascinated Watkins because in spring it disappears from sight only to reappear in autumn. It was thus for him resonantly evocative of the existential condition of the spiritual world – running so deep beneath the surface of our temporal existence that it is invisible for most of the time but then suddenly manifests itself in some physical detail or in some poetic image. For Watkins the secret, hidden spiritual grammar of the world could not be grasped by rational consciousness. It could be grasped only by the means made available by the great arts, particularly by poetry. Poems were unique forms of human understanding. At their greatest, they were forms of anamnesis – that is, they enabled us to remember what we never knew we knew. And in the autumn reappearance of Bishopston Stream Watkins felt he was witnessing the kind of revelation that poetry alone could capture:

> Crossing an open space, haunted in June by mayflies,
> Into the gloom of trees you wind through Bishopston Valley,
> Darting, kingfisher-blue, carrying a streak of silver
> Fished from oblivion. (*CP*, 315–16)

In some of the very best of Watkins's Gower poems one still feels the tremors, the distant aftershock, of that catastrophic psychic earthquake he had once suffered, a reminder that his imagination was still most authentic when it remembered that it had been originally quickened into poetry by terror and panic. Words had, after all, first come to him not out of light but out of darkness. So, by running his fingers along the 'horny quill' of a feather picked up from a Gower beach, he is given swift, deep, but safe access to his own existential angst:

> Sheer from wide air to the wilderness
> The victim fell, and lay;
> The starlike bone is fathomless,
> Lost among wind and spray
> This lonely, isolated thing
> Trembles amid their sound. (*CP*, 120–1)

Just for once, Watkins permits himself to see a world so precipitously fallen into loss, pain and suffering that it is beyond the consolatory hope of resurrection. Not that his poetry is always incapable of rendering that redemptive vision powerfully. He can be a spellbindingly affirmative poet, witness the Vaughan-like visionary sheen of lines like the following:

> I praise God with my breath
> As hares leap, fishes swim,
> And bees bring honey to the hive.
>
> The yew shuts out that sky
> And the dumbfounded well
> Hides within its stone

> The colours' trance; they shone
> Pure, but the stones give cry
> Answering what no colours spell. (*CP*, 102)

Watkins's 'stones [that] give cry' surely belong to the same holy ground as the stones of Henry Vaughan that remain contrastingly dumb because they are lost 'deep in admiration'; just as Watkins's well, in its turn, is 'dumbfounded' by what the stones cry. But what is it that they cry? Here again the parallels with Vaughan are striking. The cry of the stones breaks the spirit-imprisoning trance of their own seductive, en-trancing beauty of colour. Because their cry is a cry of vision, a cry of spiritual self-realisation and release, a cry of revelation. It is the cry of primal recognition of that pristine source of all colour, that 'original white, by which the ravishing bird looks wan', as Watkins puts it in his magnificent poem 'Music of Colours: White Blossom' (*CP*, 101). This is an example of Watkins's metaphysic of sound – the attenuation of 'swan' to 'wan' verbally emblematises the difference between mortal and divine standards of purity and thus highlights man's impoverished sense of what constitutes perfection. Man mistakes what is at best 'wan' for the authentic 'swan'. 'White Blossom' is the first in the suite of three great 'Music of Colours' poems that so excited Ceri Richards into memorable image.

Like Vaughan's, then, Watkins's is a sacramental vision of a natural world in which bright shoots of everlastingness are so movingly ubiquitous. And Watkins seems even to share Vaughan's love of turning rhyme itself into both a sonic and visual emblem of covert spiritual harmony. In the passage we're considering, 'stone' is made to form an eye-rhyme with 'shone', thus transforming an inert physical object ('stone') into one that was energised ('shone') when it became instinct with spiritual luminosity.

Watkins's deepest conscious need was to celebrate eternity's love for the productions of time, as his hero Blake poignantly put it. Particularly compelling, because so arrestingly untypical, is the third and final poem in the series, 'Music of Colours: Dragonfoil and the Furnace of Colours' (*CP*, 322–5). For me, this is one of the very few poems that make visible, and therefore make intelligible, Watkins's surprising passion for Keats, rather than for the Platonist Shelley, even though this poem is about the gorgeous colours that stain the white radiance of eternity:

Where were these born then, nurtured of the white light?
Dragonfly, kingfisher breaking from the white bones,
Snows never seen, nor blackthorn boughs in winter,
Lit by what brand of a perpetual summer,
These and the field flowers?

All is entranced here, mazed amid the wheatfield
Mustardseed, chicory, sky of the cornflower
Deepening in sunlight, singing of the reapers,
Music of colours swaying in the light breeze,
Flame wind of poppies.

Aflame with the plenitude of its life, summer is here so gloriously full
of itself that it is forgetful of all but the sumptuous abundance of the
mortal present. But amid it all, a Watkins heady with high summer
still persists in hearing,

Far off, continually, . . . the breakers
Falling, destroying, secret, while the rainbow,
Flying in spray, perpetuates the white light.

In other words, a Watkins drunk, as a poet must perhaps be, on the
sensuous delights of mortal mutable existence nevertheless never forgets
that it can never fully satisfy humanity's essentially spiritual nature.

I've already characterised Cefn Bryn as a local landsker, a linguistic
marker, a cultural boundary. But it is also the divide between two
dramatically contrasting landscapes, each with its distinctive beauties.
To the north, as we know, the estuarine coast is low-lying marshland,
waterlands and great tidal mudflats where Penclawdd cockle-pickers
used, at least, to go for their rich pickings. To the south, the coastline
is magnificently craggy, and each of the innumerable little bays seems
to have its story of smugglers and of shipwrecks. Naturally native to
this latter region is one of Watkins's favourite poetic forms, the ballad,
that had traditionally supplied whole communities and classes with
an anonymous popular voice for commemorating collective experiences
and truths. This isn't the place to start detailing the extensive modern
history of the ballad, from the eighteenth century's fascination with
supposedly primitive folk forms to the sophisticated concerns of great
modernist poets like W. B. Yeats and W. H. Auden. Suffice it to say
that Watkins was as aware of this high literary tradition as he was of

the local south Gower tradition of ballad composition. It seems clear
he was attracted to it because it seemed to give unsophisticated, direct,
unmediated expression to ordinary, general, universal human experience. The ballad form could thus be used to testify impersonally and
authoritatively to the grand eternal truths of human existence, as
Watkins, as we've seen, conceived them to be.

Many of his ballads are obsessed with the sea, its terrifying powers,
its human wrecks. This is how 'Ballad of the Equinox' begins:

> Pwlldu – an eternal place!
> The black stream under the stones
> Carries the bones of the dead,
> The starved, the talkative bones.
>
> There the great shingle-bank
> Props a theatrical scene
> Where guess the generous dead
> What lovers' words may mean.
>
> When the sun and the moon are level
> And the sky has a fish's scales
> I stand by the foxy foam
> On that groaning shingle of Wales.
>
> Beyond Hunt's moonlike bay,
> That pockmarked crescent of rocks,
> White horses, dead white horses,
> Priests of the equinox,
>
> Deride my lonely curse,
> And the moon rides over, pale,
> Where the wicked wet dog in the hearse
> And the devil in the wind prevail. (*CP*, 189–90)

Here, as repeatedly in the powerful series of Ballads, the sea becomes
the dread realm of the dead, and Watkins's mind becomes haunted
by their clamorous, threatening ghosts. Those unappeasable, voracious
ghosts, in their turn, are expressions of the psychic terrors that had
caused the young Watkins's cataclysmic and catastrophic mental
collapse. The drowned are revenants, come back to mock Watkins

with the possibility that life may be meaningless after all, matter totally devoid of spirit: it is the devil in the wind that threatens to prevail. But in other ballads Watkins fights back, struggling to reassert his Christian Platonist faith in a spiritually redeemed universe. As he writes in the very conclusion of 'Ballad of Crawley Woods',

> Though long he lay in death's embrace,
>   That tree and wall were true.
> The rose in that rose-window
>   Knew every leaf that grew.
> For him each single drop of dew
>   Trembled, a world of praise.
> The secret of the dead he knew
>   None but their Christ can raise. (*CP*, 193)

Here, then, he lays the uneasy ghost of the drowned by summoning up an exorcising vision instead of the dead released from death and risen to new spiritual life by the great redeemer, Christ. This is how he summed up his mature philosophy in a prose note to *The Death Bell*:

> unredeemed man, through acquisitiveness, wills his own perdition . . . but redeemed man, falling through time deliberately, is raised by loss. The resurrection of the body is assured, not by the instinct of self-preservation, but by the moment of loss, of the whole man's recurrent willingness to lose himself to an act of love. (*CP*, 216)

After reading Watkins, I am left with the realisation that I would not wish to be without a dozen or more of the best poems he wrote; and that is surely a decent survival rate for any writer of quality. With all his limitations, he was a fine poet and deserves far better than to be ignored. When he died, Ceri Richards felt that the cliffs of Gower themselves had been stricken with grief: 'Now that he is not there any more the landscape seems deprived and inarticulate.' But as I tread those same cliffs in these later years, my neighbour's poetry is for me still a cherished, abiding, landscape-altering presence, and he a figure whose continuing value is literally brought home to me by the print Ceri Richards produced in his memory and which now hangs in humble homage on my bedroom wall.

(Not previously published in this form.)

Notes

[1]   All quotations are from Vernon Watkins, *Collected Poems* (Ipswich: Golgonooza Press, 1986).

[2]   See, for instance, Richard Burns, *Ceri Richards and Dylan Thomas: Keys to Transformation* (Wellingborough: Enitharmon Press, 1981).

[3]   For Richards's response to Thomas, see, for instance, *Ceri Richards: Drawings to Dylan Thomas's Poetry* (Wellingborough: Enitharmon Press, 1980).

[4]   Vernon Watkins, *Dylan Thomas: Letters to Vernon Watkins* (London: Dent, 1957), p. 38. See another of Thomas's comments to Watkins on the opening of one of the latter's poems: 'all the wheels and drums are put in motion: a poem is about to begin. I see the workman's clothes, I hear the whistle blowing in the poem-factory' (p. 29).

[5]   'Taliesin in Gower' (*CP*, p. 184), 'Taliesin and the Spring of Vision' (*CP*, pp. 224–5), 'Taliesin's Voyage' (*CP*, pp. 316–18), 'Taliesin and the Mockers' (*CP*, pp. 318–21), 'Taliesin at Pwlldu' (*CP*, p. 353), 'Sea Chant: Taliesin to Venus' (*CP*, pp. 354–5).

[6]   Patrick McGuinness (ed.), Lynette Roberts, *Diaries, Letters and Recollections* (Manchester: Carcanet, 2008), p. 176.

[7]   Charles Williams, *Taliessin through Logres: The Region of the Summer Stars; and Arthurian Torso* (London: William B. Eerdmans, 1974).

[8]   See 'Digging the Past' (*CP*, pp. 381–4) and 'The Red Lady' (ibid., pp. 384–5).

[9]   Watkins specifically links Taliesin with the birth of Venus/Aphrodite in 'Sea Chant' (*CP*, p. 354).

10

'Dubious affinities': Leslie Norris's Welsh–English Translations

Albert took up his flute and began to play.
'You always play beautifully,' Lucille said, 'but the music is sad.'
'It helps me,' said Albert. 'It's instead of crying.'[1]

Albert is a little boy; Lucille, a dachshund (with chutzpah), his closest friend and confidante. Together they set out on a bewitching adventure to recover the best Christmas present Albert's mother had ever had – a delicate gold medallion desolatingly lost when she was eight years old. Published when Leslie Norris was eighty, *Albert and the Angels* is a delightful story for children. Hardly central to his oeuvre, it is nevertheless the most charming late evidence of his consummate artistry as a storyteller (not to mention his special relationship with animals). It is also obliquely revealing of his generous, melancholy imagination. Death-haunted yet life-affirming, it was always pre-occupied by, and therefore with, the past – to a dangerous degree, perhaps, for his well-being as a poet. A major project unfinished at Norris's death was a verse autobiography loosely modelled on Words-worth's *Prelude*.[2] It was the celebrated 'spots of time' passages that had first ignited his youthful passion for poetry, thus instigating the growth of his own poetic mind. Therefore, in modelling the memorial-ising poetry of his final years on these passages that were not only precious relics of his memory but also intense retrospectives broodingly concerned with their own mysterious origins, he was suggesting the infinitely regressive, inherently elusive, nature of memory itself. In the process he was in effect sending his final, fond regards to Edward Thomas, the formative influence on his mature poetry. It was Thomas, after all, who had ended his superb poem 'Old Man' by confessing himself to be terminally baffled by his own most intimately formative past. His intense effort at recollection had succeeded only in locating 'An avenue dark, nameless, without end'.

What is it, therefore, that we have in *Albert and the Angels*, with its dream of a recovery of a gold medallion lost for a lifetime, but an old poet's wistful fantasy of impossibly perfect, total recall? Is this touching children's story that, of course, ends happily, not haunted by the willed innocence of old age's belief in the possibility of complete recovery of a lost past; of rendering it as palpable, as sensuously tangible, as when it was the present?[3] And what do we have in most of Norris's mature poetry but the sad flute song of adult experience that inevitably puts an end to such innocence? That poetry is the product of an adult consciousness for which only the sweetly elegiac and sensuously restorative music of verse can provide a measure of consolation for what is otherwise irrecoverable lost. Thus can a story like *Albert and the Angels* – work in a genre untypical of Norris and seemingly marginal to his most important achievements – prove unexpectedly revealing of his central preoccupations as a writer. Emboldened by such a perception, this essay will concern itself with another of his occasional and seemingly incidental productions: his translations of a small body of poems from the Welsh language.

* * *

Over the course of his career as a writer, Leslie Norris published fourteen translations from the Welsh. Of these, eleven were from the legendary golden age of the poets of the gentry (*c*.1285–*c*.1525), including ten versions of classic poems by Dafydd ap Gwilym (*fl.* 1315/20–1350/70), who was not only the outstanding poet of his remarkable period but probably the greatest of all Welsh poets (not excluding Dylan Thomas). The eleventh poem in this 'set' was a translation of an elegy for Dafydd by his old sparring-partner, Gruffydd Gryg; and Norris himself elegised the poet after a fashion in his 'A Message for Dafydd ap Gwilym'. The first of his translations to be published came from an even earlier period of the Middle Ages: 'The Old Age of Llywarch' is a powerful survival from the ninth century and may represent a fragment from a lost saga. And Norris turned to the twentieth century to complete his portfolio, translating two poems by Gwenallt, a searing poet of Welsh industrial experience.

Norris's translations began to appear in the wake of Tony Conran's collection of translations, *The Penguin Book of Welsh Verse*, a watershed 1967 publication that excited some of the English-language poets of post-war Wales into a cultural self-revaluation resulting in a creative realignment of their work. No academic scholar, Conran was a remarkably innovative late-modernist poet, already beginning to develop into a major writer, and buried in the brilliant introduction to his volume (which covered all of Welsh poetry from the sixth to the twentieth century) was a practising poet's manifesto. His particular fascination was with the way in which the defining values of a unique high Welsh 'civilisation', emerging in the sixth century, were thereafter inscribed for almost a thousand years in the rhythm, sound and imagery of its strict-metre poetry.

Conran was later to admit that behind his translation project lay a pressing desire to connect, as an Anglophone Welsh poet, with an ancient and modern Wales from which he felt painfully excluded as a monoglot English-speaker. He conceived of himself and his (and Norris's) generation of 'Anglo-Welsh' poets as internal exiles:

> Threatened by both the ruling-class English intelligentsia we were trained [by the anglicised and Anglocentric system] to serve, and by the native Welsh culture that we felt we had the birthright, we tried to make room for ourselves. We wrote elegies for lost Wales. We proclaimed that the Dragon has two tongues. We translated Welsh poetry.[4]

To translate from the Welsh was, for him, not merely to serve a technical apprenticeship, as an aspiring Welsh modernist poet, in a variety of strange, imaginatively stimulating, forms and metres. It was to have his eyes permanently opened to a conception of the poet's role, and practice, fundamentally different from that deeply embedded in the English poetic tradition. He was excited by his discovery of

> the special relationship the poet has with his public in Wales, which is very different from the minority audience he expects to find in England. The Welsh poet is still a leader in his community, a national figure who appears at public functions and is constantly called upon to give his opinions on questions of the day.[5]

All this reinforced his budding resolution to write a culturally committed poetry. It should, he felt, be a poetry answerable, however covertly and obliquely, to the pressing needs of a contemporary Wales where a young generation of writers, intellectuals and political leaders was beginning to respond militantly to their country's long politico-cultural subordination to England, forming in the process a common front between the long-divided Welsh-language and English-language cultures of Wales. Conran conceived of his Welsh–English translations in part as a contribution to this process, while they also enabled his own development into a meaningfully Welsh poet writing through the medium of English.

But what has all this to do with Leslie Norris? What relation does Conran's example bear to Norris's own poetic stance and practice, particularly as intermittent translator from the Welsh? Crudely put, Conran was the kind of committedly Welsh anglophone poet that Norris was both implicitly and explicitly concerned to define himself against. Nowhere is their polarised relationship more evident than in Conran's outraged response to Norris's 'The Dead', a translation of Gwenallt's 'Y Meirwon'. It was natural for a poet like Norris, who had, as an adult, so mournfully lived in his brooding imagination through the slow post-industrial decline of his boyhood Merthyr (a world-leader in the development of nineteenth-century industrial society), to feel magnetically drawn to Gwenallt's mid-twentieth-century elegy for his own remarkable Welsh-speaking industrial community in a neighbouring south Wales valley, a few dozen miles to the west. So, given such deep instinctive affinities, what was it in Norris's translation that had so offended Conran?

For answer, one need only set Conran's version of a crucial passage from 'Y Meirwon' next to Norris's. It forms the conclusion of a poem full of anger at the 'explosion and flood' that 'changed us often into savages/ Fighting catastrophic and devilish powers', an early experience that taught Gwenallt 'Collects of red revolt and litanies of wrong' (*Penguin Book*, 252). Such are the feelings aroused in him as he recalls the obscenely violent exploitation of a decent, God-fearing working class by the predatory world of savage industrial capitalism. The human suffering etched indelibly into his young consciousness was instanced by the plight of his neighbours, who were called 'the Martyrs// Because they came from Merthyr Tydfil, the Town of furnaces'.[6] In Norris's version, Gwenallt's poem then ends pianissimo, on a modestly personal note:

> Here on Flower Sunday, in a soiled
>
> Acre of graves, I lay down my gasping roses
> And lilies pale as ice as one who knows
> Nothing certain, nothing; unless it is
> My own small place and people, agony and sacrifice.

Implicated in such a significantly modified ending is a 'betrayal' of the original that Conran finds unforgivable. His own version of the same passage faithfully conveys , by contrast, the authentic, unsubduable communal voice of 'Y Meirwon', with its principled refusal to be reconciled to the injustices of its past:

> Between the premature stones and the curb yet unripened,
> We gather the old blasphemings, curses of funerals past.
>
> Our Utopia vanished from the top of Gellionnen,
> Our abstract humanity's classless, defrontiered reign,
> And today nothing is left at the deep root of the mind
> Save family and neighbourhood, man's sacrifice and pain.
>
> (*Penguin Book*, 252)

And once alerted to the textual modifications of which Norris is 'guilty', what becomes evident is how extensive and radical they are, and how they all tend in the same direction – rendering the original unaccommodated text more acceptable in polite company, domesticating its discursive political wildness, draining off the raw energy of its social outrage: in short, 'sivilizing' it to perdition, as Huck Finn might have put it. There is no mention in Norris's version of 'the leopard of industry'; of 'the hootering death: the dusty, smokeful, drunken death'; of 'Mute and brave women with a fistful of blood-money,/ With a bucketful of death, forever the rankling loss' (*Penguin Book*, 252). Moreover, for Gwenallt's movingly accusatory gesture of placing 'on their graves a bunch/ Of silicotic roses and lilies pale as gas' (*Penguin Book*, 252), Norris substitutes the altogether blander, and reassuringly 'poetic', 'gasping roses/ And lilies pale as ice' – which is more reminiscent of the set of *La Traviata* than of the terrible industrial squalor of the lower Swansea valley. When rather euphemistically mentioning 'Death brutally invoked' he even describes it as 'death from the factory': *factory*! – Norris very well knew that

Gwenallt's world was that of the terrible fiery floor of the tinplate works where his father had been burned to a cinder by the spillage from an overhead ladle brimful of molten metal. In that community, the mines had filled the lungs of his childhood friends either with immediately deadly gas or with the dust that so slowly and cruelly stifled breath. Conran, by contrast, faithfully records how 'We crept in the Bibled parlours, and peeped with awe/ At cinders of flesh in the coffin, and ashes of wrong' (*Penguin Book*, 252).

These modifications are worth highlighting, along with their implications, not only for themselves but because they point up one limitation consistently to be found in Norris's faultlessly temperate poetry: its perpetual anxiety not to offend, not to raise its voice, not to be caught out in any infelicities of expression or discordances of discourse, not to disturb the carefully preserved decorum of its persona. Norris's poetry seems to have its psychic thermostat always set to the same even temperature, possibly – one might sympathetically speculate – because he was a little afraid of otherwise losing self-control. A late poem such as 'The Ballad of Self and Self' certainly hints at disturbing inner divisions of the kind explored in Edward Thomas's 'The Other'. But whereas the movingly precarious equilibrium of Thomas's poetry is that of a lost soul, otherwise unbalanced by its terrible, disorientating struggles with depression, Norris's poems never venture inwards (or outwards) any deeper than can be reached by a pleasing, controllable melancholy: the very conventionality of their structure and the predictable evenness of their tone seems to signify a determination (if not an anxiety) to stay within the reassuring bounds of the familiar.

As for Conran's critical response to Norris's translation of 'the Dead', it highlights another feature central to all his poetry.

> Norris gives us personal sadness and protest that seems as much directed at the human condition as at deplorable economic exploitation [. . . his translation] tabulates the cost of fashioning for himself an uncommitted 'voice' in the English manner. The detachment of exile or 'Britishness' is one option for an Anglo-Welsh writer; but, just as much as any other option in Wales, to choose it means a self-wounding limitation on the power to see life clearly and see it whole.[7]

Setting aside the political animus (characteristic of its period) and a rival poet's self-interest vested in these remarks, they still offer a shrewd insight into Norris's chosen stance, and chosen persona, as a poet.

Shortly before his death, he responded, with characteristic kindness and modesty, to a series of questions put to him by a student of mine at Swansea, Linda Evans. These responses are very revealing. 'My work and my life', he informed her, 'are recognizably lived at the edge of affairs, so the owl [in his poem 'Bath'] and I are one, aware of our vulnerability and our position as sufferers and onlookers' (*Recollections*, 23). He identifies here the passively receptive relation to his subjects in which he chooses to stand in his many poems about places, people, living creatures and the natural world. Like the Wordsworth of 'The Solitary Reaper' (a lyric with which he felt an instinctive affinity), and indeed like the reaper herself who works 'single in the field', he was, for all his extraordinary talent for sociability, a loner at heart, his boon companions being his dogs. Deeply disinclined to be a 'joiner', he also no doubt felt his gifts as a poet could be developed only through careful protection of his status as solitary, ruminative and meditative observer. Therefore, as a poet, he felt primarily drawn to other poets (such as Edward Thomas and Norris's close friend in West Sussex, Ted Walker) who had developed a subtle poetic style and language suitable for the expression of such a sensibility. Conran was accordingly right to draw attention to Norris's overwhelming debts to a characteristically English tradition of writing, and Norris himself quite properly made no apologies for them and took no trouble to conceal them.

He was moreover fully aware of how unrepresentative he was in these regards of the Merthyr to which he nevertheless remained so inalienably attached in nostalgic memory. 'The men and women of Merthyr have been fighting for years', he informed Linda Evans, 'against political injustice, against the rain, against poverty so complete that the only defence was to band together to jeer at it' (*Recollections*, 20). Then, distinctively positioning his own immediate family outside the highly politicised world of Merthyr proletarian society ('I am the child of farmers and gardeners'), he indicates not only that he would never wish to retire there, but that such had never been his ambition, even when he was a young man. His dream had ever been to live 'on some small holding at the outskirts of the town, with some animals – sheep, perhaps – and a pack of terriers'. These comments should be connected to others he made in like spirit. When he emphasises that 'I never felt like a Welsh poet in exile' (*Recollections*, 28), he could almost be distancing himself directly from Conran's remarks about the different forms of exile endured by 'Anglo-Welsh' poets of his generation. According to Conran, this had engendered a traumatic sense of cultural and personal displacement remediable only through their use of poetry (including translation) as a means of relocating themselves within their communities and within the ancient continuities of their culture. In his responses to Evans, Norris quite explicitly rejects this socialised sense of place and personal identity. 'The poems I write may be placed anywhere I have been', he informs her: 'Place is important to me . . . but as manifestations of the living world. I am not aware of visible, tangible boundaries' (*Recollections*, 28–9).

And yet, as his subtle late poem 'Borders' indicates, the creative conditions out of which he wrote were significantly more complex and conflicted than that. While still imaging himself as an inveterate crosser of boundaries, he now recognises that it is not a process similar to the easy flow of water he had noticed, as a boy, under the bridge separating Glamorgan from Breconshire:

> Beneath,
>   the river's neutral water
> moved on
>   to other boundaries

By stepping the lines he points up the contrast between the troubled flow of the human mind and the river's smooth one-way progression. As is made clear elsewhere in the poem, any human crossing of boundaries promotes a counter-movement (of memory – the essence, of course, of Norris's poetry); a reflex action of the imagination in acknowledgement of what can never be really left behind – of what, indeed, paradoxically acquires a new immediacy in our lives by virtue of no longer being present. But whereas Conran specifically images a boundary as a place of (d)ejection, of internal and external rupture, a point of entry into painful 'exile' from the 'true' home of one's selfhood, Norris instead conceives of the act of crossing a border in terms that emphasise the paradox of a 'wholeness' actually constituted by division:

> I was whole
> But felt an unseen line
> Divide me . . .

> I have always lived that way,
> Crossed borders resolutely
> While looking over my shoulder. (209)

This double movement is a fair summary of the trajectory of his imagination, and of his carefully cultivated progress as a socially uncommitted man and poet. And it explains why, of course, he should be concerned to protect himself, through his strategic (mis)translation of 'The Dead', from any historically deep and rooted attachments to a specific place and its people.

* * *

'I did not think I was a Welsh poet', he admitted to Linda Evans, 'but a poet and a Welshman' (*Recollections*, 28). This throws light on the construction of his mature volumes, where his 'Sussex' poems (and later his American poems) are interspersed with his poems about Wales and his Merthyr experiences to make clear his own, decentred and dispersed personality. His remark also helps us understand the nature of his interest in Dafydd ap Gwilym, who served for Norris not as a Welsh national icon, or as a signifier of the importance of the Welsh language, but rather as one valuable source (among many) of poetic reinvigoration. This is made clear in 'A Message for Dafydd ap Gwilym', at the heart of which lies a very self-revealing passage. He chooses to approach Dafydd via a recollection of a childhood scene. Invited to read 'The Solitary Reaper' aloud in class, so well had he done so that the teacher had mistakenly supposed he had already learnt it by heart 'to spout at some eisteddfod'. The accusation is a telling one – the authorities' implicit attempt to 'place' Norris's love of English poetry safely within the contexts of a distinctively Welsh cultural event. Inwardly, the boy indignantly rejects any such culturally confining manoeuvre. What had made him so instantly 'inward' with a poem previously unknown to him, he insists, was his instinctive appreciation of its remarkable way with language: 'It's the words, of course', he admits to Dafydd, 'we can't leave them.' And as that inclusive use of 'we' indicates, he conceives of Dafydd and himself as occupying this same ground; the ground common to all poets. Regard-less of their separation by different languages (Dafydd's Welsh, Norris's English), it is to the wonder and riches of language itself that both are irresistibly drawn. And there are yet further ties that bind them:

> I've written, too, of those
> Manifestations of the natural world,
> Birchtrees, birdsong, the inconvenient
> Snow, so often your concern. (182)

By such means, Norris detaches Dafydd from his specific cultural contexts, from the language of which he was the supreme poetic master, from his historically specific responses to the natural world, and thus from all those features that 'place' him at a distance in his essential foreignness. And in the process he lays down the terms (both enabling and disabling) for his own engagement as translator with Dafydd.

'Like you, I am from the south', Norris informs his Dafydd.

>   like you
> I had (in youth) the pale hair
> You boast of; in youth
> I was slender and thin-faced.
> For these dubious affinities, Dafydd,
> I tell you – though you have no need to ask –
> Dafydd, you are not dead, you will not die. (183)

That last, limp, line has a hang-dog air of embarrassment at its own presumption, as if Norris was very well aware of the dubious propriety of guaranteeing a poet whose genius was inseparable from that of the Welsh language survival in the usurping language of English beyond the life of his native tongue.

Since the political reverberations of this kind of genially appropriative approach to Dafydd ap Gwilym are unlikely to be audible to many outside Wales, it seems sensible to augment them here. By the 1960s the number of Welsh-speakers in Wales had declined from the roughly fifty per cent of the population they had represented at the beginning of the century to around twenty per cent. The situation was evidently critical and in a celebrated radio lecture in 1962, Saunders Lewis, a leading Welsh-language writer and nationalist reader, had stressed the likelihood of the language's imminent demise, after the best part of two millennia, unless steps were urgently taken to remedy the gross politico-cultural imbalances between it and English.[8] In response, a spontaneous 'resistance' movement arose amongst young students who formed themselves into the activists of Cymdeithas yr Iaith Gymraeg (the Welsh Language Society). Targeting the fact that, ever since the Act of Union of England and Wales in 1536, the Welsh language had been denied official, legal status in its own country, the youngsters embarked on a peaceful, symbolic, programme of law-breaking (chiefly involving the pulling down of monoglot English road signs), and were duly imprisoned for their pains. In other words, from the 1960s onwards for a decade and more, the whole future of the Welsh language and its culture became a highly fraught issue, in the light of which the anglophone Norris's untroubled claiming of acquaintance with, and poetic descent from, Dafydd ap Gwilym was liable to assume a controversial political complexion.

In such a context, to remain politically uncommitted could itself seem tantamount to taking a political stand. And Norris's implicit supposition, as translator, that Dafydd ap Gwilym could be comfort-ably 'normalised' – that is, rendered into English without any undue disturbance to any of the prevailing conventions of English writing – could seem like an act of linguistic colonisation. Here, again, Norris's concept of Welsh–English translation contrasts sharply with that of Conran. In a remarkable poem prefacing the second edition of his collection of translations, he styled himself 'The Good Thief', and insisted that 'to translate a poem' was not 'treason', but 'to walk in its [foreign] land'.[9] He was underlining the point he'd made decades earlier; that through the act of translation, English had to be made foreign to itself before it could begin to mediate the different world view inscribed in the Welsh-language literary tradition at its greatest. It is, of course, the kind of point that would not have been lost on Pound.

* * *

But before turning to Norris's translations of Dafydd ap Gwilym's *cywyddau*, it would be useful first to consider his version of 'The Old Age of Llywarch Hen', because, like 'The Dead', it instances how ready he was to adjust his Welsh sources to bring them into line with his own poetic needs, talents and concerns. Llywarch, an old 'crook-backed' warrior, has sent each of his sons in turn to his death in a vain attempt to regain the family's lost kingdom, and now, in a lament laced with anger, frustration, resentment and self-contempt, reflects on his own impotence. His heavily monosyllabic, and correspondingly strongly accentuated, song, its limiting, inexorably recurrent rhymes mirroring Llywarch's restricted circumstances, conveys the bleakness of his world and situation:

> Wyf hen; wyf unig, wyf annelwig oer
>> Gwedi gwely ceinmyg,
> Wyf truan, wyf tri dyblyg.[10]

Something of this harshness is captured by the distinguished American translator, Joseph Clancy:

> Wind brisk; white the fringe of the trees,
>> Stag bold; hillside hard.
> Frail the old man, rouses slowly.[11]

The imagistic terseness of this conducts us into a world irreducibly remote yet familiar. Norris, in contrast, produces a modern, bourgeois, domesticated version of what was a heroic world:

> I see in the evening the fire-smoke climb
> And the earlier dusk send the children home
> To their cool beds, their milk, their mothers' warm
>
> Love in the hospitable room of youth. (14)

A poetry relaxing, sometimes all too readily, into the reassuring comfort of nostalgia: this is a staple characteristic of Norris's writing. His instinct when translating Llywarch Hen is, therefore, to let his verse expand into sentiments totally foreign to the old warrior but congenial to Norris himself.

> Crutch there, do you hear the loud winter?
> Young men go to the inn, singing as they enter,
> But here in my room is the world's lonely centre
>
> Where the voices of the young are the voices
> of ghosts

Norris's capture of the imprisoning couplet that concludes each of Llywarch's stanzas is unfailingly deft, but in his hands its effect is to suggest the soft folds of sad memory, and by using enjambement Norris allows his verse to escape into the freedom of wistful recollection. The overall impression is of a Hemingway who has suddenly metamorphosed into a soft-core Proust.

* * *

And so to Dafydd ap Gwilym. According to Rob Buchert, 'at one time [Leslie] intended to make a complete translation of the ap Gwilym oeuvre, but abandoned the idea, deciding that some of the originals weren't worth the effort'.[12] It's an intriguing thought. It would have been easier to believe that he found the whole of Dafydd (including his *cywydd* to his penis) altogether too much to handle. One must accept, of course, that Norris could never have hoped to capture in his translations those unruly and unpredictable energies of Dafydd's verse that are generated by the nuclear fission of vowels and consonants made possible only by *cynghanedd*. That granted, there remains the question of what kind of Dafydd ap Gwilym we encounter in Norris's versions; and the answer is a Dafydd created very much in Norris's own image.[13]

However, his poetic relationship to Dafydd is interestingly different from his relationship to Llywarch. Whereas he comfortably assimilates the latter to the familiar norms of his customary style, Dafydd's poetry licenses and releases in him modes of feeling and expression nowhere else to be found in his poetry. This results in some notably attractive writing, as in the following example from 'The Thrush Singing':

> Brook-clear, carol-call, day-bright,
> Music lucid as light
> He sang again and again,
> Of happiness without pain. (100)

Although in that last line one feels the gravitational pull towards the depressive that is omnipresent in Norris's poetry and wholly absent from Dafydd's, the first two lines, in particular, convey an unguarded rapture one does not readily associate with Norris. The effect is created not only by the compound words but also by the way he here modifies the *cywydd* couplet (seven-syllable lines grouped into pairs in which the final, rhyming syllables alternate between the masculine and feminine in accentuation). Norris is notably dexterous at handling this unusual form in English, but here he deliberately shortens the second line to six syllables as well as substituting for the densely accented, and primarily spondaic, previous line an altogether lighter, prevailingly trochaic rhythm. The effect is like the clearing of the air to which 'lucid' alludes. There is no hint here of the elegiac anapaests of which Norris tends otherwise to be over-fond – Dafydd ap Gwilym's vision and poetic doesn't allow of that.

A different kind of lightness also enters Norris's verse – the lightness of wit. It surfaces, for instance, in Dafydd's poem to the fox:

> the curse of our kennel,
> A sly fox, red animal,
> Sitting there on his haunches
> As tame as a tortoise. (155)

Later in the poem this humour turns comic, as Dafydd indulges in one of his favourite devices – self-mocking invective:

> Then my fury at that fox,
> That marauder of meek-ducks,
> That harrier of fat hens,
> That glutton of goose-pens! (156)

There is for Norris an unwonted gusto in this writing, and it is quickly succeeded by an equally uncharacteristic turn of his verse towards the grotesque, as he tracks Dafydd's quicksilver movements and captures his shape-shifting poetic persona:

> He glows against the gravel.
> Ape-faced he flits the furrows,
> Stalking like a stupid goose. (156)

One of Dafydd's most virtuosic features is his ability to turn *barddas*, classic strict-metre poetry with the strictest and most complex body of required poetic devices, into a medium for apparently unfettered spontaneity and improvisation. Whereas Norris cannot, of course, convey this productive tension, he is at times able to capture the brio of Dafydd's response to the natural world, as in the following stanza from his version of 'The Fox':

> Scaring crows at the hill's rim,
> Acre-leaper, red as flame,
> Observed by the birds' high eyes,
> A dragon from old stories,
> A tumult among feathers,

> A red pelt, a torch of furs,
> Traveller in earth's hollow
> Red glow at a closed window,
> A copper-box with quick tread,
> Bloody pincers in his head. (156)

He has even managed to convey something of the exhilarating changes of direction of the original by mixing obediently perfect rhyme ('tread/head') with a range of deliberately imperfect, or off-centre, rhymes ('rim/flame'; 'eyes/stories'; 'feathers/furs'). In thus suggesting the elusiveness of the creature, the way it eludes full capture even by the imagination, he is able to register the completely untameable 'otherness' of the natural world better, perhaps, than anywhere else in his poetry.

In his reply to Linda Evans's questions, Norris confessed that he had been

> consistent in writing elegies, not only for friends, but also for the passing of the natural world. I am by temperament a man for whom life is the great miracle, and the possibility, but not the inevitability, of eternity exists in the visibility and the sensuous recognition of the living principle. So in my small, individual way I make sure that I honour it in what words I have. (*Recollections*, 19)

He attributed this elegiac, cautiously mystical turn in his approach to nature to the early influence of Wordsworth. Reading his translations of Dafydd ap Gwilym, one wonders what sort of poet he might have become had his earliest, most formative, encounters been with Dafydd's poetry instead. Dafydd's world is a wild one in constant motion. It never stays still long enough for him to ponder it at his leisure. It is no place for leisurely reflection and rumination. To enter that emotionally and linguistically mobile world, however briefly, seems to me to have been both a lesson and a tonic for Norris.

By adopting the persona of Dafydd ap Gwilym, Norris was able also to free himself not only from old, and otherwise ingrained, poetic habits but from certain inhibitions. His poem 'The Owl', he confided to Linda Evans, was a 'hidden love poem, since I am not capable of writing such a poem openly, for anyone to read' (*Recollections*, 23). By contrast, Dafydd ap Gwilym was as great a love poet as may be found in any language, and wholly up-front about it. It's intriguing, therefore, that Norris should have chosen to translate such a poem as

'The Spear', a brilliantly idiosyncratic, typically tongue-in-cheek, improvisation on the courtly love convention of the fatal wounding of the lover by his mistress's beauty. In Norris's version, it opens as follows:

> I saw her there, her fair hair
> Pale as foam, as white water,
> From to head to toe perfection
> More radiant than day-dawn. (157)

There are at least the glimmerings, in those opening two lines, of a sensuous, and indeed erotic, response entirely foreign to Norris's usual poetic sensibility, as the supple, cupping, phrasing seems to enact ('there. . .hair; her. . . hair; fair. . .foam') a sonic moulding of the girl's physical beauty. And with like unexpected effect, and perhaps for the same instinctively self-liberating reason, Norris turns to one of Dafydd ap Gwilym's genuinely devout religious poems:

> Sanguis Christi, salva me.
>> Christ's blood, lest for wildness – I am sent
>> Into the wilderness,
>> Then rise, light of God's praise,
>> And keep me from drunkenness. (162)

In its way, this is quite a tour de force, as it approximates, at least in skeletal form (minus the internal sonic texture), to an englyn, one of the classic forms of *barddas* (classical strict-metre poetry). Whereas the first line is taken from the Latin mass, the next four constitute the englyn itself. This consists of four lines that are expected to be roughly ten, six and seven syllables in length respectively. The first line is split into two unequal parts, the rhyming word ('wildness') occurring at the end of the first part, while the second part is treated as the effective beginning of the second line. In the englyn proper, it is required that this physically 'split' line be sonically united by a single approved pattern of recurrent sounds. While retaining some, at least, of these definitive features of the englyn, Norris has also managed to construct a genuinely affecting English poem of intense spiritual petition.

* * *

These, then, are some of the notable consequences for Norris of his adoption of Dafydd ap Gwilym as his persona and of Dafydd's poetry as his model. Not that he was by any means alone among poets of his post-war generation to be interested in Dafydd, Harri Webb and Dannie Abse, for example, being others with the same enthusiasm. But of greatest significant in the present context is the use made of Dafydd ap Gwilym by Glyn Jones, one of Norris's very closest friends. Born in Merthyr, educated at the Cyfarthfa Castle School, a lifelong devotee of his childhood locality, Jones – poet, novelist, short-story writer and occasional essayist and critic – was Norris's Welsh alter ego. Born in 1905, and therefore sixteen years older than Norris, Jones had been drawn, in the early 1930s, into briefly close friendship with Dylan Thomas through their common passion – exotic by the standards of industrial and puritan south Wales – for outré forms of art and of writing. Unlike the bohemian and cosmopolitan Thomas, however, Jones remained all his life undemonstratively conventional in conduct, extremely modest about his own substantial talents, and invariably loyal and generous in his many friendships with others. In his enigmatic person he blended a violent imagination with a great courtesy, considerateness and gentleness of personal bearing. Several of his short stories remain neglected classics of the comic grotesque, and he was also a restlessly innovative poet of considerable imaginative daring. Unlike Norris, he remained firmly Wales-based and Wales-committed throughout his long life and troubled to relearn Welsh in his twenties in order to gain access to a body of literature he regarded as of primary importance, not only within the European tradition, but also specifically for modern anglophone Welsh writers such as himself.

In 1973 Norris published an attractive brief study of his friend's life and work. It is studded with generalisations about 'Anglo-Welsh' writers that, while questionable in themselves, amount to an oblique self-portrait of Norris. Thus he claims that 'a passion for the visible is an Anglo-Welsh characteristic', resulting in Jones's case in a poetry that is 'at once lyrical and precise, highly individual yet immediate and immensely accurate'.[14] 'The Welsh', he elsewhere asserts, 'have often been slow developers as poets; or rather, however good they have been in their youth, retain the capacity for growth and change and development even into old age, a marvellous faculty, forbidden to most English poets' (*Glyn Jones*, 83). And he appreciates how Jones 'relies on a largely intuitive approach, feeling and realising the texture of his sentences as if they were woven and coloured' (*Glyn Jones*, 29).

But while Norris thus seems implicitly to identify himself, too, as an
'Anglo-Welsh' poet, there are places where he is evidently concerned
to place a distance between himself and the culture in which his friend
seemed to him perhaps over-securely embedded.

> Certainly [Glyn Jones] is the very personification of the Anglo-Welsh
> writer, for he draws upon the traditions of both literatures, he can use
> both languages; and he is truly a Welshman writing in English of men
> and matters which are wholly Welsh. As he says of himself, 'While using
> cheerfully enough the English language, I have never written in it a word
> about any country other than Wales or any people other than the Welsh
> people.' (*Glyn Jones*, 11)

As a young, belatedly modernist writer in the early 1930s, Glyn Jones
had been galvanised by his discovery in Dafydd ap Gwilym's writing
of a kind of Welsh proto-modernist style. This discovery was to prove
of long-lasting consequence for the development of his own aesthetic
as a writer. But while thus feeling the deepest creative affinity with
Dafydd, he also felt considerable guilt about such an association.
Dafydd had been an aristocrat serving a highly hierarchical society,
whereas Jones was a committed socialist; and whereas Dafydd's
language had been Welsh, that of Jones was English, the very language
that threatened to relegate Dafydd and his whole culture to oblivion.
His relation to Dafydd ap Gwilym was, therefore, in its tense ambivalence, opposite in character to that of Norris. The deep mixture of
his feelings is captured in his splendid poem, 'Henffych [Ave], Ddafydd',
which begins with a cautious indictment of him for failing to notice
'the taeog's [serf's] toiling'.[15] Ever an 'indifferent agitator', Dafydd
wilfully ignored 'Culture's brutal nourishing'.

But then the tone changes as the poet confesses how awe-struck,
not to say love-struck, he is by Dafydd's prowess:

> I first read your words dazzled,
> Heart's skin suddenly too small,
> Merthyr's hair shirt forgotten
> And that blade through my rib-cage.
> In ecstasy, despairing,
> A seablue road through Dyfed
> I walked, the wind's current bed. (75)

In Dafydd ap Gwilym, Glyn Jones recognises a

> spinther, maker, more,
> Rain-finery's fisherman,
> Netter of downpour's glitter.

'Spinther' is one of those glitteringly exotic words Jones (like his friend Dylan Thomas) so delighted in seizing, like a poetic magpie, to decorate his own textual nest. It is a term, so rare that it's not even included in the *Shorter Oxford English Dictionary*, from Gnostic writings, meaning a splinter, or spark, of divine light emanating from the Perfect Man and entering a human consciousness. In using it Jones not only brilliantly acknowledges Dafydd as the divine source of his own imaginative insights but also proves Dafydd's influence upon him by demonstrating the very same passion for the jewelled qualities of words that is a hallmark of Dafydd's own writing. And the sense of creative affinity between them was all the stronger for Jones's appreciation of the way in which the constant changes of register and virtuosic play with vocabulary in Dafydd's poetry suggested a multilingual world not far removed from the hybrid society he, too, had known from his Merthyr childhood, when his friends had included boys whose origins were variously Welsh, English, Irish, Maltese and Jewish. In such a setting, the ludic liquefactions of language were foregrounded. It was in these, Jones accurately detected, that Dafydd ap Gwilym had so incomparably revelled and it was these same linguistic features that he, too, was perfectly equipped (by his Merthyr background) to deploy in his translations of Dafydd's work. Hence the spirited opening of his translation of 'Le Jaloux': 'Daily I feel down, doleful,/ A girl calls my love-talk bull!' (*Collected Poems*, 53). And hence, too, his cheekily demotic rendering of the opening lines of that most celebrated of Dafydd's *cywyddau*, 'The Girls of Llanbadarn':

> I'm about in my doubles, mad, may the whole female
> Population of this parish have scabs.
> I'm wasting my time here, I have never managed
> To fix a date with a single girl yet.
> Not with a decent, easy-going lovely,
> Nor with a little toots, or even a housewife, or a hag.
>   (*Collected Poems*, 225)

Contrast this with Norris's altogether more constrained, and linguistically straitened, version:

> Plague take them, every female!
> With longing I'm bent double,
> Yet not one of them, not one,
> Is kind to my condition.
> Golden girl, wise wife, harsh witch,
> All reject my patronage. (159)

A like difference emerges if one places a passage from Glyn Jones's translation from 'The Seagull' (in which the bird becomes a love-messenger) next to Norris's version. This is the former:

> Girl-glorified you shall be, pandered to,
> Gaining that castle mass, her fortalice.
> Scout them out, seagull, those glowing battlements,
> Reconnoitre her, the Eigr-complexioned.
> Repeat my pleas, my citations, go
> Girlward, gull, where I ache to be chosen.
> She solus, pluck up courage, accost her,
> Stress your finesse to the fastidious one;
> Use honeyed diplomacy, hinting
> I cannot remain extant without her. (*Collected Poems*, 52)

And this Norris's attempt:

> Wide praise is for you and her;
> Circle that castle tower,
> Search till you see her, seagull,
> Bright as Eigr on that wall.
> Take all my pleading to her,
> Tell her my life I offer.
> Tell her, should she be alone –
> Gently with that gentle one –
> If she will not take me, I
> Losing her, must surely die. (158)

What seems to be restraining Norris here is that sense of poetic 'good taste' he began to absorb fatally early, when he was first exposed to the work of Wordsworth and others at his Cyfarthfa Castle School. And unlike Jones, he never reached out to alternative models, available not least in the Welsh-language poetic tradition, that might well have rendered his mature poetry less cautiously conventional, rhythmically monochrome and conversationally understated in the fashion of the English tradition of ruminative nature poetry than it was too often inclined to be. America might well have had a liberating effect on him – one thinks of A. R. Ammons's fine comment in 'Corsons Inlet':

> I see narrow orders, limited tightness, but will
> not run to that easy victory:
> still around the looser, wider forces work.[16]

But while his eventual exposure to the USA certainly helped loosen up his poetry a little, it came far too late in his career to affect his poetics of rather comfortable and predictable closure in any fundamental way.

Part of the reason for the relative conservatism of his tone and the caution of his poetic discourse might well have been his understandable reaction against a dangerous youthful addiction to Dylan Thomas's 'colour of saying'. He touches on this in what was, perhaps, his signature poem, 'More than Half Way There', clearly intended to confirm the emergence of his mature poetic. It reflects on the difference between his 'young voice [that] told/ Of swallows' ruby eyes between such trees/ As the cool moon allowed' and his present more temperate utterance. 'The common/ Blackbird sings and I accept this marvel', he quietly notes, while recognising that the protection of any 'true voice . . ./ Means constant vigilance': 'I am alert lest an old voice soften/ What needs to be said' (25). And a visit to Dylan Thomas's grave at Laugharne prompts him to a similar meditation on internal change, in a poem that on occasion deliberately echoes, in its dispassionate way, the impassioned rhetoric of Thomas himself:

> So I'll not denounce this death
> Nor embitter the ordinary air
> With blown words that my breath
> Is now too small to wear.

Having thus briefly paid his respects to the at-times blowsy poet of 'A Refusal to Mourn', Norris is then careful to inoculate himself against the infectious extravagance of such rhetoric by soberly noting how 'Smoothly the plain day ends' (180). The mature Norris believed, no doubt correctly, that his development into a credible poet had necessitated a move away from Dylan Thomas, but his translations from Dafydd ap Gwilym provided him with a safely distanced way of deploying a bolder poetic than his normally cautious self would allow. Those translations also leave one feeling his poetry might have benefited from more regular excursions in such directions. Within his limits, Norris was a fine, humane, attractive and accomplished poet. But, given his not inconsiderable gifts, he should, one reluctantly and sadly feels, have been capable of so much more.

(Published in *Literature and Belief*: 29 + 30.1 [Utah: Brigham Young University, 2009–10].)

Notes

[1] Leslie Norris, *Albert and the Angels* (New York: Farrar, Straus and Giroux, 2000).

[2] 'For many years I have been collecting such poems and am nearing the end when they will form one long poem written in sections, rather like Wordsworth's "spots" (his word) of time in "The Prelude" without the boring philosophical bits'. Leslie Norris, *Recollections* (Provo: Tryst Press, 2006), p. 77.

[3] 'When I was perhaps fifteen, I read Wordsworth's "There was a Boy" in my school anthology, I read it with the greatest satisfaction, and believed at once that the purpose of poetry was to preserve, perhaps even to reanimate, lives (in every sense) – which for the poet continued to live. The poem was not one which had been set for us to read, but this was an important development in my poetic theory and I suppose I still believe it' (*Recollections*, p. 19).

[4] 'Anglo-Welsh Manqué: On the Selected Poems of Bobi Jones', *Planet*, 76 (1989), 68.

[5] Anthony Conran, trans., *The Penguin Book of Welsh Verse* (Harmondsworth: Penguin Books, 1967), p. 72.

[6] Leslie Norris, *Collected Poems* (Bridgend: Seren, 1996), p. 252. All subsequent quotations will be from this volume, unless otherwise identified.

[7] Tony Conran, *Frontiers in Anglo-Welsh Poetry* (Cardiff: University of Wales Press, 1997), pp. 231–3.

[8] Translated as 'The Fate of the Language', in Alun R. Jones and Gwyn Thomas, *Presenting Saunders Lewis* (Cardiff: University of Wales Press, 1973), p. 127.

[9] Tony Conran, *Welsh Verse* (Bridgend: Seren, 2003).

10 Thomas Parry (ed.), *The Oxford Book of Welsh Verse* (London: Oxford University Press, 1962), p. 10.

11 Joseph P. Clancy, trans., *Medieval Welsh Poems* (Dublin: Four Courts Press, 2003), p. 88.

12 'Publisher's Note', Leslie Norris, *Translations* (Provo: Tryst Press, 2006). This volume also includes lecture notes by Norris about Dafydd ap Gwilym which, while interesting, are not without several basic inaccuracies.

13 Anyone interested in the very numerous English-language translations of Dafydd ap Gwilym, and in the wider subject of Welsh–English literary translation, can find a comprehensive listing in S. Rhian Reynolds (ed.), *A Bibliography of Welsh–English Literary Translation* (Cardiff: University of Wales Press, 2005).

14 Leslie Norris, *Glyn Jones* (Cardiff: University of Wales Press; Writers of Wales Series, 1973), p. 22.

15 Meic Stephens (ed.), *The Collected Poems of Glyn Jones* (Cardiff: University of Wales Press, 1996), p. 75.

16 'Corsons Inlet', in A. R. Ammons, *The Selected Poems: Expanded Edition* (New York: W. W. Norton, 1986), p. 46.

11

'STAYING TO MIND THINGS': GILLIAN CLARKE'S EARLY POETRY[1]

The account any poet chooses to offer of himself is always fascinating, and in our time all the more so, perhaps, when that self is a herself. In her poem 'Llŷr', Gillian Clarke traces her origins as a poet back to Stratford. There, in what elsewhere she has called one of Shakespeare's 'father–daughter plays',[2] she was 'taught the significance of little words'.[3] And what significance they turned out to have. With its tragic demonstrations of how dangerous it may be for woman, in a man's world, either to speak or to remain silent, and its painfully glorious demonstration of the way the English language may eloquently appropriate and distort indigenous Welsh materials, *King Lear* provided the ten-year-old Clarke with an 'object lesson' that was eventually to set her up for life. Almost fifty years later she was to find in writings such as Eavan Boland's remarkable *Object Lessons* powerful confirmation of central aspects of her own early history as a women poet. 'As I read the poems of the [Irish] tradition,' wrote Boland, 'it could often seem to me that I was entering a beautiful and perilous world filled with my own silence.'[4] But long before reading words such as these, Clarke had had to find ways of empowering herself to write; ways of granting herself permission to be a poet; ways of coming to understand that

> for me poetry is a rhythmic way of thinking, but it is a thought informed by the heart, informed by the body, informed by the whole self and the whole life lived, so that being a woman and being Welsh are inescapably expressed in the art of poetry.[5]

Absent from the poem 'Llŷr' is the aunt who, Clarke subsequently explained in an essay, had actually taken her ten-year-old niece on that fateful outing. Written out of the text, shouldered verbally aside by Shakespeare, Lear, Laughton and Olivier, that aunt now seems to stand for the female self that Clarke eventually discovered needed to be 'outed'. Thus identified, Auntie Phyllis (to give her her real name) may also conveniently stand for the need to relocate the sources of poetry in the traditional domain of the female. In a world where poetry is Shakespeare, and therefore male, Shakespeare's very language nevertheless runs 'like a nursery rhythm' in Gillian Clarke's head – the connecting of it with the traditionally 'female' preserve of the nursery (that crucial early nurturing space) pointedly redresses the gender balance.

In the magnificent concluding peroration of *A Room of One's Own*, Virginia Woolf urges women to realise that '[Shakespeare's dead sister] lives in you and in me, and in many other women who are not here tonight, for they are washing up the dishes and putting the children to bed'.[6] Gillian Clarke is making an analogous point when she takes Shakespeare back to his nursery, and to hers, describing her genesis as a poet in the process. As she has explained, her own love-affair with language began with nursery rhymes, playground games, biblical language and Welsh hymns (*HPW*, 124). And before ever she encountered Lear or Cordelia (and how intricately the one name there echoes and recasts the other), she had already identified with Branwen, the daughter of Lear's prototype, the Welsh king Llŷr. Moreover, in another example of breaking the male monopoly over the creative imagination, Clarke recalls how, on first hearing the phrase 'The isle is full of noises' spoken in a stage production of *The Tempest*, she recognised it as arising from, and applying to, her own wartime experience as a child:

> My father's radio was the voice of the radio-teller. Later, when I was ten, I was to hear Shakespeare's words, and would at once know they were describing the 'sounds and sweet airs' of Fforest. It was not difficult to imagine my grandmother's farm as an isle full of noises, cut off by the sea, poor roads, weather and the family from bombs, sirens, and air raids, though not from the rumours of war. Life into language equals fiction. (*HPW*, 124)

Her grandmother's farm thus becomes the setting for *The Tempest*, with Clarke implicitly acting Prospero on her 'island'. In admitting that she has been writing such '"fiction"[. . .] all my life', Clarke is of course tacitly admitting that she has always been a poet. But hers was a gradual and phased awakening to that fact, since her society neglected to offer her the means to authentic self-recognition. Poetry seemed largely the preserve of the male, and such was the manifest authority of the great masters whose work she studied while reading English at University College, Cardiff, that Clarke was into her thirties before she found the confidence to publish her work.

True, she had kept a diary since she was fifteen, a form of writing that was well suited to her early life as young wife and as mother to three children whose needs monopolised her attention. But then in 1970–1 she stumbled upon a new identity, and with it she entered upon a new existence, almost unawares:

> I threw my first poems in the bin because I was unaware they were poems. I suppose it was because I hadn't read anything in print that was like what I was writing. I think we all need models, and I was both Welsh and a woman. The world wasn't very interested in either. Have you noticed how late in their careers women get published? Both Ruth Bidgood and Jean Earle, whose work I like, were published late in their lives. I read *Poetry Wales*, and I saw things there that spoke to half of me, the Welsh part. It would never have occurred to me to send work to London. My former husband posted some poems off to *Poetry Wales* because I had said 'I could write as well as this.' Meic Stephens, the editor at that time, wrote back accepting them.[7]

This simple statement is dense with quiet details that turn it into the most poignant of parables about the developing of Welsh women's writing. Poetry's failure to recognise itself, in the absence of any objective confirmation of its status; a woman's dependence on men for identity and opportunity; these and other features of the case make it troublingly exemplary.

Joseph Conrad has a striking remark by Novalis as epigraph to *Lord Jim*: 'It is certain any conviction gains infinitely the moment another soul will believe in it.' *Poetry Wales*, a magazine founded by Meic Stephens in 1965, partly to allow English-language poets to contribute to the revitalised nationalist culture of the period, helped provide Welsh poets with self-belief and thus sponsored an important new generation of Welsh writers. It so happens that the author of the first poem in the first issue was Alison Bielski, and such writers as

Ruth Bidgood and Sally Roberts (Jones) (the only woman featured in Bryn Griffiths's important 1967 anthology *Welsh Voices*) also figured prominently in the early numbers, but the contributors were preponderantly male, consistent with the gender profile of the literary culture of the period. Beginning with Gillian Clarke's significant appearance in 1970, however, a change began to occur. And just as it is appropriate that Meic Stephens, the mover and shaker of the poetry scene in Wales during the later 1960s, should (with Sam Adams) have acted as male midwife to this new development, so is it appropriate that Roland Mathias, a major influence on the ideological restructuring of Anglo-Welsh literature in the post-war period, should have so readily and rapidly provided Gillian Clarke (first as contributor and then as editor) with the opportunity of redesigning *The Anglo-Welsh Review*. Jeremy Hooker, a poet and critic himself at that time emerging as an important new talent on the Anglo-Welsh scene, was another who was quick to recognise Clarke's potential. And in choosing four of her poems for his *Poems '71* volume he set a pattern to be followed for several years by his successors as selectors of the best poems to have appeared in Wales.

By (presumably) a coincidence, the first poem Gillian Clarke ever published in *Poetry Wales* was about the coming alive of a dead self.[8] 'Beech Buds' likens the experience to the putting of dry, bare twigs in water:

> From the hard,
> Brittle wood came tenderness and life, numerous
> Damp, green butterflies, transparently veined,
> Opening like a tree that is alive.

It also so happens that, with its naively unguarded exclamations ('I feel so happy'), its conspicuous evidence of delicate sensibility, and its implicit representation of the female self as dependent on male sustenance, the poem could have been read by males as reassuringly, stereotypically 'feminine'. A similar reassurance seems to radiate from 'Nightride' and 'Sailing', with their emphasis respectively on warmly protective and anxious maternal care.

In its immediate difference, though, a fourth poem from that very first set, 'The Fox', not only suggests a much more edgy and self-troubled sensibility than may previously have been apparent but also has the power to persuade us to reread those other poems with an altogether less complacent eye. It is the kind and the quality of the sensuous writing in these poems that now comes into startling focus. A child's head is seen as 'nodding on its stalk' in 'Nightride'; in 'Beech Buds' twigs dipped in water produce 'bubbles/ Of silver against the light'; and in 'The Fox', a hill is set 'flying free and horizontal from the plane of symmetry'. In such lines the senses are as it were given their head; that is, they are granted a mind, an intelligence, and with it a life, of their own. They set us free to feel how we come to both ripeness and vulnerability in our small children; how the very air we breathe may have aesthetic as well as functional qualities; how a transgressive wildness may be inhering in the most solidly familiar mass and matter.

Yet, as early as these first published poems, Clarke ironically lays herself open to the charge of deriving her poetry from influential male models. So, in its fascination with the violent convergence of life and death as expressed through the configuration of ewes giving bloody birth, little silver skulls smeared with gore, a fox hanging red and dead from a tree, Gillian Clarke seems to be trespassing on the Gothic pastoral territory of Ted Hughes. But although at this early stage Clarke's personal touch is by no means sure ('the lambs/ Leapt away round the hill'), there is nevertheless already a sense not of mere imitation but of a conversation between poets that is also a conversation between genders. 'The Fox' is a poem not only by a woman but also about the contradictions of female 'nature'. The ewe and her lambs is contrasted not with the predatory male 'fox' (of the deliberately misleading title) but with the vixen, in whose violent death may be seen the full ambivalence of her nature – her warm flaming beauty, her role as provider of both milk *and* raw meat for her young, her dual aspect of killer and victim. Similarly, in another poem, 'Birth', the Hughes-like registering of the sticky, messy physicality of the process of calving ('Hot and slippery, the scalding/ Baby came') is offset by a human mother's empathy with the cow. This is registered both through the sensual recall of the erotic physiology of the newly maternalised body ('I could feel the soft sucking/ Of the new-born, the tugging pleasure/ Of bruised reordering, the signal/ Of milk's incoming tide') and through the diffusion of the birthing experience throughout the landscape ('The light flowed out leaving stars/ And clarity'). The latter involves a strategy of refiguring the body as world, a strategy which has traditionally been central to male love poetry but which has drawn upon uniquely female experience only in recent decades.

That Hughes was a very important presence in the mind of the
young Gillian Clarke is not, of course, to be disputed. So, too, undoubtedly was Seamus Heaney, whose significance for her – again so
frequently diminished and distorted in easy prattle about 'influence'
– she has subtly explained:

> A poet like Seamus Heaney has a tremendously feminine sensibility,
> and because Seamus Heaney is such an extremely good poet, he admitted
> possibilities that weren't there before, which women are now exploring.
> To put it another way, more women began to be published, which enabled
> us to see a poet like Seamus Heaney. I wonder whether he would have
> been so well received by an earlier generation, when feminine values
> were less noticed and admired. (*UI*, 28–9)

It is the mutuality of the indebtedness that is fruitfully insisted upon
here, and indeed Clarke demonstrates exactly what she means in the
accomplished early poem 'Lunchtime Lecture', clearly an interesting
variant on Heaney's celebrated Bog Queen poems. (Although it is
interesting to note that an English translation of 'Geneth Ifanc'
['Young Girl'], Waldo Williams's familiar Welsh-language poem
about the feelings of kinship awakened in him by the 'stone skeleton'
from the Iron Age, was printed directly following Clarke's first poems
in *Poetry Wales*.) The moment of her encounter with the skeleton of
a young female from the second or third millennium BC at once
reproduces, in an entirely different key and setting, Heaney's mental
exhumation of a long-buried life, and claims a kind of priority over
it, since there is between Clarke and her subject an intuitive understanding, based on shared gender experience, to which he can lay no
claim: 'She's a tree in winter, . . ./ I, at some other season, . . ./ We
stare at each other, dark into sightless/ Dark'.[9] It is as if Clarke had
been admitted by Heaney into a world of experience which was already
hers by right, and which her sex had in the first instance made available
to her.

In fact, the supportive presence of pioneering women writers is as
palpable in Clarke's early texts as is the influence of her prominent
male contemporaries. Sylvia Plath's 'Morning Song', the opening
poem in *Ariel* (1965),[10] seems in some way to foreshadow, and in a
sense to make possible, the poem 'Baby Sitting', with which Clarke's
first collection *Snow on the Mountain* (1971) opens. Except, of course,
that Plath's distinguishing note of raw self-exposure is missing from

Clarke's altogether more gentle and composed poem of self-knowledge. That difference seems to determine, as much as to be determined by, their respective choice of subject, with Plath owning up to her resentful attachments to her selfishly demanding brat of a baby that seems like a mere monstrous automaton of need, and Clarke, markedly less daring, reflecting guiltily on her cold, nervous imperviousness to the blind demands of a baby that is not her own. But elsewhere in *Snow on the Mountain* she, too, probes as deep as the vein of anger and resentment that can run through maternal love. In 'Catrin', she explores, in her perhaps too conciliatory way, the struggle for separateness that locks mother and teenage daughter into a newly intense relationship.

Relationships are, in fact, at the heart (in every sense) of Clarke's early poetry. Indeed, in three of the quartet of poems she originally published in *Poetry Wales* she defines herself in terms of her relationship with somebody else. Moreover, her coming into new being, as described in 'Beech Buds', is imaged as issuing directly from an immersion of self in another's 'brightness'. Such a generously joyous image of powerless indebtedness seems strikingly un-masculine, and seems, further, to anticipate that sense of female selfhood, and that view of female writing, that Gillian Clarke was later to expound in her prose. 'Men', she wrote in an important essay in the Bloodaxe catalogue,

> often observe themselves in poems. They cast themselves into roles. It is called 'being objective'. Craig Raine sees himself as Shakespeare in one poem. Seamus Heaney sees himself as Wordsworth. Less famously, men see themselves as fathers, sons, lovers, and their poems are often written from that objective, observed viewpoint.

By contrast, she goes on to argue,

> Women often move halfway into a role, the transition incomplete and felt rather than seen . . . Is it that women spend their lives in uncertainty, never quite the hunter-gatherer or the Madonna-mistress? Certainly they show a markedly greater interest in the detail and subtlety of relationships.[11]

The quartet of poems in *Poetry Wales* that signalled Gillian Clarke's arrival on the scene did not for some reason include 'The Sundial', the poem (her first for many years) that really marked the genesis of

her poetry, and which she later selected to be the title-poem of her
second (though first substantial) collection of poems. Recording a
day spent caring for her sick youngest child, this 'relationship' poem
typifies several important aspects of Clarke's early poetry.

It is a domestic piece, thus adumbrating one of the basic tenets of
that female (as opposed to feminist) poetics that Clarke began shortly
later to construct, in piecemeal fashion, through her occasional writings.
In an *Anglo-Welsh Review* editorial published in 1979 she argued that

> the likeliest subjects of female writing [are] the domestic and familiar,
> and the way of looking at relationships, places, objects, and society that
> is inclined to be minutely perceptive and detailed. It is an under-valued
> perception and 'domestic' and 'familiar' are too frequently taken to be
> derogatory words. The 'domus' is one of our society's most unheard
> messages, powerhouse as that place is for every emerging adult.[12]

Elsewhere she has retrospectively dubbed these early poems 'in-
doorscapes', indicating they were 'artlessly, instinctively written, and
that mood ended with publication'.[13] She has also drawn attention to
their 'presentness', that is their preoccupation with the pressing, though
passing, concerns of the invariably crowded domestic moment, a
feature particularly evident in a poem that starts, as does 'The Sundial',
'Owain was ill today' (*S*, 11), and a characteristic that may betray the
continuity between these early attempts at poetry and her already
well-established practice of keeping a diary of the day's events.

A less immediately evident, but ultimately perhaps more significant,
aspect of the poem is its manner of investigating the workings of the
imagination. The feverish boy has been delirious during the night,
'shouting of lions/ In the sleepless heat'. Now, still 'slightly/ Trembling
with fever', he patiently fashions a sundial out of paper, a stick and
some stones, in order to calculate 'the mathematics of sunshine'. His
mother is struck by his new-found, silent, adult-like concentration:

> he found
> Deliberation, and the slow finger
> Of light, quieter than night lions. (*S*, 11)

That aspect of the poem – its focusing on a moment when the boy
begins to probe for hidden patterns of energy and to trace invisible
rhythms of light – becomes much more apparent when it is read in

the context of the other poems in *Snow on the Mountain*, the little booklet of poems by Clarke that was published as Number Five of the *Triskel Poets* series in 1971.

The title-poem of that collection is itself full of what, on the analogy of 'The Sundial', one might call 'the mathematics of snow'. In other words, it shows how new angles on reality emerge as one struggles to find one's bearings in a world rendered strange, blankly elemental, and apparently featureless by snow. So the family, out to clamber up the snow-covered heights of the hills around Machen, fixes its attention on a bird:

> A crow cut a clean line
> Across the hill, which we grasped as a rope
> To pull us up the pale diagonal.[14]

This heightened attention to, and trust in, the draughtsmanship and texture of the visible is deeply characteristic of a poet one of whose greatest loves is the visual arts. And such a passion for form and colour is everywhere evident in her work – so in the wake of a vixen's death all the reds in a day that had begun 'warm with colour' grow cold, and, elsewhere, a cow standing up creates the chiaroscuro effect of 'cool/ Flanks, like white flowers in the dark' (*SM*, 22). But it is not only that Clarke is a painterly poet; she is also a poet for whom language itself is a thickly sensuous medium, a medium to the enchantment of which one needs almost languorously to submit, so that it can then be intuitively worked, as a painter works paint, until unexpected forms of meaning seem miraculously to appear. As she has explained, 'After pen and paper, the beauty of the empty cleanness, there is energy. It sets me thinking. I try the paper to see what the words will do. It must be like drawing . . . try the line, see what happens.'[15] The echo of Paul Klee's celebrated description of drawing as taking a line for a walk is unmistakeable here.

The new discoveries that come only through the suspension of conventional rational intelligence and its spuriously authoritative categories of description have been a constant preoccupation of Clarke's over the years. She has, for instance, confessed her attraction to

> the new nature poems [which] are scientific rather than lyrical, concerned but not romantic. They aim to match the precision of metaphor and

word-patterns to the clarity of the fact. They relish the patterning of
things, the connections between the worlds of nature and ideas. (*OSL*,
292)

The analogy with her own work is evident, except that her means of
achieving the same ends are somewhat different. She has always on
the one hand been drawn to mythopoeic descriptions, whose devastating power to re-form reality she has repeatedly distinguished from
arbitrary fantasy (her son's night-lions) while on the other being
attracted to rhythms and patterns (of both sound and perception)
that involve profound realignments of reason.

So 'Community', the concluding poem in *Snow on the Mountain*,
appropriately speaks of how, in company,

> one can stand aside and watch
> The spatial movement, understanding
> Edge forward, falter and change
> Form. *(SM*, 30)

Elsewhere in the collection, too, deepening understanding is troped
in terms of forms described in space. 'Lines' centres on the way a
scene, and with it the day, is intersected diagonally by the wavering
edge of a washing line, which comes to represent 'That wound of the
divided/ Mind' (*SM*, 20). 'Waterfall' is about following the path that

> led me under the fall to feel
> The arc of the river and the mountain's exact
> Weight; the roar of rain and lapwings
> Leaving: water-beat, heart-fall in accord. (*SM*, 14)

And already embryonically apparent in these early poems is 'that
sense of moving from one image to another as if searching, as if not
fully committed to a role, the metaphor not seen but felt' (*H-g*, 20).
So memories of giving birth register as a feeling of 'satisfaction/
Fall[ing] like a clean sheet around me' (*SM*, 22), and the head of a
dead curlew chick 'Loll[s] from the snapped stem of its neck/ Like the
hung clock of a dandelion/ Wasting its seed' (*SM*, 24).

Remarks such as the above about images and metaphors are really
fragments of Gillian Clarke's female poetics, a poetics, grounded in
her developing understanding of female experience, upon which she

has been unsystematically at work, virtually since she began to publish her poems. So, for instance, her own early awareness of having constantly to shift roles from wife to mother to housewife to teacher to editor to poet underlies her emphasis on the provisional, exploratory and tentative nature of the stances and images women tend fluidly to produce in their writings: such, she suggests, is also the magically unpredictable and unstable world which the Mabinogion conjures up for us. This has further led her to reflect on the subversively shifting sense of perspective and scale that a woman's constantly changing role, or theatre of operations, entails. For Clarke, therefore, a woman is naturally possessed of a power to tilt the world off its familiar axis, that convulsive power of the artistic imagination that has traditionally been figured through stories of giants like Bendigeidfran. Similarly, her association of poetry with energies and rhythms of intuition that are anterior to consciousness relates in part to her theory of female psychological development:

> The girl-child often has an early advantage in language-skills, is likely to talk earlier, to learn to read sooner than a boy and to prefer imaginative literature. Words store memory, 'Nothing is until it has a word' ('Llŷr' 1982). Women oftener record memories of babyhood than men and thus draw more deeply on the first physical, animal sensations of infancy, where body and mind are single, fact and imagination indivisible. It is not clear that men never share this characteristic, as Heaney proves, but that it is rarer in men, and might even be said to be commonplace in women. (*OSL*, 288)

The ascertainable truth of this statement probably matters less than its capacity, as belief or modern myth, to enable or to empower women to write. Indeed, Clarke's own writing, at first womanly only in fairly superficial though significant ways, could be said to have been deepened and enriched through that continuing exploration of female identity she has undertaken primarily in her poetry and secondarily in her complementary prose.

That awakening to herself as poet, which entailed new explorations of herself as woman, seems further to have involved, in Gillian Clarke's case, the beginning of a process of personal reintegration which was grounded, so to speak, at Blaen Cwrt, the dilapidated farm cottage in rural west Wales that came into her possession in the early 1970s. Indeed, the importance of this location is perceptively noted by Sam

Adams in his Introduction to *Snow on the Mountain*, a document that is a valuable record of how Clarke's emergence as a poet was at that time viewed by an individual closely connected with it and with her:

> The revival of her creative interest in poetry coincided with the finding of a cottage in Cardiganshire where the family now spend as much time as possible. Many of her poems are about this quieter world, far removed from the suburbia of Cardiff, much more closely associated with the rhythms of the seasons. Here she observes the constantly changing patterns of nature, the integration of rural landscape, bird and beast. All this she records with superb delicacy and tact, finding in her experience of motherhood analogies for the fertility of the natural world and the pangs of birth and separation. She takes as her main themes areas of life infrequently explored in poetry and very rarely indeed illuminated with such honesty and insight – the interplay of relationships within the family, and the family observed against the background of nature.

Only later, with the publication not only of *The King of Britain's Daughter* but also of two important essays associated with the writing of that volume's title sequence, did it become possible to understand fully what that part of Ceredigion in which Blaen Cwrt is situated actually means to Gillian Clarke.[16] For her it represents her idyllic childhood retreat, that spot of time (to adopt, and adapt Wordsworth's celebrated phrase) where her artistic sensibility was nurtured, where she grew unawares into a writer, where the tensions between her parents (symbolised, as she has put it, by their quarrels over the Welsh language) could be magically suspended, where she felt snugly secluded and yet (thanks to her radio-engineer father) tuned in to the wavelength of the whole wide world, where the landscape was haunted and sculpted by giant imagination, and where she felt as ladied by her grandmother and nature as the boy Dylan Thomas had felt lorded at Fern Hill. Although her actual home, both as a child and later as a wife and mother, was in Cardiff, she was most really and truly at home in west Wales. As she has written,

> The fact that literature, from nursery rhyme and fairy story onwards, was so closely associated with the natural world, has played a strong part in making me a country person, not an urban one, even during the long years of my life spent in the city. Literature hallowed the natural with the supernatural. It made the stones sing. It populated the

countryside with animals, seen and unseen. It made natural phenomena reverberate with mythological meaning, turned a rocking stone to a giant's apple, a rock pool to a footprint. (*OSL*, 280)

It would be wrong to bring all these insights with which Clarke provided us in the nineties to bear uncritically on her poetry of the 1970s – wrong not least because as she has made clear it is only by painful degrees that she herself came to understand her childhood, and its locations, in these terms. Nevertheless, to read her early poem 'Blaen Cwrt' with a judicious degree of hindsight is not only to appreciate anew the terms in which it consciously celebrates a re-discovered community with place, and a place with its own unique community, it is also to sense for the first time the unconscious feelings working like yeast and helping the phrases swell to such a rich fullness of meaning.

'Blaen Cwrt', too, is a 'relationship' poem, beginning as it does by addressing an interlocutor: 'You ask how it is. I will tell you' (*SM*, 10). And this is appropriate since the poem as a whole is about 'relating', is indeed about a place that in an important sense really exists only in Clarke's relating to it, which in turn is inscribed in her relating of it. Equally, it exists only as a place held in common – the stress throughout is on the first person plural, the language is one of encounter with environment ('Holding a thick root/ I press my bucket through the surface/ Of the water'), the similes are social connectives ('Our fingers curl on/ Enamel mugs of tea, like ploughmen'), the syntax is a homogenising device ('All is ochre and earth and cloud-green/ Nettles'), and everywhere there is the semiotics of coexistence ('Some of the smoke/ Rises against the ploughed, brown field/ As a sign to our neighbours in the/ Four folds of the valley that we are in'). Integration of the self, and simultaneous integration into a community of people and nature, are the poem's implicit themes, made explicit in the concluding lines:

> It has all the first
> Necessities for a high standard
> Of civilised living: silence inside
> A circle of sound, water and fire,
> Light on uncountable miles of mountain

> From a big, unpredictable sky,
> Two rooms, waking and sleeping,
> Two languages, two centuries of past
> To ponder on, and the basic need
> To work hard in order to survive. (*SM*, 10)

Dealing, as it so obviously does, with the theme of 'belonging' – a central topos of the 1960s, almost obsessively figured throughout that decade as a search for 'roots' – 'Blaen Cwrt' is in danger of appearing to be a dated product of its time. That it can still nevertheless command attention through the power and the measured dignity of its speech may be due partly to those unconscious feelings that, as Clarke later enabled us to see, were secretly animating her attachment to the cottage. For instance, the way these concluding lines seek to contain and pacify instability ('a big, unpredictable sky'), and their resemblance to an epithalamium – a celebration of the marriage between Wales's two cultures – acquires a poignancy when read in the light of the tensions in Clarke's early family background.

Moreover, the poem is very much a portrait of that artist Clarke had, at the time of writing, newly come to realise she was. Her visual acuity, her painterly eye for colour and texture, are abundantly evident throughout ('The stones clear in the rain/ Giving their colours. It's not easy/ There are no brochure blues or boiled sweet/ Reds'). The point, as in several of Wordsworth's greatest poems, is that only to the patiently loving attention of one who is inward with it does this scene 'give' its colour and reveal itself as beautiful. And again like the Wordsworth of 'Michael', Clarke insists that only to those who know it well will this place entrust its history:

> The wattle and daub
> Chimney hood has decayed away, slowly
> Creeping to dust, chalking the slate
> Floor with stories.

Moreover, by so clearly emphasising at the outset her intention to 'tell' her reader/ listener not about Blaen Cwrt but literally 'how it is' Clarke is demonstrating the power of language and the authority to be a poet that is vested in her by this place. In this respect, the poem is her signature text because (in spite of my references to Wordsworth) the kind of sensuous immersion in, and receptive submission to, the ancient peculiarities of a landscape that is registered in 'Blaen Cwrt' is associated in Gillian Clarke's mind with a 'feminine' sensibility. Thus the poem may be read as a celebration of a feminised – and indeed feminising – landscape, centring on the implicit demonstration that Clarke's way of moving in and setting up home is not the male's way of taking possession of a property. Rather, she tentatively feels her way, adapting herself gently to what's there, taking new shape from it, just as

> Some of the smoke seeps through the stones
> Into the barn where it curls like fern
> On the walls.

When Gillian Clarke moved permanently to Blaen Cwrt in 1984 it marked a new phase in her life as a woman and as a writer. Her children were now grown up and she was free to accept a Welsh Arts Council sponsored writer's residency at St David's University College, Lampeter. She described this as 'a change of life . . . without fracture or disruption. It seems to me that I have turned to face the already known, to know it more profoundly.'[17] But as she also wryly noted:

> In 1978 I wrote a long poem ('Letter from a far country') about a woman who, in the spirit of feminist rebellion, threatens to leave home and family, although in the end, seduced by memory, tradition and the ties of family life, she stays. However, as one friend remarked, on hearing of my present adventure, 'So the prophecy of "Letter" is fulfilled.'

Until the early 1980s, however, Clarke continued to be circumstanced in those ways upon which she so expressively reflects in 'Letter from a far country'.

Broadcast as a half-hour radio poem in 1978 but not published until 1982, that work is now accepted as a landmark text in Welsh writing in English. And, most notably in her preface to the selection of her work published in *Six Women Poets*, Clarke herself has written informatively about the poem. She has explained that it was composed 'easily in between 10 and 15 hours spread over five late-night sessions when my sons' drums and guitars had fallen silent for the night', and has noted that the poem is both a celebration of life's good things – clean sheets, the smell of baking, orderliness – with which my mother and grandmother surrounded me [– and] a small contribution towards feminist protest, a meditation on traditional woman's work written in the form of an imaginary letter, the sort of letter you write in your mind and never post.

That letter, she adds, 'is a letter from a fictitious woman to all men. The "far country" is childhood, womanhood, Wales, the beautiful country where the warriors, kings and presidents don't live, the private place where we all grow up.' More pointedly, she reveals that the poem arose out of a feeling of anger and frustration at the way

the earth – birth, death, caring, nurturing, teaching, nursing, home-making, were in women's hands, while the world – public life, money, government, organisation, judgement, war, were in the hands of men. This would, perhaps, suit us well enough, if only both kinds of work were equally valued, but we all know they are not.[18]

In those phrases from 'Blaen Cwrt' that deliberately override the difference between men's and women's work ('Our fingers curl on/ Enamel mugs of tea, like ploughmen') linger, perhaps, memories of early sex discrimination such as those registered in 'Letter':

To be out with the men, at work,
I had longed to carry their tea,
for the feminine privilege,
for the male right to the field.
Even that small task made me bleed. (*LFC*, 12–13)

And just as, later in the poem, women's bleeding becomes both a painful monthly fact and a metaphor for the equivocal biological and cultural terms on which woman is granted her unique powers of creativity, so 'Letter from a far country' proceeds by recuperating aspects of female experience that males have traditionally stigmatised, and by reconceiving forms of living and writing that had previously borne the imprint only of the male imagination. Such regenerations of form are also, of course, re-genderings of form. Indeed, not only does the poem force a redefinition of the 'long poem' as a genre, revealing the inherently gendered and contingent character of its supposedly intrinsic kinds of subject-matter and structure, it is also written in a flexible, and therefore unemphatic, three-stress line that seems pointedly to stop short of the full fig of the masculine iambic pentameter.

It is also important to remember that 'Letter from a far country' was commissioned for broadcast on radio, and that it therefore belongs to the 'genre' so famously and definitively represented in Wales by *Under Milk Wood*. The very rhythm of that work's celebrated opening – 'It is spring, moonless night in the small town, starless and bible-black'[19] – seems echoed in Clarke's:

> They have gone. The silence resettles
> slowly as dust on the sunlit
> surfaces of the furniture. (*LFC*, 7)

Echo, indeed, seems the operative word when writing about 'Letter'. If *Under Milk Wood* is a 'Play for Voices', then Clarke's work is a Poem for Echoes. Not only is her poem about the resonances between past and present, it repeatedly figures the imagination itself as an echo-chamber and it turns words into echoes of each other, in lines like 'the ruined warehouse where the owls stare' (*LFC*, 9). 'Listen!', she writes, again adopting one of Dylan Thomas's favourite rhetorical strategies, 'to the starlings glistening on a March morning!' (*LFC*, 10). Yes, both Thomas and Clarke are inspired users of 'alliteration and assonance', if we must trundle out those tired terms, but the significance of the fact lies in the radically different ways in which these devices speak the mind of these two poets so decisively divided by temperament and gender. And what is really at issue is their fundamentally opposed ways of conceiving of language.

'The poet is the father of his poem, its mother is a language; one could list poems as race horses are listed – *out of L by P*,' wrote W. H. Auden, demonstrating how easily a male author betrays his gender when writing about writing.[20] But elsewhere in his essays Auden more usefully distinguishes between a poet who 'thinks of the poem he is writing as something already latent in the language which he has to reveal', and one who 'thinks of language as a plastic passive medium upon which he imposes his artistic conception' (*SE*, 134). Absolute though such a distinction undoubtedly is – and applicable though Auden would have it be only to 'formal' and 'free verse' poets respectively – it does help us understand Clarke's obstetric relationship to language in 'Letter from a far country', a relationship that is, of course, inseparable from her encouraging receptivity to the past, as that is present alike in place and in woman's ambiguously 'given' place. It is evident that, as she confessed elsewhere, 'I love to find clues in language and stories to show old complexities.'[21]

For Gillian Clarke, 'Letter from a far country' was in many respects a threshold poem; it marked a liminal stage in her life both as woman and as writer. On the other hand, *The Sundial* – her first substantial collection of poems, published after the writing but before the publication of 'Letter' – is more of a summation of her work to that date, and a retrospective exhibition of her achievements. The volume's title is well-chosen; language throughout the book struggles to track heat and light, to catch in its sounds and cadences 'the savage roar of the trapped sun/ Seeding the earth against the stop of winter' (*S*, 27). And in the concluding poems in *The Sundial* death is repeatedly viewed in this light, as in the visionary, not to say apocalyptic, last verse of 'Harvest at Mynachlog':

> We are quiet again, holding our cups
> In turn for the tilting milk, sad, hearing
> The sun roar like a rush of grain
> Engulfing all winged things that live
> One moment in the eclipsing light. (*S*, 50)

Reading some of these poems is sometimes like stepping into one of the light-storms of a painting by Turner or being caught in the energy field of one of Van Gogh's quivering canvases. Not that Clarke's imagery is all of light; she is attracted equally to the headlong liquefactions of water, seeing the river in her poem 'At Ystrad Fflur', 'ra[cing] for the south too full/ of summer rain for safety' (*S*, 22). The provenance of such writing is mixed, connecting back as it does with Romantic vitalism (in both its nineteenth-century and twentieth-century modernist forms), the hyperbolic Welsh praise tradition, and the feminist poetics of fecundity. Other aspects of that poetics are apparent when Gillian Clarke beautifully notices at Ystrad Fflur 'a river blossoming on stone'. The phrase both conveys a sense of female in relation to male (with a sidelong glance at Moses?) and suggests hard matter's hidden other self – the secret sap which runs through the veins of rock. And in this last respect it connects with the language and imagery of concavity that recurs in *The Sundial*, the caves and skulls and shells that turn some of her poems into verbal equivalents

of paintings by Georgia O'Keefe, to whose work she was later to
address a poem. Several of the poems in *The Sundial* carry the signs (and stigmata)
of female consciousness as characterised by Clarke in her prose
writings. In her essay 'The King of Britain's Daughter' she later recalled
how 'as a child I used to play a game which I called "big and little"'
(*HPW*, 123). In other words she saw how a stone could become a
planet and the setting sun a pebble about to drop. Grown up, she was
to realise that much of woman's life involved such abrupt changes in
scale, a constant movement between interior and exterior, domestic
and public, family and world. No better example of the habit of
imagination thus inculcated could be found than her perception, in
'Two Points of View', of the resting red combine harvester (that macho
machine) as standing 'still and powerful/ As a ladybird resting between
flight' (*S*, 46), or of her Blakean vision (yes, men can see this way too,
as she would readily admit) of the curlew:

> She dips her bill in the rim of the sea.
> Her beak is the ellipse
> of a world much smaller
> than that far section of the sea's
> circumference. (*S*, 36)

Another of the qualities of her female vision is apparent in 'In Pisgah
Graveyard', where 'The warmth tumbles here like a giant sun/ Flower
dying and full of glossy seed' (*S*, 27). There, not unlike Virginia Woolf,
she demonstrates such a sensitivity to atmosphere (of places or relationships) that it is as if she possessed the poetic equivalent of a psychic's
gift for perceiving 'aura' or as if she could feel the amniotic fluid of
life.

'In Pisgah Graveyard' is in part an elegy for Dewi Emrys, that most
maverick of Welsh-language poets of the twentieth century. There,
next to a 'poet's grave that tidies his wild life', she feels a deep affinity
with one whose passion for language was so unbridled:

> This roughest stone of all, a sand-stone pod
> Bursting with words, is Dewi Emrys's grave.
> And all around the living corn concedes
> Fecundity to him. (*S*, 27)

In these images, so suggestively bisexual in nature, can be sensed a generous acknowledgement of indebtedness to, and kinship with, the male poets of Wales's past. This bond, which is also a double bind, closely resembles those feelings towards the male writers of Ireland that Eavan Boland so carefully and caringly expresses in *Object Lessons*:

> As I read the poems of the tradition, it could often seem to me that I was entering a beautiful and perilous world filled with my own silence. As I struggled to become my own subject – in poems I could hardly write and in a literary tradition which blurred the feminine and the national – these poems were enabling and illuminating. As a woman I felt some mute and anxious kinship with those erotic subjects which were appropriated; as a poet I felt confirmed by the very powers of expression which appropriated them. (*OL*, 237–8)

Several poems in *The Sundial* implicitly explore Clarke's place in the male-voice chorus of Welsh poetry. In 'Dyddgu Replies to Dafydd' she enables the mute object of the praise of Wales's greatest poet to become a speaking subject, and she thus empowers a woman to speak her own differently erotic love poem, to yearn for

> when the wind whitens the tender
> underbelly of the March grass
> thick as pillows under the oaks. (*S*, 21)

And in the companion poem 'At Ystrad Fflur', Gillian Clarke quietly claims, in the name of her female self, not only the place where Dafydd ap Gwilym is buried but also the traditions of praise poetry and *canu bro* which had previously been virtually a Welsh male preserve. In her poem the landscape becomes vividly female in body, culminating in a sensation of how

> desire runs
> Like sparks in stubble through the memory
> of the place, and a yellow mustard field
> is a sheet of flame in the heart. (*S*, 23)

It is almost as if it has taken a woman to recognise, and in that sense fully to awaken, the riotous 'desire' that is pent-up in this location, that latent passion which is the true legacy of Dafydd ap Gwilym and which is the hidden blazon of puritanically and politically oppressed Wales.

Of course, Gillian Clarke's poetry in *The Sundial* is not always so startlingly and convincingly vivid. Her poetics of deliquescence and of liquefaction, her extravagantly sensuous language, and the ringing diapason of her affirmations can sometimes seem altogether too lush and luscious. And she herself put her finger on the dangers and difficulties inherent in her early practice in an uncharacteristically impatient review of *Conundrums*, Jan Morris's book about changing sex. While emphasising (perhaps too uncritically for her own good as a poet) that 'to be female is to live a woman's life, an essentially seasonal, physical, body-conscious life from an early age', she also properly objects to Morris's sentimental view of the female nature: 'I must insist that we come good, bad and indifferent, placid or passionate, gentle or fierce, as men do.'[22] What one sometimes feels the want of in *The Sundial* is precisely such a full mediation, through the medium of poetry, of women's complex fate, her incorrigibly human, as well as gendered, nature.

Nevertheless, the abiding impression left from reading Gillian Clarke's early poetry is one of exhilaration at the headlong, head (and body) strong energy of its innovativeness. She was to go on, of course, to a new phase which also amounted in her case to a new life, and in the process she not only consolidated her talent but also developed and extended it. But there can still be felt in her early writing all the unrepeatable vigour of the adventure and excitement of self-discovery. It was then that self-awakening was achieved by 'shak[ing] words awake', and that poetry first became for her 'an unconscious act of revelation'.[23] And behind that whole process lay the determination, as she put it in 'Letter from a far country', to be – both as woman and as poet, but in such very different senses – the girl who 'stays. To mind things' (*LFC*, 8).

(Published in Menna Elfyn [ed.], *Trying the Line: A Volume of Tribute to Gillian Clarke* [Llandysul: Gomer, 1997].)

Notes

[1]   I am very grateful to Dr Diane Green for providing me with a bibliography of
      Gillian Clarke's writings and xeroxes of several of the more inaccessible items.
[2]   'The King of Britain's Daughter', in Tony Curtis (ed.), *How Poets Work*
      (Bridgend: Seren, 1996), pp. 122–6. Hereafter *HPW*.
[3]   *Letter from a Far Country* (Manchester: Carcanet, 1982), p. 27. Hereafter *LFC*.
[4]   Eavan Boland, *Object Lessons: The Life of the Woman and the Poet in Our
      Time* (Manchester: Carcanet, 1995). Quotations from the London: Vintage
      edition, p. 232. Hereafter *OL*.
[5]   'Beginning with Bendigeidfran', in Jane Aaron, Teresa Rees, Sandra Betts
      and Moira Vincentelli (eds), *Our Sisters' Land* (Cardiff: University of Wales
      Press, 1994), pp. 287–93. Hereafter *OSL*.
[6]   Virginia Woolf, *A Room of One's Own*, ed. Morag Shiach (Oxford: Oxford
      University Press, World's Classics, 1992), p. 148.
[7]   'Interview with Gillian Clarke', in David T. Lloyd (ed.), *The Urgency of Identity:
      Contemporary English-language Poetry from Wales* (Evanston, IL: Northwestern
      University Press, 1994), p. 29. Hereafter *UI*.
[8]   Gillian Clarke's poetry first appeared in *Poetry Wales*, 6/1 (1970), 18–20.
[9]   'Lunchtime Lecture', *The Sundial* (Llandysul: Gomer, 1978), p. 13. Hereafter *S*.
[10] 'Morning Song', *Ariel* (London: Faber, 1965).
[11] 'Hunter-gatherer or Madonna mistress?', *Bloodaxe Catalogue, 1986–7*, p. 20.
      Hereafter *H-g*.
[12] Editorial, *The Anglo-Welsh Review* (1979).
[13] Introduction to her own work, in Meic Stephens (ed.), *The Bright Field: An
      Anthology of Contemporary Poetry from Wales* (Manchester: Carcanet, 1991),
      p. 54. Hereafter *BF*.
[14] 'Snow on the Mountain', in *Snow on the Mountain* (Swansea and Llandybïe:
      Christopher Davies, 1971), Triskel Poets Series, Number Five, p. 18. Hereafter *SM*.
[15] Interview with Gillian Clarke, in Susan Butler (ed.), *Common Ground: Poets in
      a Welsh Landscape* (Bridgend: Poetry Wales Press, 1995), p. 198. Hereafter *CG*.
[16] The two essays are 'Beginning with Bendigeidfran' and 'The King of Britain's
      Daughter' (see above).
[17] 'In Literary Residence', *Llais Llyfrau/Book News from Wales* (1984).
[18] 'Gillian Clarke: The Poet's Introduction', in Judith Kinsman (ed.), *Six Women
      Poets* (Oxford: Oxford University Press, 1992), p. 1.
[19] *Under Milk Wood*, ed. Daniel Jones (London: Dent, Everyman edition, 1992),
      p. 1. I have, of course, omitted the opening line: 'To begin at the beginning.'
[20] 'D. H. Lawrence', in W. H. Auden, *Selected Essays* (London: Faber, 1964),
      p. 31. Hereafter *SE*.
[21] '*Letting in the Rumour*: a letter from a far country, by Gillian Clarke', *Poetry
      Book Society Bulletin*, 141 (1989), 14.
[22] Review of Jan Morris, *Conundrum*, in *The Anglo-Welsh Review*, 53 (1974), 259.
[23] The phrases are taken from 'Writer's Diary', *Llais Llyfrau/Book News from
      Wales* (Spring 1993), 4.

INDEX